CICS Clients Unmasked

Guido De Simoni
Alan Hollingshead
Walter Krischker
Tie Ping Liu

INTERNATIONAL TECHNICAL SUPPORT ORGANIZATION
SAN JOSE, CALIFORNIA 95120

PRENTICE HALL PTR
UPPER SADDLE RIVER, NEW JERSEY 07458

© Copyright International Business Machines Corporation 1995, 1996. All rights reserved.

Note to U.S. Government Users — Documentation related to restricted rights — Use, duplication, or disclosure is subject to restrictions set forth in GSA ADP Schedule Contract with IBM Corp.

This edition applies to Version 1.0 of the IBM CICS Clients product set, and to all subsequent releases and modifications until otherwise indicated in new editions.

Comments about ITSO Technical Bulletins may be addressed to:
IBM Corporation ITSO, 471/80-E2, 650 Harry Road, San Jose, California 95120-6099

 Published by Prentice Hall PTR
Prentice-Hall, Inc.
A Simon & Schuster Company
Upper Saddle River, NJ 07458

Acquisitions Editor: Michael E. Meehan
Manufacturing Manager: Alexis R. Heydt
Cover Design: Andreas Bitterer, Design Source
Copy Editors: Maggie Cutler, Pamela Puckett
Production Supervision: Ann Sullivan

The publisher offers discounts on this book when ordered in bulk quantities. For more information, contact:
Corporate Sales Department, Prentice Hall PTR, One Lake Street, Upper Saddle River, NJ 07458
Phone: 800-382-3419; FAX: 201-236-7141; E-mail (Internet): corpsales@prenhall.com

Printed in the United States of America

10 9 8 7 6 5 4 3 2 1

ISBN 0-13-569237-7

Prentice-Hall International (UK) Limited, *London*
Prentice-Hall of Australia Pty. Limited, *Sydney*
Prentice-Hall Canada Inc., *Toronto*
Prentice-Hall Hispanoamericana, S.A., *Mexico*
Prentice-Hall of India Private Limited, *New Delhi*
Prentice-Hall of Japan, Inc., *Tokyo*
Simon & Schuster Asia Pte. Ltd., *Singapore*
Editora Prentice-Hall do Brasil, Ltda., *Rio de Janeiro*

To my family who encouraged me, in particular to my relatives in California who inspired me.

Alan

To my wife Christa, our precious son Nicolas, and my friend Frank.

Walter

To my wife Li Jun.

Tie Ping

To my family for supporting my adventure in California, to my father still looking after me from a different perspective. To my friends Rosanna, Paulette, and Franco for being always "specially" there.

Guido

Contents

Figures xiii

Special Notices xix

Foreword xxiii

Preface xxvii
How This Document Is Organized xxix
Related Publications xxxii
International Technical Support Organization on the World Wide Web xxxiii
International Technical Support Organization on the Internet xxxiii
About the Authors xxxiv
Acknowledgments xxxiv

Chapter 1. IBM CICS Clients 1
CICS: The Application Server 2
   High-Level Functions for Application Use 2
   Client-Server Models 3
CICS Clients within the CICS Family 7
Architecture of the CICS Clients 10
   CICS External Call Interface 11
   CICS External Presentation Interface 11
   CICS 3270 Terminal Emulator 12
   CICS 3270 Client Printer Support 12
   Client Control 13
Benefits of Using IBM CICS Clients 13
Network Configurations 16
   NetBIOS 16
   TCP/IP 16
   APPC 17
   Gateways for APPC Communications 18
   Multiple Protocol Configurations 21
   Mobile Communications 21
Performance 22
Migration from CICS OS/2 Distributed Feature Clients 22
Associated Tools and Products 23
Additional Information 24

Chapter 2. Sample Configurations: Overview 25
SNA Configurations 27
TCP/IP Configurations 27
NetBIOS Configurations 28
Printer Configurations 28

Chapter 3. CICS/ESA • CICS Client for OS/2 Using CM/2 29
Software Checklist 30
Definitions Checklist 31

Matching Definitions 32
Sample Definitions 32
    VTAM 32
    CICS/ESA 34
    Communications Manager/2 36
    Local Node Characteristics 38
    Change Number of Sessions 45
    CICSCLI.INI 46
Testing Your Configuration 47

Chapter 4. CICS/ESA • Token-Ring • Client Using APPC NS/Windows 49
Software Checklist 50
Definitions Checklist 51
Matching Definitions 52
Sample Definitions 53
    VTAM 53
    CICS/ESA 54
    APPC NS/Windows 56
    CICSCLI.INI 62
Testing Your Configuration 63

Chapter 5. CICS/ESA • NetWare for SAA Gateway • CICS Clients 65
Definitions Checklist 67
Matching Definitions 68
Sample Definitions 68
    VTAM 68
    CICS/ESA 70
    NetWare for SAA Gateway 72
    DOS Client 73
    Windows Client 73
    CICSCLI.INI 74
Testing Your Configuration 75

Chapter 6. CICS/VSE • SDLC • CICS Client for OS/2 Using CM/2 77
Software Checklist 78
Definitions Checklist 79
Matching Definitions 80
Sample Definitions 80
    VTAM 80
    CICS/VSE 83
    Communications Manager/2 85
    CICSCLI.INI 92
Testing Your Configuration 93

Chapter 7. CICS/VSE • SDLC • Client Using APPC NS/Windows 95
Software Checklist 96
Definitions Checklist 97
Matching Definitions 98
Sample Definitions 98
    VTAM 98

CICS/VSE	101
APPC NS/Windows	103
CICSCLI.INI	108
Testing Your Configuration	109

Chapter 8. CICS/VSE • Ethernet • Client Using APPC NS/Windows 111

Software Checklist	112
Definitions Checklist	113
Matching Definitions	114
Sample Definitions	115
VTAM	115
CICS/VSE	120
LAN Support Program	122
APPC NS/Windows	123
CICSCLI.INI	127
Testing Your Configuration	128

Chapter 9. CICS/VSE • CM/2 APPN Gateway • APPC NS/Windows 131

Software Checklist	132
Definitions Checklist	133
Matching Definitions	135
Sample Definitions	135
VTAM	135
CICS/VSE	138
Communications Manager/2	140
APPC NS/Windows	146
CICSCLI.INI	149
Testing Your Configuration	150

Chapter 10. CICS for OS/2 • CICS Client Using TCP/IP for OS/2 153

Software Checklist	154
Definitions Checklist	155
Matching Definitions	156
Sample Definitions	156
TCP/IP for OS/2 V2.0 on Server	156
CICS for OS/2 on Server	160
TCP/IP for OS/2 V2.0 on Client	161
CICSCLI.INI for CICS Client for OS/2	162
Testing Your Configuration	162

Chapter 11. CICS for OS/2 • CICS Client for Macintosh • TCP/IP 165

Software Checklist	166
Definitions Checklist	167
Matching Definitions	168
Sample Definitions	168
TCP/IP for OS/2 V2.0 on Server	168
CICS for OS/2 on Server	172
MacTCP on Client	173
CICSCLI.INI for CICS Client for Macintosh	176
Testing Your Configuration	177

Chapter 12. CICS/6000 • CICS Client for OS/2 Using TCP/IP for OS/2 179
Software Checklist 181
Definitions Checklist 181
Matching Definitions 182
Sample Definitions 183
    TCP/IP for AIX/6000 183
    CICS/6000. 185
    TCP/IP for OS/2 186
    CICSCLI.INI 189
Testing Your Configuration 189

Chapter 13. CICS/6000 • Clients for DOS and Windows • TCP/IP for DOS. 191
Software Checklist 193
Definitions Checklist 193
Matching Definitions 195
Sample Definitions 195
    TCP/IP for AIX/6000 195
    CICS/6000. 197
    TCP/IP for DOS 198
    CICSCLI.INI 201
Testing Your Configuration 202

Chapter 14. CICS for Windows NT • PC/TCP • Clients Using TCP/IP 205
Software Checklist 206
Definitions Checklist 207
Matching Definitions 208
Enabling TCP/IP on the Windows NT Server 208
Sample Definitions 209
    CICS for Windows NT Definitions 209
    LAN Support Program. 210
    PC/TCP for DOS/Windows. 210
    CICSCLI.INI 212
Testing Your Configuration 213

Chapter 15. CICS for Window NT • LAN WorkPlace • TCP/IP. 215
Software Checklist 216
Definitions Checklist 217
Matching Definitions 218
Enabling TCP/IP on the Windows NT Server 218
Sample Definitions 218
    CICS for Windows NT Definitions 219
    LAN WorkPlace 219
    CICSCLI.INI 222
Testing Your Configuration 223

Chapter 16. CICS for OS/2 • CICS Client for OS/2 Using NetBIOS 225
Software Checklist 226
Definitions Checklist 227
Matching Definitions 228
Enabling NetBIOS Support 228

Sample Definitions 229
   CICS for OS/2 229
   CICSCLI.INI for CICS Client for OS/2 230
Testing Your Configuration 231

Chapter 17. CICS for OS/2 • CICS Client for DOS/Windows • NetBIOS ... 233
Software Checklist 234
Definitions Checklist 235
Matching Definitions 236
Enabling NetBIOS 236
Sample Definitions 237
   CICS for OS/2 237
   LAN Support Program 238
   CICSCLI.INI 243
Testing Your Configuration 244

Chapter 18. CICS 3270 Client Printer Configurations 245
Method 1: Client Printer Attached to a CICS for OS/2 Server 246
   CICS for OS/2 Definitions 247
   CICS Client CICSCLI.INI Definition 247
   CICS Client CICSPRNT Command 248
Method 2: Client Printer Attached to a CICS for OS/2 Server
Running User Exit 21 248
   User Exit 21 249
   CICS for OS/2 Definitions 249
   CICS Client CICSCLI.INI Definition 250
   CICS Client CICSPRNT Command 251
   Testing Your Printer Configuration 252
   Matching Definitions 252
   Multiple Printers 253
Method 3: Client Printer Attached to a CICS/6000 Server 253
   CICS/6000 Definitions 253
   CICS Client CICSCLI.INI Definition 254
   CICS Client CICSPRNT Command 255
   Testing Your Configuration 255

Chapter 19. External Call Interface 257
ECI Model 258
Program Link Calls 258
   Synchronous Program Link Calls 259
   Asynchronous Program Link Calls 262
Status Information Calls 265
   Synchronous 266
   Asynchronous 267
Reply Solicitation Calls 268
Managing Logical Units of Work 269
   ECI Facilities 269
   Single Program Link Call within One LUW 270
   Sequence of Program Link Calls within One LUW 271
Multiple Asynchronous Calls Accessing Multiple CICS Servers 273

ECI Asynchronous Implementation with Callback 274
Sample Implementation. 277
    Sample Program Functions. 277
    Portability and Compatibility Considerations 279
    Running the Sample Program. 279
Further Information. 281

Chapter 20. External Presentation Interface 283
EPI Model 284
Application Flow. 284
    Initialization. 285
    Starting Transaction 285
    Events Processing 286
    Termination 288
Sample Implementation. 288
    Sample Program Functions. 289
    Portability and Compatibility Considerations 289
    Running the Sample Program. 290
Further Information. 292

Chapter 21. Problem Determination 293
Tools. 294
Sources of Information 295
    Preliminary Checks 296
CICS Client Environment 296
    Starting and Stopping CICS Client Trace 297
    CICS Client Trace File. 298
    CICS Client Error Processing 298
CICS Server Environment. 299
    CICS Server Trace 300
    CICS Server Dumps. 301
    CICS Server Message Logs 301
Communications Environment 302
    Communication Traces and Dumps 303
    Other Tools and Utilities 304
CICS Client Trace Analysis 305
    Sample CICS Client Trace. 306
    ECI Application Error 307
    Connecting to CICS for Windows NT Using NetBIOS. 309
    Connecting to CICS/6000 Using TCP/IP. 311
Common Errors in a CICS Client Environment. 312
Common Errors in a CICS Server Environment 313

Appendix A. Hints and Tips 315
Establishing a Connection Between CM/2 and CICS Mainframe 316
Establishing a Connection Using APPC NS/Windows 317
Automatic Start of CICS Client. 320
Starting CICS Client for DOS 321
Starting and Stopping Your CICS Client 321
Checking the Status of Your CICS Client 322

Using CICSTERM Commands 322
CICS Client for Macintosh Operation... 323
Data Conversion: ASCII to EBCDIC... 326
Using the Ping Utility to Verify TCP/IP Connections 327
TCP/IP Port Selection 328

Appendix B. Frequently Asked Questions 331
Operating Environment... 331
Limitations 333
Compatibility and Migration 334
ECI 336

Appendix C. Common Problems: Symptoms and Solutions 339
Starting Clients and Terminals.. 340
SNA 341
TCP/IP.. 344
NetBIOS 345
ECI 346
Documentation 346

Appendix D. Programming Languages and Compilers 349

Appendix E. Sample ECI and EPI Source Code............................. 351
Client Program for the ECI Sample 351
Server Program for the ECI Sample 356
Client Program for the EPI Sample 358
Server Program for the EPI Sample 363

Appendix F. CM/2 .NDF and APPC NS/Windows NSD.INI Files 367
CM/2 .NDF File: CICS/ESA-CICS Client for OS/2 Using CM/2 368
CM/2 .NDF File: CICS/VSE-SDLC-CICS Client for OS/2 Using CM/2.............. 370
CM/2 .NDF File: CICS/VSE-CM/2 APPN Gateway-APPC NS/Windows 371
APPC Networking Services for Windows NSD.INI
File in a Token-Ring Environment 372
APPC Networking Services for Windows NSD.INI File in an SDLC Environment. 373
APPC Networking Services for Windows NSD.INI File:
CICS/VSE-Ethernet-APPC NS/Windows 373
APPC Networking Services for Windows NSD.INI File:
CICS/VSE-CM/2 APPN Gateway-APPC NS/Windows................................. 374

Appendix G. IBM 3172 Customization 377
IOCDS and VM/ESA Definitions.. 378
VSE/ESA Definitions 379

Appendix H. Configuration Worksheets 381
CICS/ESA • CICS Client for OS/2 Using CM/2 382
CICS/ESA • Token-Ring • Client Using APPC NS/Windows 384
CICS/ESA • NetWare for SAA Gateway • CICS Clients.......................... 386
CICS/VSE • SDLC • CICS Client for OS/2 Using CM/2 388
CICS/VSE • SDLC • Client Using APPC NS/Windows............................. 390

CICS/VSE • Ethernet • Client Using APPC NS/Windows 392
CICS/VSE • CM/2 APPN Gateway • APPC NS/Windows 394
CICS for OS/2 • CICS Client Using TCP/IP for OS/2. 396
CICS for OS/2 • CICS Client for Macintosh • TCP/IP. 398
CICS/6000 • CICS Client for OS/2 Using TCP/IP for OS/2 400
CICS/6000 • Client for DOS/Windows • TCP/IP for DOS 402
CICS for Windows NT • PC/TCP • Clients Using TCP/IP for OS/2 V1.2.1 404
CICS for Windows NT • LAN WorkPlace • TCP/IP. 406
CICS for OS/2 • CICS Client for OS/2 • NetBIOS. 408
CICS for OS/2 • CICS Client for DOS/Windows • NetBIOS 409

Glossary. 411

List of Abbreviations 415

Index. 417

Figures

1. Remote Data Access Model 4
2. Database Server Model 5
3. Application Server Model 6
4. CICS Client Architecture 10
5. CICS Clients on a LAN Communicating over NetBIOS 16
6. CICS Clients on a LAN Communicating over TCP/IP 17
7. CICS Clients Communicating over APPC 18
8. CICS Clients Communicating over APPC Using a CM/2 Gateway 19
9. CICS Clients Communicating over APPC Using a NetWare for SAA Gateway . 20
10. CICS Clients Communicating over APPC Using a SNAœps Gateway 20
11. CICS Client for OS/2 Communicating over NetBIOS, TCP/IP, and APPC 21
12. CICS Clients Using Mobile Communication to CICS Server 22
13. SNA Configuration Using CM/2 30
14. VTAM XID, PU, and LU Definitions: CICS/ESA-CICS Client for OS/2 Using CM/2 33
15. VTAM Logmode Definition: CICS/ESA-CICS Client for OS/2 Using CM/2 ... 33
16. VTAM APPL Definition: CICS/ESA-CICS Client for OS/2 Using CM/2 34
17. System Initialization Table Definitions: CICS/ESA-CICS Client for OS/2 Using CM/2 34
18. Install DFHISC: CICS/ESA-CICS Client for OS/2 Using CM/2 35
19. LU6.2 Connection Definition: CICS/ESA-CICS Client for OS/2 Using CM/2 35
20. LU6.2 Sessions Definition: CICS/ESA-CICS Client for OS/2 Using CM/2 36
21. Communications Manager Configuration Definition: CICS/ESA-CICS Client for OS/2 Using CM/2 37
22. Communications Manager Profile List: CICS/ESA-CICS Client for OS/2 Using CM/2 38
23. Local Node Characteristics: CICS/ESA-CICS Client for OS/2 Using CM/2 39
24. Connection to a Host: CICS/ESA-CICS Client for OS/2 Using CM/2 40
25. Partner LUs: CICS/ESA-CICS Client for OS/2 Using CM/2 41
26. Local LU Name Definition: CICS/ESA-CICS Client for OS/2 Using CM/2 .. 42
27. Mode Name Definition: CICS/ESA-CICS Client for OS/2 Using CM/2 43
28. Transaction Program Definition: CICS/ESA-CICS Client for OS/2 Using CM/2 44
29. Sample CNOS Statements: CICS/ESA-CICS Client for OS/2 Using CM/2 46
30. CICSCLI.INI Definitions: CICS/ESA-CICS Client for OS/2 Using CM/2 ... 46
31. SNA Configuration Using APPC NS/Windows 50
32. VTAM XID, PU, and LU Definitions: CICS/ESA-Token-Ring-Client Using APPC NS/Windows 53
33. VTAM Logmode Definition: CICS/ESA-Token-Ring-Client Using APPC NS/Windows 54
34. VTAM APPL Definition: CICS/ESA-Token-Ring-Client Using APPC NS/Windows 54
35. System Initialization Table Definitions: CICS/ESA-Token-Ring-Client Using APPC NS/Windows . 55
36. Install DFHISC: CICS/ESA-Token-Ring-Client Using APPC NS/Windows 55
37. LU6.2 Connection Definition: CICS/ESA-Token-Ring-Client Using APPC NS/Windows 55
38. LU6.2 Sessions Definition: CICS/ESA-Token-Ring-Client Using APPC NS/Windows 56
39. Networking Services Configuration Window 57
40. General Configuration Window 58
41. LAN Configuration Window 59
42. Define Mode Window: CICS/ESA-Token-Ring-Client Using APPC NS/Windows . 60
43. Define Transaction Program Window: CICS/ESA-Token-Ring-Client Using APPC NS/Windows ... 61
44. CICSCLI.INI Definitions: CICS/ESA-Token-Ring-Client Using APPC NS/Windows 62
45. VTAM XID, PU, and LU Definitions: CICS/ESA-NetWare for SAA Gateway-CICS Clients 69
46. VTAM Logmode Definition: CICS/ESA-NetWare for SAA Gateway-CICS Clients 69
47. VTAM APPL Definition: CICS/ESA-NetWare for SAA Gateway-CICS Clients . 70
48. System Initialization Table Definitions: CICS/ESA-NetWare for SAA Gateway-CICS Clients . 70
49. Install DFHISC: CICS/ESA-NetWare for SAA Gateway-CICS Clients 71
50. LU6.2 Connection Definition: CICS/ESA-NetWare for SAA Gateway-CICS Clients 71
51. LU6.2 Sessions Definition: CICS/ESA-NetWare for SAA Gateway-CICS Clients 72
52. CICSCLI.INI Definitions: CICS/ESA-NetWare for SAA Gateway-CICS Clients 74
53. SDLC Configuration: CICS/VSE-SDLC-CICS Client for OS/2 Using CM/2 ... 78
54. VTAM Startup Procedure ATCSTR04.B 81
55. PU, ADDR, and LU Definitions in VTAM CA Major Node 82
56. VTAM APPL Major Node Definition: CICS/VSE-SDLC-CICS Client for OS/2 Using CM/2 82
57. System Initialization Table Definitions: CICS/VSE-SDLC-CICS Client for OS/2 Using CM/2 . 83
58. Install DFHISC: CICS/VSE-SDLC-CICS Client for OS/2 Using CM/2 83

59.	LU6.2 Connection Definition: CICS/VSE-SDLC-CICS Client for OS/2 Using CM/2	84
60.	LU6.2 Sessions Definition: CICS/VSE-SDLC-CICS Client for OS/2 using CM/2	85
61.	Communications Manager Configuration Definition Window	86
62.	Communications Manager Profile List Window	86
63.	SDLC DLC Adapter Parameters Window	87
64.	Local Node Characteristics Window	88
65.	Connection to a Host Window	89
66.	Partner LUs Window	90
67.	Local LU Name Definition Window	91
68.	Sample CNOS Statements: CICS/VSE-SDLC-CICS Client for OS/2 Using CM/2	92
69.	CICSCLI.INI Definitions: CICS/VSE-SDLC-CICS Client for OS/2 Using CM/2	93
70.	SDLC Configuration Using APPC NS/Windows	96
71.	VTAM Startup Procedure ATCSTR04.B: CICS/VSE-SDLC-Client Using APPC NS/Windows	99
72.	PU, ADDR, and LU Definitions in VTAM CA Major Node: CICS/VSE-SDLC-Client Using APPC NS/Windows	100
73.	VTAM APPL Major Node Definition: CICS/VSE-SDLC-Client Using APPC NS/Windows	100
74.	System Initialization Table Definitions: CICS/VSE-SDLC-Client Using APPC NS/Windows	101
75.	Install DFHISC: CICS/VSE-SDLC-Client Using APPC NS/Windows	101
76.	LU6.2 Connection Definition: CICS/VSE-SDLC-Client Using APPC NS/Windows	102
77.	LU6.2 Sessions Definition: CICS/VSE-SDLC-Client Using APPC NS/Windows	103
78.	Networking Services Configuration Window: CICS/VSE-SDLC-Client Using APPC NS/Windows	104
79.	General Configuration Window	105
80.	Remote Configuration Window: CICS/VSE-SDLC-Client Using APPC NS/Windows	106
81.	Select Modem Type Window	107
82.	CICSCLI.INI Definitions: CICS/VSE-SDLC-Client Using APPC NS/Windows	108
83.	Ethernet Configuration: CICS/VSE-Ethernet-Client Using APPC NS/Windows	112
84.	VSE/VTAM XCA Major Node for the IBM 3172	116
85.	VTAM XID, PU, LU and DIALNO Definitions	116
86.	VTAM APPL Definition: CICS/VSE-Ethernet-Client Using APPC NS/Windows	117
87.	VTAM Startup Procedure ATCSTR04.B: CICS/VSE-Ethernet-Client Using APPC NS/Windows	118
88.	IBM 3172 ICP Configuration	119
89.	System Initialization Table Definitions: CICS/VSE-Ethernet-Client Using APPC NS/Windows	120
90.	Install DFHISC: CICS/VSE-Ethernet-Client Using APPC NS/Windows	120
91.	LU6.2 Connection Definition: CICS/VSE-Ethernet-Client Using APPC NS/Windows	121
92.	LU6.2 Sessions Definition: CICS/VSE-Ethernet-Client Using APPC NS/Windows	122
93.	CONFIG.SYS Definitions: LAN Support Program	123
94.	Networking Services Configuration Window: CICS/VSE-Ethernet-Client Using APPC NS/Windows	124
95.	General Configuration Window: CICS/VSE-Ethernet-Client Using APPC NS/Windows	125
96.	LAN Configuration Window: CICS/VSE-Ethernet-Client Using APPC NS/Windows	126
97.	CICSCLI.INI Definitions: CICS/VSE-Ethernet-Client Using APPC NS/Windows	127
98.	CM/2 APPN Gateway Configuration: CICS/VSE-CM/2 APPN Gateway-APPC NS/Windows	132
99.	VTAM Startup Procedure ATCSTR04.B: CICS/VSE-CM/2 APPN Gateway-APPC NS/Windows	136
100.	PU, ADDR, and LU Definitions in VTAM CA Major Node: CICS/VSE-CM/2 APPN Gateway-APPC NS/Windows	137
101.	VTAM APPL Major Node Definition: CICS/VSE-CM/2 APPN Gateway-APPC NS/Windows	137
102.	System Initialization Table Definitions: CICS/VSE-CM/2 APPN Gateway-APPC NS/Windows	138
103.	Install DFHISC: CICS/VSE-CM/2 APPN Gateway-APPC NS/Windows	138
104.	LU6.2 Connection Definition: CICS/VSE-CM/2 APPN Gateway-APPC NS/Windows	139
105.	LU6.2 Sessions Definition: CICS/VSE-CM/2 APPN Gateway-APPC NS/Windows	140
106.	Communications Manager Configuration Definition Window: CICS/VSE-CM/2 APPN Gateway-APPC NS/Windows	141
107.	Communications Manager Profile List Window: CICS/VSE-CM/2 APPN Gateway-APPC NS/Windows	141
108.	SDLC DLC Adapter Parameters Window: CICS/VSE-CM/2 APPN Gateway-APPC NS/Windows	142
109.	Local Node Characteristics Window: CICS/VSE-CM/2 APPN Gateway-APPC NS/Windows	143
110.	Connection to a Host Window: CICS/VSE-CM/2 APPN Gateway-APPC NS/Windows	144
111.	Partner LUs Window: CICS/VSE-CM/2 APPN Gateway-APPC NS/Windows	145
112.	Communications Manager Profile List: CICS/VSE-CM/2 APPN Gateway-APPC NS/Windows	146
113.	Networking Services Configuration Window: CICS/VSE-CM/2 APPN	

Gateway-APPC NS/Windows 147
114. General Configuration Window: CICS/VSE-CM/2 APPN Gateway-APPC NS/Windows 148
115. LAN Configuration Window: CICS/VSE-CM/2 APPN Gateway-APPC NS/Windows 149
116. CICSCLI.INI Definitions: CICS/VSE-CM/2 APPN Gateway-APPC NS/Windows 150
117. TCP/IP Configuration: CICS for OS/2-CICS Client Using TCP/IP for OS/2 154
118. TCP/IP for OS/2 Configure Network Interface Parameters 157
119. TCP/IP for OS/2 Routing Information 158
120. TCP/IP for OS/2 Services Definitions 159
121. Port Number Definition in Services File 160
122. SIT Parameters to Enable TCP/IP Support for CICS for OS/2 161
123. TCP/IP Messages in CICS for OS/2 Message Log 161
124. CICSCLI.INI Definitions: CICS for OS/2-CICS Client Using TCP/IP for OS/2 162
125. TCP/IP Configuration Using MacTCP 166
126. TCP/IP for OS/2 Configure Network Interface Parameters: CICS for OS/2-CICS Client
for Macintosh-TCP/IP 169
127. TCP/IP for OS/2 Routing Information: CICS for OS/2-CICS Client for Macintosh-TCP/IP 170
128. TCP/IP for OS/2 Services Definitions: CICS for OS/2-CICS Client for Macintosh-TCP/IP 171
129. Port Number Definition in Services File: CICS for OS/2-CICS Client for Macintosh-TCP/IP 172
130. SIT Parameters to Enable TCP/IP Support for CICS for OS/2: CICS for OS/2-CICS Client
for Macintosh-TCP/IP 173
131. TCP/IP Messages in CICS for OS/2 Message Log: CICS for OS/2-CICS Client
for Macintosh-TCP/IP 173
132. MacTCP Token-Ring Panel 174
133. MacTCP Configuration Panel 174
134. Workstation IP Address: MacTCP 175
135. MacTCP Configuration Panel with IP Address 176
136. CICSCLI.INI Definitions: CICS for OS/2-CICS Client for Macintosh-TCP/IP 176
137. TCP/IP Configuration: CICS/6000-CICS Client for OS/2 Using TCP/IP for OS/2 180
138. TCP/IP for AIX/6000 Definitions 184
139. TCP/IP for AIX/6000 Name Resolution Definitions 184
140. TCP Service Entry 185
141. CICS/6000 Listener Definition 186
142. TCP/IP for OS/2 Installation and Network Configuration 187
143. TCP/IP for OS/2 Name Resolution Definitions: CICS/6000-CICS Client for OS/2
Using TCP/IP for OS/2   188
144. CICSCLI.INI Definitions: CICS/6000-CICS Client for OS/2 Using TCP/IP for OS/2 189
145. TCP/IP Configuration: CICS/6000-Clients for DOS and Windows-TCP/IP for DOS 192
146. TCP/IP for AIX/6000 Definitions: CICS/6000-Clients for DOS and Windows-TCP/IP for DOS .. 196
147. TCP Service Entry: CICS/6000-Clients for DOS and Windows-TCP/IP for DOS 197
148. CICS/6000 Listener Definition: CICS/6000-Clients for DOS and Windows-TCP/IP for DOS ... 198
149. CONFIG.SYS Entries 199
150. AUTOEXEC.BAT Entries 199
151. TCP/IP for DOS Network Configuration Definitions Panel 200
152. TCP/IP for DOS Name Resolution Definitions Panel 201
153. CICSCLI.INI Definitions: CICS/6000-Clients for DOS and Windows-TCP/IP for DOS 202
154. TCP/IP Configuration Using PC/TCP from FTP Inc. 206
155. TCP/IP Definitions: CICS for Windows NT Server 210
156. PC/TCP for DOS/Windows IP Configuration 211
157. PC/TCP for DOS/Windows DNS Configuration 212
158. CICSCLI.INI Definitions: CICS for Windows NT-PC/TCP-Clients Using TCP/IP 213
159. Configuration Using Novell's LAN WorkPlace 216
160. LAN WorkPlace Configuration File: NET.CFG 221
161. CICSCLI.INI Definitions: CICS for Windows NT-LAN WorkPlace-TCP/IP 222
162. NetBIOS Configuration 226
163. Enabling NetBIOS Support: NTS/2 229
164. NetBIOS Definitions: CICS for OS/2 Server 230
165. CICSCLI.INI Definitions: CICS for OS/2-CICS Client for OS/2 Using NetBIOS 231
166. NetBIOS Configuration: CICS for OS/2-CICS Client for DOS/Windows-NetBIOS 234
167. Enabling NetBIOS Support: CICS for OS/2-CICS Client for DOS/Windows-NetBIOS .. 237
168. NetBIOS Definitions: CICS for OS/2-CICS Client for DOS/Windows-NetBIOS 238

169.	Environment Information: LAN Support Program	240
170.	Process Adapter Option Diskette: LAN Support Program	240
171.	Current Configuration Panel: LAN Support Program	241
172.	NetBIOS Active Confirmation: DOS System Bootup	241
173.	CONFIG.SYS File: DOS Workstation	242
174.	CICSCLI.INI Definitions: CICS for OS/2-CICS Client for DOS/Windows-NetBIOS	243
175.	Printer Configuration	246
176.	Client Printer TCT Definition (Method 1): CICS for OS/2	247
177.	Client Printer TCT Definition (Method 2): CICS for OS/2	250
178.	CICS ECI Model	258
179.	CICS ECI Program Link Calls	259
180.	Synchronous ECI Program Flow	260
181.	Sample Synchronous ECI Program in COBOL	262
182.	Asynchronous ECI Program Flow	263
183.	Simple Example of an Asynchronous ECI Program in C	264
184.	Sample Synchronous Status Information Call	267
185.	Sequence of Program Link Calls in the Same LUW	272
186.	Multiple Asynchronous Calls Accessing Multiple Servers	274
187.	Example of an Asynchronous Program Link Call with Callback	275
188.	Modification for Client Sample Program	278
189.	ECI Test Window: Sample Program Messages	280
190.	CICS EPI Model	284
191.	EPI Initialization	285
192.	EPI Starting Transaction	286
193.	EPI Events Processing	287
194.	EPI Termination	288
195.	EPI Test Window Sample Program Messages	291
196.	Sample CICS Client Error Log	298
197.	CICS Client Error Message Pop-up Window	299
198.	CICS for OS/2 Message Log	302
199.	Sample CICS Client Trace	306
200.	CICS Client Trace Showing ECI Application Error	308
201.	CICS Client Trace: Connecting to a CICS for Windows NT Server	309
202.	CICS Client Trace: Using an Invalid Port Number	311
203.	Local LU Control: APPC NS/Windows	318
204.	Connections Window Showing No Active LU Sessions	319
205.	Activate LU Sessions: APPC NS/Windows	319
206.	Connections Window Showing Active LU Sessions	320
207.	Inactive CICS Client for Macintosh	323
208.	Selecting the List Option: CICS Client for Macintosh	324
209.	Connection Status List: CICS Client for Macintosh	324
210.	Messages Returned from Ping Utility	327
211.	Port Selection Summary	329
212.	IBM 3172 IOCDS Entries	378
213.	VM/ESA Auto-Sense Definitions in SYSTEM CONFIG File	378
214.	VM Directory Entry for VSE/ESA Machine	379
215.	VSE IPL Procedure to Add the IBM 3172	379

Tables

1. Communications and Functions between CICS Clients and CICS Servers. 8
2. SNA Configurations 27
3. TCP/IP Configurations 27
4. NetBIOS Configurations 28
5. Printer Configurations. 28
6. Matching Definitions: CICS/ESA-CICS Client for OS/2 Using CM/2 32
7. Matching Definitions: CICS/ESA-Token-Ring-Client Using APPC NS/Windows . . . 52
8. Matching Definitions: CICS/ESA-NetWare for SAA Gateway-CICS Clients 68
9. Matching Definitions: CICS/VSE-SDLC-CICS Client for OS/2 Using CM/2 80
10. Matching Definitions: CICS/VSE-SDLC-Client Using APPC NS/Windows 98
11. Matching Definitions: CICS/VSE-Ethernet-Client Using APPC NS/Windows 114
12. Matching Definitions: CICS/VSE-CM/2 APPN Gateway-APPC NS/Windows 135
13. Matching Definitions: CICS for OS/2-CICS Client Using TCP/IP for OS/2 156
14. Matching Definitions: CICS for OS/2-CICS Client for Macintosh-TCP/IP 168
15. Matching Definitions: CICS/6000-CICS Client for OS/2 Using TCP/IP for OS/2. . . 182
16. Matching Definitions: CICS/6000-Clients for DOS and Windows-TCP/IP for DOS. 195
17. Matching Definitions: CICS for Windows NT-PC/TCP-Clients Using TCP/IP 208
18. Matching Definitions: CICS for Windows NT-LAN WorkPlace-TCP/IP 218
19. Matching Definitions: CICS for OS/2-CICS Client for OS/2 Using NetBIOS. 228
20. Matching Definitions: CICS for OS/2-CICS Client for DOS/Windows-NetBIOS . . . 236
21. Matching Definitions: CICS 3270 Client Printer Configurations 252
22. Multiple Asynchronous Calls Accessing Multiple Servers. 273
23. CICS for OS/2 and CICS for Windows NT: Functional Differences 335
24. Language Compilers Supported by CICS Clients 350

Special Notices

This publication will help customers, sales representatives, systems engineers, programmers, service engineers, and anyone else who is interested in client/server networks. The information in this publication is not intended as the specification of any programming interfaces that are provided by IBM CICS Clients or any of the CICS family server products. See the PUBLICATIONS section of the IBM Programming Announcement for IBM CICS Clients V1.0 for more information about what publications are considered to be product documentation.

References in this publication to IBM products, programs or services do not imply that IBM intends to make these available in all countries in which IBM operates. Any reference to an IBM product, program, or service is not intended to state or imply that only IBM's product, program, or service may be used. Any functionally equivalent program that does not infringe any of IBM's intellectual property rights may be used instead of the IBM product, program, or service.

Information in this book was developed in conjunction with the use of the equipment specified, and is limited in application to those specific hardware and software products and levels.

IBM may have patents or pending patent applications covering subject matter in this document. The furnishing of this document does not give the reader any license to these patents. License inquiries may be sent, in writing, to the IBM Director of Licensing, IBM Corporation, 500 Columbus Avenue, Thornwood, NY 10594 USA.

The information contained in this document has not been submitted to any formal IBM test and is distributed AS IS. The information about non-IBM (VENDOR) products in this manual has been supplied by the vendor and IBM assumes no responsibility for its accuracy or completeness. The use of this information or the implementation of any of these techniques is a customer responsibility and depends on the customer's ability to evaluate and integrate them into the customer's operational environment. While each item may have been reviewed by IBM for accuracy in a specific situation, there is no guarantee that the same or similar results will be obtained elsewhere. Customers attempting to adapt these techniques to their own environments do so at their own risk.

Any performance data contained in this document was determined in a controlled environment; therefore, the results that may be obtained in other operating environments amy vary significantly. Users of this document should verify the applicable data for their specific environment.

The following document contains examples of data and reports used in daily business operations. To illustrate them as completely as possible, the examples contain he names of individuals, companies, brands, and products. All of these names are fictitious and any similarity to the names and addresses used by an actual business enterprise is entirely coincidental.

Reference to PTF numbers that have not been released through the normal distribution process does not imply general availability. The purpose of including these reference number is to alert IBM customers to specific information relative to the implementation of the PTF when it becomes available to each customer according tot he normal distribution process.

The following terms are trademarks of the International Business Machines Corporation in the United States and/or other countries:

ACF/VTAM	Advanced Peer-to-Peer Networking
AIX/6000	APPN
C Set ++	CICS
CICS OS/2	CICS for Windows/NT
CICS for OS/2	CICS/ESA
CICS/MVS	CICS/VSE
CICS/400	CICS/6000
COBOL/2	DB2
Enterprise Systems Architecture/390	ESA/390
FAA	First Failure Support Technology/2
IBM	LAN Distance
MVS/ESA	NetView
Operating System/2	OS/2
Personal System/2	PS/2
RACF	RISC System/6000
RS/6000	SAA
ThinkPad	VisualAge
VisualGen	VisualSet
VSE/ESA	VTAM
WIN-OS/2	

The following terms are trademarks of other companies:

Windows is a registered trademark of Microsoft Corporation.

PC Direct is a trademark of Ziff Communications Company and is used by IBM Corporation under license.

UNIX is a registered trademark in the United States and other countries licensed exclusively through X/Open Company Limited.

Apple Computer Inc.	Apple, AppleTalk, LocalTalk, Macintosh MacTCP, MPW, System 7, SNA•ps
Digital Equipment Corporation	AXP, DEC
Hewlett Packard Company	HP
Micro Focus Limited	Micro Focus
Microsoft Corporation	Microsoft, Windows, Windows NT
Motorola	Motorola
Novell, Inc.	Novell, NetWare, LAN Workplace
Open Software Foundation	OSF/1

Other trademarks are trademarks of their respective companies.

Foreword

Customer Information Control System (CICS) is a major success story for both IBM and our customers. The technology has evolved from being the de facto transaction processor on the IBM 390 to its current position as a thriving family of products implemented on a range of IBM and non-IBM platforms.

CICS controls "line of business" applications in all areas of industry across the globe. Virtually everyone in the world has come into contact with CICS in one way or another—banking services, tax returns, and government services, to name a few. There can be no better testament to it's functional value andreliability than statements from some of our largest corporate enterprises that their entire business relies on CICS.

What is CICS, why is it so important, and more specifically how is it positioned to capitalize on the computing trends of the future?

As a transaction processor, CICS provides the key services necessary for any industrial strength application server:

- ❏ An application programming interface that enables easy, platform independent access to core facilities such as presentation services, files, databases, and operating system functions
- ❏ Easy communications to remote platforms for access to data or programs
- ❏ Data integrity and secure access to resources—even if the data updates are split across numerous platforms!
- ❏ Application run-time services. Scalability, workload balancing, performance, systems management, and problem determination and the ability to schedule and prioritize applications.
- ❏ Client/server functions enabling modern workstation interfaces (GUI, multimedia) to be placed on new, or existing, applications.

This book focuses on the product's client/server functions. Today, CICS is implemented on MVS/ESA, VSE/ESA, OS/400, AIX, OS/2, Windows NT, DEC OSF1, and HP-UX. You can expect to see more platforms appearing in the future. The "mainframe" family members exploit the latest, exciting CMOS-based 390 technology. The UNIX and Intel-based systems are not ports of CICS/ESA, but thet are designed to the same specification while exploiting the native characteristics of each platform. The family offers portability of applications to any platform. All implementations support the CICS API and basic mapping support, enabling you to capitalize on your investment in these applications. The implementations also fully support CICS intersystem communications—function shipping, transaction routing, and distributed transaction processing.

These features position the CICS architecture as a compelling candidate for those looking for a pervasive, reliable, client/server middleware.

The CICS Clients are the most recent addition to the family. They are a series of lightweight, desktop products that enables workstation connectivity directly to any CICS server. The Clients are currently implemented on DOS, Windows, OS/2, and Apple Macintosh. Like the servers, this list will grow—OS/2 for PowerPC, Windows NT, and Windows95 versions can be expected in the future. The Clients support two programmable interfaces: the external presentation interface (EPI), which allows you to place a modern workstation interface on an existing 3270 CICS transaction (without requiring to change the transaction's logic), and the external call interface (ECI) designed for new client/server applications, where the presentation logic on the client is cleanly separated from the business logic (a CICS program) running on the server.

CICS clients and servers offer you one of the most functional and flexible middleware architectures available for creating client/server solutions. The implementation is pervasive—on a range of IBM and non-IBM clients and servers that is expanding all the time, you can move between a "two-tier" (client to mainframe) or "three-tier" (client to distributed server to mainframe) implementation without having to change the application's design or logic. The architecture realizes that your requirement may not be just for new applications (ECI); it also addresses the needs of those who want to implement new interfaces on existing applications (EPI).

The story has not ended. IBM is committed to the CICS family, listening to your requirements and addressing your needs. We are currently focused on how we can reduce your cost of computing by exploiting parallel systems, improving systems management through single point of definition, and dynamic workload balancing. We have an impressive, growing, array of application development tools available from IBM (VisualAge, VisualGen) and non-IBM vendors that support ECI and EPI client development and the development of CICS server logic. You will be seeing object interfaces for both the Client ECI, EPI APIs, and the server CICS API; access to the Internet, and improved integration with workstation technologies such as Lotus applications.

CICS Clients Unmasked is an invaluable read for existing CICS customers or those evaluating client/server technology.

The book describes in an easy-to-read manner the client/server CICS functions and how the programming interfaces (ECI and EPI) can be used. It details all potential configurations, including tried and tested examples to help you set up connections quickly to either your mainframe or a distributed server. The book has been written by experienced programmers and designers who understand what their fellow programmers and designers want to get of a publication like this. This understanding is highlighted in the chapters on performance information, problem determination, frequently asked questions, and hints and tips.

In closing, I would like to urge those customers who are evaluating technology to read this book and match our experience, technical features, and reliability against your business requirements for a client/server architecture. I hope to soon welcome you into our growing family of satisfied customers.

Have fun!

Rob Lamb

Transaction Processing Strategy Manager

IBM Hursley

roblamb@winvmd.vnet.ibm.com

January 1996

Preface

With the continual change in the business climate, many organizations are seeking flexible client-server solutions to improve their competitive position in the marketplace.

To help companies today and in the future, CICS, an application server handling thousands of transactions daily for most big businesses in the world, has introduced the IBM CICS Clients into its large family.

With the announcement of the CICS Clients family of products, IBM has delivered on its "any-client-to-any-server" strategy for transaction processing; the first CICS transaction processing software clients that will enable PC users to connect to any computer server that runs CICS software. The new CICS Clients give the customer and independent software vendors the opportunity to access and exploit business-critical information directly from their standard desktop packages.

Customers who already have CICS installed can now, with the new IBM CICS Clients, extend their transaction processing to client-server operation with a minimum of investment and new programming.

The IBM CICS Clients are a family of products for workstations running a range of operating systems, capable of communicating through several protocols and a range of supported communications products directly with CICS servers on all platforms. The CICS Clients bring the benefits of client-server operation to the entire CICS family of application servers.

The new CICS Clients family of products comprises:

- CICS Client for **DOS**
- CICS Client for **Windows**
- CICS Client for **OS/2**
- CICS Client for **Macintosh**.

CICS Clients support provides the advantage of the established CICS external call interface (ECI), External Presentation Interface, and 3270 terminal emulation to enable workstations to access CICS application programs and functions running on CICS servers.

The advantages of client-server operations include the ability to exploit productivity-enhancing workstation facilities such as a graphical user interface or multimedia interface, and to exchange data directly between CICS and personal productivity applications (for example, a spreadsheet) used at the workstation.

Whether you run a small office, have several branches, or maintain a large enterprise network with many different platforms, CICS Clients enable the optimum solution to exploiting the potential of client-server systems to provide **integrated business solutions**.

CICS Clients:

- Enable existing CICS customers to move easily and inexpensively into client-server computing in a simple and low-risk way.
- Allow exploitation of existing and future workstation investments anywhere in an enterprise to gain access to CICS applications and data on all CICS platforms with integrity and security.
- Can access other CICS platforms directly, without a CICS server on the desktop.
- Protect customer investment in existing CICS applications designed for use with 3270 devices and allow those applications to interface with workstation facilities and productivity aids.
- Enable all benefits of new interfaces, such as GUI and multimedia, to be added to running applications without any change to the application.
- Enable seamless integration of desktop productivity applications (for example, spreadsheets) and enterprise applications and data on a CICS server.
- Interface industry devices (such as image scanners and barcode readers) conveniently.
- Enable local printers attached to desktop workstations to be used for printing output sent from CICS server applications.

The announcement of the CICS Clients is consistent with the IBM Open Blueprint, which is the market-leading approach for open, distributed computing. Since the Open Blueprint incorporates a range of standards, it offers the best assurance that businesses can build, run, and manage distributed applications in a diverse, multivendor environment.

This document is suitable for:

Customers	To visualize the enormous potential CICS Clients have to offer.
Sales representatives	To understand the flexibility of the CICS Clients.
Systems engineers	To help configure the different products.

Programmers	To try out the fully documented application sample programs.
Service engineers	To aid in problem determination.

How This Document Is Organized

The document is organized as follows:

❑ **Chapter 1, "IBM CICS Clients"**

This chapter positions the IBM CICS Clients within the CICS family and highlights the benefits and flexibility of using CICS Clients within various network configurations. A list of associated vendor tools and products is provided.

❑ **Chapter 2, "Sample Configurations: Overview"**

In this chapter we provide an overview of the configuration chapters that follow. Included is a table listing the configurations.

❑ **Chapter 3, "CICS/ESA • CICS Client for OS/2 Using CM/2"**

A working configuration showing a CICS Client for OS/2 connecting to a CICS/ESA V3.3 server over a token-ring. The client uses SNA supplied by Communications Manager/2.

❑ **Chapter 4, "CICS/ESA • Token-Ring • Client Using APPC NS/Windows"**

A working configuration showing a CICS Client for Windows connecting to a CICS/ESA V3.3 server over a token-ring. The client uses SNA supplied by APPC Networking Services for Windows.

❑ **Chapter 5, "CICS/ESA • NetWare for SAA Gateway • CICS Clients"**

Two working configurations showing a CICS Client for Windows and CICS Client for DOS connecting to a CICS mainframe through a Novell NetWare for SAA gateway.

❑ **Chapter 6, "CICS/VSE • SDLC • CICS Client for OS/2 Using CM/2"**

A working configuration showing a CICS Client for OS/2 connecting to a CICS/VSE V2.2 server over SDLC. The client uses SNA supplied by Communications Manager/2.

❑ **Chapter 7, "CICS/VSE • SDLC • Client Using APPC NS/Windows"**

A working configuration showing a CICS Client for Windows connecting to a CICS/VSE V2.2 server over SDLC. The client uses SNA supplied by APPC Networking Services for Windows.

How This Document Is Organized

❑ **Chapter 8, "CICS/VSE • Ethernet • Client Using APPC NS/Windows"**

A working configuration showing a CICS Client for Windows connecting to a CICS/VSE V2.2 server over Ethernet. The client uses SNA supplied by APPC Networking Services for Windows.

❑ **Chapter 9, "CICS/VSE • CM/2 APPN Gateway • APPC NS/Windows"**

A working configuration showing a CICS Client for Windows connecting to a CICS/VSE V2.2 server through a CM/2 APPN OS/2 gateway. For the CICS Client for Windows the SNA LU6.2 communication is supplied by APPC Networking Services for Windows.

❑ **Chapter 10, "CICS for OS/2 • CICS Client Using TCP/IP for OS/2"**

A working configuration showing a CICS Client for OS/2 connecting to a CICS for OS/2 server using IBM's TCP/IP for OS/2.

❑ **Chapter 11, "CICS for OS/2 • CICS Client for Macintosh • TCP/IP"**

A working configuration showing a CICS Client for Macintosh connecting to a CICS for OS/2 server. The client uses MacTCP.

❑ **Chapter 12, "CICS/6000 • CICS Client for OS/2 Using TCP/IP for OS/2"**

A working configuration showing a CICS Client for OS/2 connecting to a CICS for AIX server using TCP/IP.

❑ **Chapter 13, "CICS/6000 • Clients for DOS and Windows • TCP/IP for DOS"**

A working configuration showing a CICS Client for DOS/Windows connecting to a CICS for AIX server. The client uses IBM's TCP/IP for DOS.

❑ **Chapter 14, "CICS for Windows NT • PC/TCP • Clients Using TCP/IP"**

A working configuration showing a CICS Client for DOS/Windows connecting to a CICS for Windows NT server. The client uses PC/TCP from FTP Software for TCP/IP communication.

❑ **Chapter 15, "CICS for Window NT • LAN WorkPlace • TCP/IP"**

A working configuration showing a CICS Client for DOS/Windows connecting to a CICS for Windows NT server. The client uses Novell's LAN WorkPlace for TCP/IP communication.

❑ **Chapter 16, "CICS for OS/2 • CICS Client for OS/2 Using NetBIOS"**

A working configuration showing a CICS Client for OS/2 connecting to a CICS for OS/2 server using NetBIOS.

❏ **Chapter 17, "CICS for OS/2 • CICS Client for DOS/Windows • NetBIOS"**

A working configuration showing a CICS Client for DOS connecting to a CICS for OS/2 server using NetBIOS. This configuration also is suitable for a CICS Client for Windows.

❏ **Chapter 18, "CICS 3270 Client Printer Configurations"**

Three working configurations showing CICS Clients connecting to CICS servers. The second configuration uses the CICS for OS/2 user exit 21 (TCS Autoinstall).

❏ **Chapter 19, "External Call Interface"**

In this chapter we discuss the external call interface (ECI) and include a sample implementation.

❏ **Chapter 20, "External Presentation Interface"**

In this chapter we discuss the external programming interface (EPI) and include a sample implementation.

❏ **Chapter 21, "Problem Determination"**

In this chapter we discuss the tools available and sources of information for problem determination in a CICS Client environment.

❏ **Appendix A, "Hints and Tips"**

This appendix contains useful hints and tips to aid programmers, systems engineers, and service engineers. It covers basic CICS Client commands, CM/2 and APPC NS/Windows operations, plus ASCII to EBCDIC data conversion for ECI applications.

❏ **Appendix B, "Frequently Asked Questions"**

In this appendix we answer some of the more frequently asked questions about installing and customizing a CICS Client and a CICS Server environment.

❏ **Appendix C, "Common Problems: Symptoms and Solutions"**

In this appendix we discuss some common network configuration problems and suggest solutions to help resolve them.

❏ **Appendix D, "Programming Languages and Compilers"**

This appendix lists the compilers and languages that can be used for ECI and EPI applications.

❏ **Appendix E, "Sample ECI and EPI Source Code"**

This appendix provides the client and server source code used for the sample implementations, as discussed in Sample Implementation on page 277 and Sample Implementation on page 288.

❑ **Appendix F, "CM/2 .NDF and APPC NS/Windows NSD.INI Files"**

This appendix contains the CM/2 .NDF and APPC NS/Windows NSD.INI definition files used in the SNA sample configurations.

❑ **Appendix G, "IBM 3172 Customization"**

This appendix describes how to customize the IBM 3172 Interconnect Controller for an Ethernet adapter.

❑ **Appendix H, "Configuration Worksheets"**

To aid in configuring a network, in this appendix we provide a worksheet for each configuration described in this book.

Related Publications

The publications listed in this section are considered particularly suitable for a more detailed discussion of the topics covered in this document.

❑ *CICS Clients Administration, Version 1*, SC33-1436
❑ *CICS Family: Client/Server Programming*, SC33-1435
❑ *CICS Family: Interproduct Communication*, SC33-0824
❑ *CICS OS/2 V2 Problem Determination*, SC26-8135
❑ *CICS/ESA Facilities and Planning Guide*, SC33-0654
❑ *CICS/ESA Problem Determination Guide*, SC33-0678
❑ *OS/2 LAN Server: Local Area Network Support Program User's Guide, Version 3.0*, S96F-8436
❑ *LAN Technical Reference IEEE 802.2 and NetBIOS Application Program Interfaces*, SC30-3587
❑ *IBM 3172 Interconnect Controller Program Version 3.3 User's Guide*, SC30-3572
❑ R. Lamb, *Cooperative Processing Using CICS*. New York: McGraw-Hill, Inc. (1993)
❑ *AIX CICS/6000 Installation and Configuration: A Guide to Implementation*, GG24-4091

A complete list of International Technical Support Organization publications, with a brief description of each, may be found in:

International Technical Support Organization Bibliography of Redbooks, GG24-3070.

To get a catalog of ITSO technical publications (known as "redbooks"), VNET users may type:

```
TOOLS SENDTO WTSCPOK TOOLS REDBOOKS GET REDBOOKS CATALOG
```

―― **How to Order ITSO Technical Publications** ――――――――

IBM employees in the USA may order ITSO books and CD-ROMs using PUBORDER. Customers in the USA may order by calling 1-800-879-2755 or by faxing 1-800-284-4721. Visa and Master Card are accepted. Outside the USA, customers should contact their local IBM office.

Customers may order hardcopy ITSO books individually or in customized sets, called GBOFs, which relate to specific functions of interest. IBM employees and customers may also order ITSO books in online format on CD-ROM collections, which contain books on a variety of products.

International Technical Support Organization on the World Wide Web

Internet users may find additional material about new redbooks on the ITSO World Wide Web homepage. Point your web browser to the following page:

http://www.redbooks.ibm.com/redbooks

IBM internal users may also download redbooks or scan through redbook abstracts. Point your web browser to the internal IBM Redbooks homepage:

http://w3.itsc.pok.ibm.com/redbooks/redbooks.html

International Technical Support Organization on the Internet

If you do not have World Wide Web access, you can obtain the list of all current redbooks through the Internet by anonymous FTP to:

ftp.almaden.ibm.com
cd /redbooks
get itsopub.txt

All users of ITSO publications are encouraged to provide feedback to improve quality over time. Send questions about and feedback on redbooks to:

- REDBOOK at WTSCPOK
- REDBOOK@VNET.IBM.COM
- USIB5FWN at IBMMAIL

About the Authors

Guido De Simoni, from IBM Italy, works at the IBM International Technical Support Organization in San Jose, California. You can reach him by e-mail at gds@vnet.ibm.com.

Alan Hollingshead works in Hursley, United Kingdom, at the IBM Laboratories. His e-mail address is hollingshead@vnet.ibm.com.

Walter Krischker is a freelance consultant in Stuttgart, Germany. His e-mail address is walter.krischker@t-online.de.

Tie Ping Liu works for IBM China in Bejing. You can send him e-mail at liutp@vnet.ibm.com.

Acknowledgments

This book would not have been possible without the help of the following people who contributed information, resources, and technical advice: Rob Lamb, Tim Baldwin and Paul Warren, IBM Hursley Laboratories, and Hugh Smith, IBM ITSO San Jose. Thanks to Carlos Bittrich, IBM Peru, and Werner Stieber, IBM Germany for the significant contribution to VSE related chapters.

Special thanks to everyone at the ITSO San Jose Center, in particular Elsa Barron, Mary Comianos, and Alan Tippett for their continuous support and to Andi Bitterer for driving me to a *real book*. Thanks also to Jim McNair, Bob Yelavich, IBM United States, and John Wade, IBM United Kingdom for reviewing the first draft document, and to Maggie Cutler for the timely editing.

1

IBM CICS Clients

This chapter covers the following topics:
- "CICS: The Application Server" on page 2
- "CICS Clients within the CICS Family" on page 7
- Communications and Functions between CICS Clients and CICS Servers (Table 1 on page 8)
- "Architecture of the CICS Clients" on page 10
- "Benefits of Using IBM CICS Clients" on page 13
- "Network Configurations" on page 16
- "Performance" on page 22
- "Migration from CICS OS/2 Distributed Feature Clients" on page 22
- "Associated Tools and Products" on page 23
- "Additional Information" on page 24

Customer Information Control System (CICS) is IBM's industry-leading transaction processing software. It provides a high-performance software environment in which to run business applications, and helps solve the portability, interoperability, and scalability issues customers face when deploying applications across a multivendor network.

IBM CICS Clients V1.0 software runs on OS/2, Windows, DOS, and Macintosh. The CICS Clients can directly access all CICS software servers, which scale from workstations to mainframe systems, and support a variety of local area network (LAN) environments including OS/2, NetWare, AppleTalk, and TokenTalk.

Before we describe the IBM CICS Clients in detail (see "CICS Clients within the CICS Family" on page 7), we discuss how the CICS Clients complement the CICS servers for an ideal application server environment that provides excellent integrity and performance suitable for all businesses.

CICS: The Application Server

CICS is a family of licensed programs providing services for transaction processing on both IBM and non-IBM systems. CICS provides a rich set of easy-to-use communication facilities, as well as transaction processing services on platforms ranging from a stand-alone workstation to the largest ESA/390 processors.

IBM CICS Clients are members of the CICS family and provide CICS workstation-based client support to CICS servers. IBM CICS Clients support is provided for DOS, OS/2, Macintosh, and Windows.

There are more than 50,000 CICS licenses worldwide, and an estimated 300,000 programmers have CICS skills. Vendor applications use CICS across multiple platforms. CICS is used by 90 percent of Fortune 500 companies and in more than 90 countries.

High-Level Functions for Application Use

CICS has a rich and widely used application programming interface (API). The CICS API provides business applications with easy access to many application functions (such as security, scheduling, screen access, and communications handling), while adding value to the overall applications through applicationwide functions (such as integrity, reliability, recovery, and performance). Use of the API conceals from the application many of the complexities and dependencies of underlying functions, which in turn allows application developers to be more productive.

CICS: The Application Server

These high-level functions are provided across the CICS family, encompassing IBM and non-IBM platforms. More importantly, the applications are easily portable across these platforms, providing a broad level of investment protection and flexibility of platform, database, and communications software choice.

Client-Server Models

Client-server computing is a form of distributed processing where a client requests tasks to be fulfilled by a server. The client and server can remain transparent to each other in terms of location and platform, yet they interact seamlessly.

Client-server usage today is primarily limited to departmental productivity applications spread across relatively small numbers of concurrently active users. As client-server moves to the world of mainstream commercial application processing, there will be a need to support the local environments of escalating numbers of users across different departments with integrity, reliability, and performance. Such support requires a software environment for applications that is different from the departmental decision support implementations today.

Whatever software environment is chosen, it must have the flexibility to allow applications to grow with the business, across available platforms and technologies. It must enable businesses to gain the new features they need in their applications as productively and efficiently as possible, while continuing to provide high levels of quality of service.

Client-server can be implemented in a number of different models. Industry experts categorize these models in anywhere from three to seven different groups. However, the three most common are:

❑ Remote data access model

❑ Database server model

❑ Application server model

Remote Data Access Model

The remote data access model (see Figure 1 on page 4) is by far the most common today in departmental client-server computing. It consists of a LAN of end-user workstations running a variety of departmental support applications (for example, Lotus 1-2-3, Microsoft Word). A data server workstation on the LAN allows information to be stored in a place where other members of the department can share it. In the remote data access model, the application logic and screen handling are run in the end-user workstations, and data requests are routed to the data server.

CICS: The Application Server

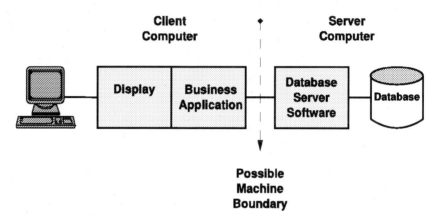

Figure 1. Remote Data Access Model

The remote data access model is by far the easiest to implement and understand, and has definite benefits when used for departmental support applications. However, if this model is used for mainstream commercial application processing (for example, mission-critical applications, large numbers of users), it breaks down. Network traffic becomes intense (as every request for data must flow around the LAN and back), and security and administration concerns become serious because the application resides in the end-user workstation.

Consider, for instance, an application on 1000 end-user workstations. If the application needs to be changed, how will it be updated on every workstation? And what if some workstations are mobile and hence not always connected to the LAN? What if the end user alters the application, either accidentally or maliciously? From a sociological perspective, because the application lives in the end-user workstation, most people consider their workstations on their desks as THEIR property, rather than the property of the business. They may have private software on their workstations, they may have made their own hardware modifications to memory and storage. In short, the end-user workstation cannot be regarded as a trusted environment and hence is not the place to put mission-critical application code.

Database Server Model

The database server model (see Figure 2 on page 5) addresses some of the drawbacks of the remote data access model, but it still has limitations in addressing the needs of commercial computing. The database server model allows for some of the business application to run in the database server workstation rather than in the end-user workstation. This approach ensures more efficient use of the network, because multiple data requests can be carried out before the system sends back an answer across the LAN to the end-user workstation, using, for example, such facilities as stored procedures and triggers.

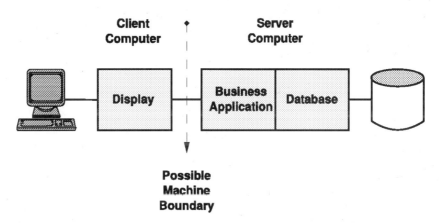

Figure 2. Database Server Model

One drawback of the database server model is that only the data portion of the application can be moved out of the end-user workstation, and even that is often impractical when more than one database type is used (for example, DB2 and Oracle). In addition, most of the stored procedure implementations do not work with other database managers (that is, they are proprietary), thus limiting considerably the flexibility of application implementation.

Even when a large portion of the application can be placed in the database server there can be additional problems. In a high-usage, high-load environment the database server is often a key performance throttle, and placing application code and the related processing in the same workstation as the database server simply increases the pressure on that workstation's performance.

Possibly the most critical drawback is that the database server model is quite naturally data-oriented. Because the application is in part running under control of the database resource manager, it is viewed from a data perspective. This lack of an application-centric view can become a major inhibitor to business growth. In essence, there is no software component to provide services across the application and the various resources it uses, no coordination of changes to different resource types, and no application level statistics.

Application Server Model

The application server model (see Figure 3 on page 6) is the client-server approach best suited to running mainstream commercial applications. With this model, although the screen handling is run from the end-user workstation, the business application is run in an application server workstation on the LAN. The application is accessed through a thin layer of client code in the end-user workstation.

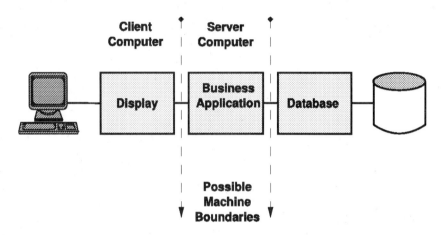

Figure 3. Application Server Model

In the application server model the business application runs in an application-oriented environment (such as CICS) on a server on the LAN and is therefore not present in the end-user workstation. This approach ensures that the business application is in a trusted environment, well away from the end-user workstation. Resources used by the business application are accessed through the application environment software (CICS). Thus, the various application services that CICS provides are available across the entire application encompassing all of the various resources being used. If the application, for example, changes a database and a flat file in the same business step, the application environment can ensure that the changes are kept in synch, and integrity is thus maintained across these different resource types.

As load increases, the application server model can allow the setting up of multiple application servers on the LAN, and those servers also can provide gateways to other connected systems, for example, LANs or mainframes.

Summary

The application server model offers the maximum flexibility and the best level of "future proofing," while providing an environment with excellent integrity and performance characteristics. CICS, the application server that has handled mainstream commercial computing applications for many of the big businesses in the world for many years, is the only choice!

CICS Clients within the CICS Family

The IBM CICS Clients family comprises workstation products that communicate with the entire family of CICS application servers. CICS Clients therefore bring the advantages of client-server operation to transaction processing.

The IBM CICS Clients V1.0 family comprises:

- IBM CICS Client for DOS
- IBM CICS Client for OS/2
- IBM CICS Client for Windows
- IBM CICS Client for Macintosh

The CICS Clients can communicate with the following CICS server products:

- CICS for OS/2 V2.0.1 and higher
- CICS for Windows NT V2
- CICS on Open Systems, that is:
  - CICS/6000
  - CICS for HP/9000
  - CICS for DEC OSF/1 AXP
- CICS/400 V3.1
- CICS/ESA V4.1 and higher
- CICS/ESA V3.3
- CICS/MVS V2.1.2
- CICS/VSE V2.2 and higher

IBM CICS Clients V1.0 supports three communication protocols:

NetBIOS Network Basic Input/Output System (NetBIOS) is a communication interface for the IBM LAN and Novell NetWare LAN environments. NetBIOS is used for connections between CICS Clients and CICS for OS/2 and CICS for Windows NT servers.

Note: CICS Client for Macintosh does not support the use of NetBIOS.

TCP/IP   Transmission Control Protocol/Internet Protocol (TCP/IP) originated from the UNIX operating system, but is now supported by a magnitude of operating systems including AIX, OS/2, VM, MVS, DOS, and Apple Macintosh. TCP/IP is used for connections between CICS Clients and CICS for OS/2, CICS for Windows NT, and CICS on Open Systems.

APPC   Advanced-Program-to-Program Communication (APPC) is a commonly used term for the verbs and services included in the Systems Network Architecture (SNA) Logical Unit type 6.2 (LU6.2). An LU6.2 communication session provides device-independent application-to-application communication. APPC is used for connections between CICS Clients and mainframe CICS servers as well as CICS/400.

Table 1 shows the protocols that can be used for each client to communicate with each server and the functions supported. For each client, one or more communication software products may provide support for a protocol. You therefore can use the products best suited to your network environment. Although all CICS Clients share the same functional qualities, some of the servers have limited support. The ECI (external call interface), EPI (external presentation interface), and Autoinstall columns show the functions that each CICS server supports.

Table 1. (Part 1 of 2) Communications and Functions between CICS Clients and CICS Servers

Server	Client	NetBIOS	TCP/IP	APPC	ECI	EPI	Auto-install
CICS for OS/2 V2+	DOS	✧	✧	—	✧	✧	✧
	Windows	✧	✧	—	✧	✧	✧
	OS/2	✧	✧	—	✧	✧	✧
	Macintosh	—	✧	—	✧	✧	✧
CICS for Windows NT V2	DOS	✧	✧	—	✧	✧	✧
	Windows	✧	✧	—	✧	✧	✧
	OS/2	✧	✧	—	✧	✧	✧
	Macintosh	—	✧	—	✧	✧	✧
CICS on Open Systems	DOS	—	✧	—	✧	✧	✧
	Windows	—	✧	—	✧	✧	✧
	OS/2	—	✧	—	✧	✧	✧
	Macintosh	—	✧	—	✧	✧	✧
CICS/400 V3.1	DOS	—	—	✧	✧	✧	✧
	Windows	—	—	✧	✧	✧	✧
	OS/2	—	—	✧	✧	✧	✧
	Macintosh	—	—	✧	✧	✧	✧

CICS Clients within the CICS Family

Table 1. (Part 2 of 2) Communications and Functions between CICS Clients and CICS Servers

Server	Client	NetBIOS	TCP/IP	APPC	ECI	EPI	Auto-install
CICS/ESA V4.1+	DOS	—	—	✧	✧	✧	✧
	Windows	—	—	✧	✧	✧	✧
	OS/2	—	—	✧	✧	✧	✧
	Macintosh	—	—	✧	✧	✧	✧
CICS/ESA V3.3	DOS	—	—	✧	✧	—	✧
	Windows	—	—	✧	✧	—	✧
	OS/2	—	—	✧	✧	—	✧
	Macintosh	—	—	✧	✧	—	✧
CICS/MVS V2.1.2	DOS	—	—	✧	✧	—	✧
	Windows	—	—	✧	✧	—	✧
	OS/2	—	—	✧	✧	—	✧
	Macintosh	—	—	✧	✧	—	✧
CICS/VSE V2.2+	DOS	—	—	✧	✧	—	✧
	Windows	—	—	✧	✧	—	✧
	OS/2	—	—	✧	✧	—	✧
	Macintosh	—	—	✧	✧	—	✧

Key:

✧ = supported

— = not supported

Notes:

- EPI always incorporates CICS 3270 terminal emulation and CICS 3270 client printer support.
- Autoinstall means you do not need to predefine the CICS Client to the CICS server; that is, control table definitions are automatically created for the client at the CICS server.
- TCP/IP communication with CICS for OS/2 requires CICS for OS/2 V2.0.1 or later.

Architecture of the CICS Clients

The architecture is the same across all CICS Clients (see Figure 4).

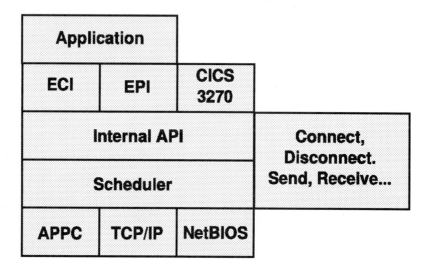

Figure 4. CICS Client Architecture

Application Your user application, for example, a spreadsheet. For the IBM CICS Clients V1.0, your **ECI** or **EPI** application can be written using the C, COBOL (not CICS Client for Macintosh), or PL/I (CICS Client for OS/2 only) programming languages.

CICS 3270 Support for your CICS 3270 terminal and printer emulators (see "CICS 3270 Terminal Emulator" on page 12 for more information).

Internal API CICS Client internal API for controlling the client functions.

Scheduler Scheduling of client tasks.

APPC, TCP/IP, NetBIOS Communication protocol code.

Connect, Disconnect Connection and disconnection of clients and client terminals.

Send, Receive	Sending and receiving of data to and from the server.

CICS External Call Interface

The CICS ECI allows CICS applications to be designed with the business logic on the CICS server and the presentation logic on the workstation-based CICS Clients.

The ECI is a remote call from a user's application on the client workstation to a CICS program on a server. ECI enables a non-CICS client application to call a CICS application, synchronously or asynchronously, as a subroutine. The client application communicates with the CICS server program using the CICS COMMAREA.

At the CICS server, the ECI looks like a distributed program link (DPL) from a partner CICS system.

CICS Clients, with the exception of CICS Client for DOS, can support an unlimited number of outstanding concurrent ECI calls to a CICS server, with no restrictions on communication protocols, functions, or whether the calls are to the same or different CICS system. In the case of CICS Client for DOS, there is a limit of 16 concurrent calls.

Using ECI, any program on the workstation can access facilities on any CICS server. ECI provides maximum flexibility for the client-server environment because you can change the client without affecting the server and vice versa.

See Chapter 19, "External Call Interface," on page 257 for more information on the ECI.

CICS External Presentation Interface

The CICS EPI allows existing CICS applications to exploit graphical user interfaces (GUIs) on workstation-based CICS clients without the need to change CICS applications.

The EPI allows a GUI front end to be added to an existing CICS application without changing the CICS application. The CICS server application sends and receives 3270 datastreams (for example, a CICS basic mapping support (BMS) transaction) to and from the client application as though it were conversing with a 3270 terminal. The client application captures this data and processes it as desired, usually displaying the data with a non-3270 presentation product such as a GUI.

Applications written with a GUI front end have proven to be easy for end users to work with and often simplify the task of learning a new application because the interface is the same no matter which facilities the application uses.

For all CICS Clients there may be up to 15 concurrent EPI calls.

See Chapter 20, "External Presentation Interface," on page 283 for more information on the EPI.

Note: Some servers do not support the EPI (see Table 1 on page 8).

CICS 3270 Terminal Emulator

CICS 3270 terminal emulator support enables a client workstation to function as a 3270 display for CICS applications, without the requirement for a separate 3270 emulator product. This support provides flexible client workstation capabilities without the need for extensive software outlay. Because each client (except CICS Client for DOS) can run multiple CICS 3270 emulation sessions, the hardware required is reduced, and end users can see multiple 3270 emulator sessions from one or more servers, all on one workstation.

By means of mapping files, you can customize the client emulator's screen color attributes and keyboard settings. Thus, users can tailor their workstations to their own preferences, or, for example, to comply with company-standard keyboard layouts.

For the CICS servers that support terminal emulation (see Table 1 on page 8) the terminals are autoinstalled; that is, you do not have to predefine the terminals to the CICS server.

CICS 3270 Client Printer Support

Client printer support is the ability to define a printer terminal on the client workstation. This support enables CICS applications running on the server to direct output to the client-attached printer.

You can direct the output to a physical printer attached, for example, to the LPT1 port, or you can specify a command to process the data into a format suitable for special-purpose printers.

CICS 3270 client printer support uses CICS 3270 emulation functions. See Table 1 on page 8 for CICS servers that currently support CICS 3270 emulation and hence CICS 3270 client printer support.

Client Control

CICS Clients provide commands and icons to:

❏ **Control the client process**
- Start or stop the client process
- Turn the client trace on or off
- Specify the client initialization file to be used
- Set up security by specifying userids and passwords for a CICS server
- List connected servers
- Enable and disable the display of messages

❏ **Control terminal emulation**
- Start or stop the terminal emulator
- Specify the initial transaction
- Define the terminal characteristics
- Specify the name of the keyboard and screen color mapping files
- Define the command used to process print requests
- Specify the name of a file used for appending print requests

❏ **Control client printer operation**
- Start or stop the client printer emulator
- Specify the initial transaction to be run against the client printer
- Define the printer terminal characteristics
- Define the command used to process print requests
- Specify the name of a file used for appending print requests

Appendix A, "Hints and Tips," on page 315 contains some basic commands for controlling CICS Clients. You can find full details on how to control your CICS Clients in the *CICS Clients: Administration* manual, which is shipped with the product but can also be ordered separately.

Benefits of Using IBM CICS Clients

CICS Clients provide you with many benefits. Here are some of the main benefits:

Easy migration CICS Clients enable existing CICS users to move easily and inexpensively into client-server computing in a low-risk way.

Benefits of Using IBM CICS Clients

Inexpensive hardware You can use existing low-function workstation hardware for your CICS Clients to gain access to CICS applications and data on all CICS platforms.

Protected investment CICS Clients protect your investment in existing CICS applications designed for use with 3270 devices by enabling the EPI to allow these applications to interface with workstation facilities and productivity aids.

Exploit GUIs With the use of CICS Clients, CICS applications can be optimized by locating the business logic on the server and the presentation logic on the client, exploiting the usability and productivity of GUIs.

Any-to-any connection Any CICS Client can connect to any CICS server.

Concurrent server access A CICS Client can concurrently access multiple CICS applications on multiple servers (see Figure 11 on page 21). The power of your client applications is considerably enhanced by their ability to access applications and databases on many servers at the same time. This ability allows CICS users on every platform to write new applications that use the client-server application server model.

Interface to non-terminal devices CICS Clients with the ECI offer a convenient method of interfacing a non-terminal device, for example, barcode readers and image scanners, with CICS.

Automatic data exchange CICS Clients provide a mechanism to enable automatic data exchange between desktop applications (for example, a spreadsheet) and data in a CICS server.

Platform advantages	Workstation clients provide you with the advantages of the platform on which they run, development tools, modern workstation interfaces (GUI, multimedia), and low cost.
Autoinstall	CICS servers can autoinstall client connections and terminals. This capability greatly facilitates your systems management (see Table 1 on page 8).
Novell networks	In addition to IBM networks, you can use networks running Novell Netware for both APPC- and NetBIOS-attached clients.
Local printers	You can use local printers attached to desktop workstations to print output sent from CICS server applications.
Security	CICS Clients provide userid and password security features.
NLS	With national language support (NLS), your end users can receive CICS Client messages in their native language. IBM CICS Clients V1.0 currently provide NLS in U.S. English, French, German, Italian, Spanish, Japanese, and simplified Chinese. (CICS Client for Macintosh does not support Japanese or simplified Chinese.)
Workstation customization	You can customize the colors of your CICS Client terminal emulator and remap your keyboard layout.
Distribution of clients	On a distributed network you can install multiple copies of the CICS Client for OS/2 and CICS Client for Windows onto many workstations using a distributed management product, for example, IBM's NetView Distribution Manager (NetView DM).

Network Configurations

CICS Clients can access CICS servers in your network in numerous ways. In this section we discuss some of these network configurations.

For a list of working examples for some of the sample configurations discussed below, see Chapter 2, "Sample Configurations: Overview," on page 25.

NetBIOS

CICS Client for DOS, CICS Client for OS/2, and CICS Client for Windows on a LAN can connect to CICS for OS/2 and CICS for Windows NT servers through NetBIOS. Figure 5 shows the CICS Clients communicating with a CICS for OS/2 server through NetBIOS.

NetBIOS Configuration

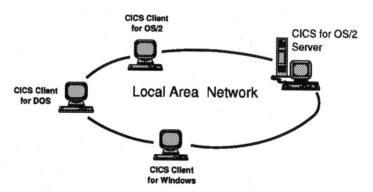

Figure 5. CICS Clients on a LAN Communicating over NetBIOS

The LAN shown in Figure 5 could be either an IBM LAN or a Novell NetWare LAN. The CICS Clients can communicate with the CICS for OS/2 server using IBM's NetBIOS or Novell's emulation of NetBIOS over the Internet Packet Exchange (IPX) protocol. See the *CICS Clients: Administration* manual for more information.

TCP/IP

Using TCP/IP, all clients on a LAN can connect to the following servers:

❑ CICS for OS/2

Network Configurations

- CICS for Windows NT
- CICS on Open Systems.

Figure 6 shows the CICS Clients communicating with a CICS/6000 server through TCP/IP.

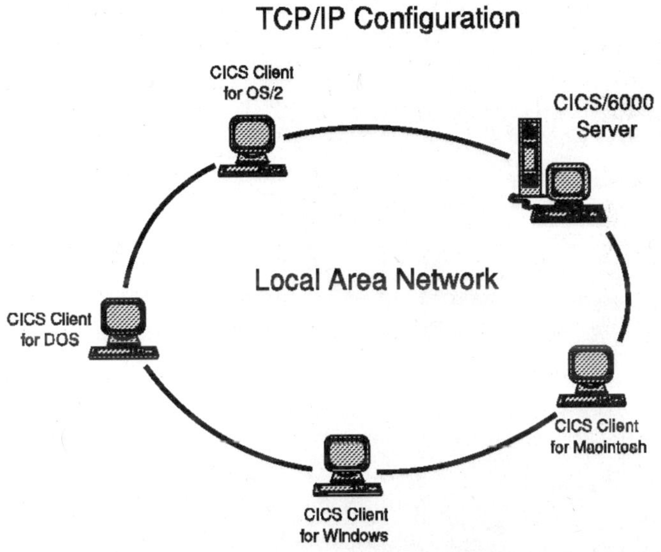

TCP/IP Configuration

Figure 6. CICS Clients on a LAN Communicating over TCP/IP

APPC

Using APPC, all clients can connect to the following servers:
- CICS/ESA V4.1 or later
- CICS/ESA V3.3
- CICS/MVS V2.1.2
- CICS/VSE V2.2 or later
- CICS/400 V3.1

This communication is commonly achieved through a LAN and a workstation acting as a SNA gateway. However, for the CICS Client for OS/2 and CICS Client for Windows it is also possible to communicate directly with a CICS mainframe or CICS/400 server without the need for a gateway workstation (see Figure 7 on page 18). Examples include CM/2 for the CICS Client for OS/2, and IBM APPC Networking Services for Windows for the CICS Client for Windows.

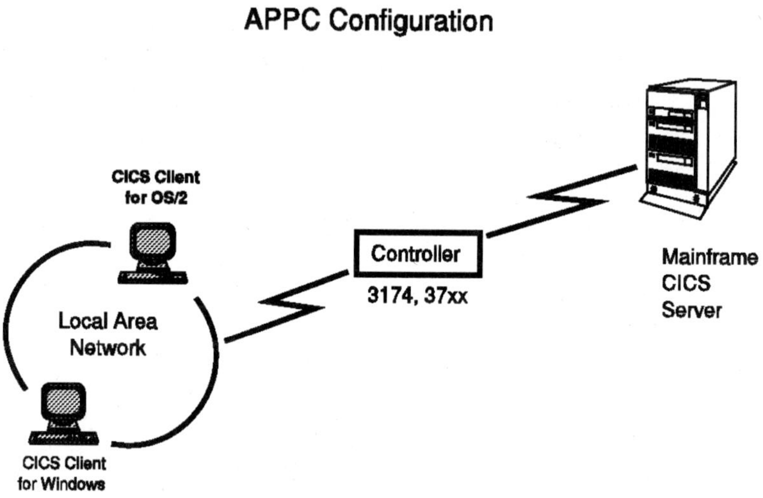

APPC Configuration

Figure 7. CICS Clients Communicating over APPC

Gateways for APPC Communications

CICS Clients communicate with mainframe CICS application servers using APPC, usually through a LAN and an SNA gateway.

A gateway is a device that connects two, possibly dissimilar, LANs or a LAN to a wide area network (WAN), midrange computer, or mainframe computer. A gateway device has its own processor and memory, and can perform protocol conversion.

The physical links from a gateway to CICS server machines can be made in a variety of ways, such as using token-ring, SDLC, or coaxial connections. For example, a gateway workstation on a LAN can be connected directly by a token-ring cable to an IBM 3745 controller, the front-end processor for a mainframe.

One of the main advantages of using a SNA gateway workstation attached to a mainframe CICS or CICS/400 machine is that it handles multiple communication sessions simultaneously. Therefore, a separate connection is not required for each CICS Client workstation.

SNA gateway software is required in the gateway workstation to provide gateway server functions to the clients on the LAN. Examples of this software include:

Communications Manager/2 for CICS Client for OS/2 and CICS Client for Windows

Novell NetWare for SAA for CICS Client for DOS and CICS Client for Windows

SNA•ps for CICS Client for Macintosh

SNA Gateway Configurations

Figure 8 shows an example of using Communications Manager/2 (CM/2) to provide gateway server functions between the CICS Clients on an IBM LAN and the mainframe CICS server.

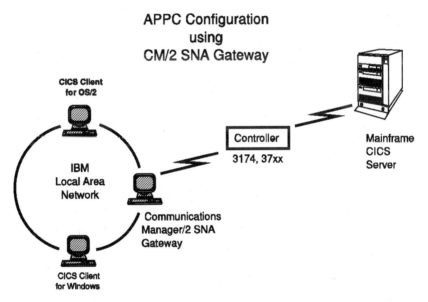

Figure 8. CICS Clients Communicating over APPC Using a CM/2 Gateway

Figure 9 on page 20 shows an example of using Novell's NetWare for SAA to provide gateway server functions between the CICS Clients on a NetWare LAN and the mainframe CICS server.

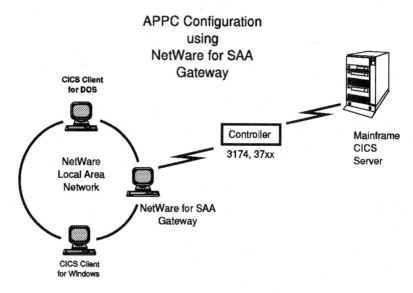

Figure 9. CICS Clients Communicating over APPC Using a NetWare for SAA Gateway

Figure 10 shows an example of using Apple Computer Inc.'s SNA•ps to provide gateway server functions between the CICS Clients on an AppleTalk LAN and the mainframe CICS server. Although this example shows an AppleTalk LAN, you can use a TokenTalk LAN instead.

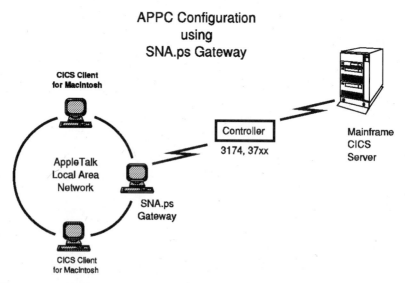

Figure 10. CICS Clients Communicating over APPC Using a SNAœps Gateway

Network Configurations

Multiple Protocol Configurations

Such is the flexibility of the CICS Clients that they can communicate with multiple servers simultaneously using the same or different communication protocols.

Figure 11 shows a CICS Client for OS/2 communicating with a CICS/6000 server using TCP/IP, a CICS for OS/2 server using NetBIOS, and a CICS mainframe using APPC, simultaneously.

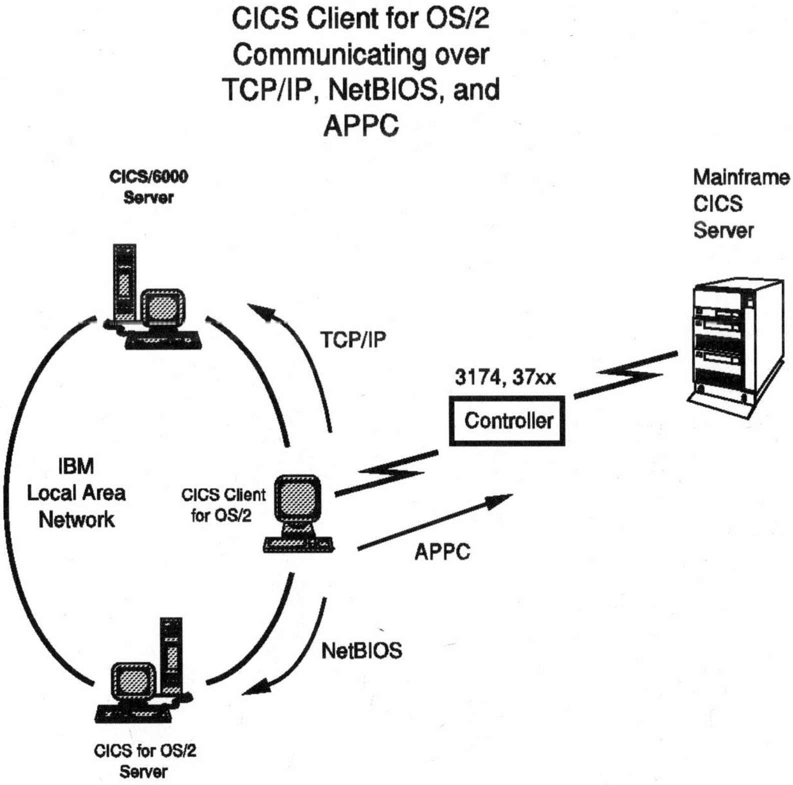

**CICS Client for OS/2
Communicating over
TCP/IP, NetBIOS, and
APPC**

Figure 11. CICS Client for OS/2 Communicating over NetBIOS, TCP/IP, and APPC

Mobile Communications

CICS Clients can communicate using mobile (also known as wireless) communications in the same way as a CICS for OS/2 server (see Figure 12 on page 22). This support uses either LAN Distance Remote for OS/2 or LAN Distance Remote for Windows. In addition, the LAN Distance Connection Server product is required on the gateway machine on the token-ring. The connection from the workstation is by modem, and the connection to the server is also by modem. The connection between the two modems can be either a cellular radio or a telephone connection.

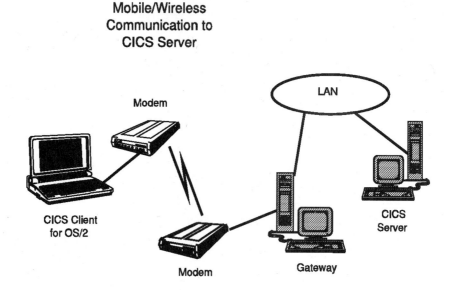

Figure 12. CICS Clients Using Mobile Communication to CICS Server

Performance

The performance of a CICS Client communicating with a CICS server is dependent on your CICS server and the type of communication protocol you are using.

By using ECI on the client workstation for presentation logic, you offload work from the server, thus increasing server performance.

With the EPI you can have 16 concurrent logical terminals on one client workstation, thus saving 15 physical 3270 terminals.

Migration from CICS OS/2 Distributed Feature Clients

The distributed feature clients, first shipped with CICS OS/2 V2.0, do not incorporate the functional enhancements of the CICS Clients family. Although they connect to the CICS for OS/2 V2.0.1 server using

NetBIOS support, they do not contain the TCP/IP or APPC support required to connect to other servers. For TCP/IP and APPC support you must have the IBM CICS Clients.

To aid migration to the CICS Clients you can use your CICS OS/2 distributed client FAARQ.INI initialization file for IBM CICS Clients connecting to the CICS for OS/2 server using NetBIOS. For more information, see the
CICS Clients: Administration manual.

Associated Tools and Products

An increasing number of workstation-based application development tools and products can be used with the CICS Clients. The list below is current as of publishing time, but for up-to-date information please contact your IBM representative.

The CICS ECI and/or EPI is supported by:

Vendor	*Product*
IBM	VisualAge
IBM	VisualGen
IBM	COBOL VisualSet for OS/2 (planned)
Digitalk	PARTS Wrapper for CICS
Lotus	Lotus Notes
KASE Systems	KASE:VIP (formerly known as Kaseworks)
Sterling Software	Key/Construction Workstation (formerly known as KnowledgeWare's ADW/Construction Workstation)
Micro Focus	COBOL Workbench CICS OS/2 Option
Micro Focus	Dialog System Professional
Network Software Associates	Visual Basic Connection for CICS
Attachmate	EXTRA! for Windows
Df Systems	CICS NEXUS

ECsoft Synapse ECvip

Intelligent Environments Europe Application Manager V4.3

Tangent DCI/PowerCICS.

Additional Information

To help evaluate the IBM CICS Clients for your own needs, see:

- *CICS Clients Administration*. The book is shipped with the product, but you also can order it separately.
- *CICS Family: Client/Server Programming*. This book accompanies all CICS server and client products.
- *Interproduct Communication*. This book describes communication among the CICS products.

2 Sample Configurations: Overview

This chapter contains the following sample configurations:
- SNA
- TCP/IP
- NetBIOS
- Printer

Each configuration contains the following information:

Software checklist Checklists for software required on both client and server machines and on gateway workstations where used.

Definitions checklist	Tables of definitions for each product required in the sample configuration. A reference key is assigned to each definition that requires a matching value in at least one other product.

Matching definitions	Table of definitions that must be the same across the different products within the sample configuration.

Sample definitions	All required definitions, as listed in the definitions checklist, are shown. For some products, detailed step-by-step examples show how to configure the definitions.

Testing your configuration	Some recommendations on how to test the different components of your configuration.

Hints and Tips provides useful information related to various products.

SNA Configurations

Table 2 lists the sample SNA configurations. The network used varies between token-ring, SDLC, and Ethernet.

Table 2. SNA Configurations

CICS Server	Product	Client	Network	Gateway	Page
CICS/ESA V3.3	VTAM CM/2 V1.1	OS/2	Token-ring	-	29
CICS/ESA V3.3	VTAM APPC NS/Windows V1.0	Windows	Token-ring	-	49
CICS/ESA V3.3	VTAM	DOS	Token-ring	NetWare for SAA	65
CICS/ESA V3.3	VTAM	Windows	Token-ring	NetWare for SAA	65
CICS/VSE V2.2	VTAM CM/2	OS/2	SDLC	-	77
CICS/VSE V2.2	VTAM APPC NS/Windows V1.0	Windows	SDLC	-	95
CICS/VSE V2.2	VTAM APPC NS/Windows V1.0	Windows	Ethernet	-	111
CICS/VSE V2.2	VTAM APPC NS/Windows V1.0 CM/2 (for Gateway)	Windows	SDLC	CM/2 APPN OS/2	131

TCP/IP Configurations

Table 3 lists the sample TCP/IP configurations. Many of the TCP/IP products on the client workstation are interchangeable.

Table 3. (Part 1 of 2) TCP/IP Configurations

Server	Product	Client	Network	Page
CICS for OS/2 V2.0.1	TCP/IP for OS/2 V2.0	OS/2	Token-ring	153
CICS for OS/2 V2.0.1	TCP/IP for OS/2 V2.0 MacTCP V2.0.4	Macintosh	Token-ring	165
CICS/6000 V1.2	TCP/IP for AIX/6000 TCP/IP for OS/2 V2.0	OS/2	Token-ring	179
CICS/6000 V1.2	TCP/IP for AIX/6000 TCP/IP for DOS V2.1.1	DOS	Token-ring	191
CICS/6000 V1.2	TCP/IP for AIX/6000 TCP/IP for DOS V2.1.1	Windows	Token-ring	191

Table 3. (Part 2 of 2) TCP/IP Configurations

Server	Product	Client	Network	Page
CICS for Windows NT V2	TCP/IP for Windows NT PC/TCP V3.0 from FTP Software	DOS	Token-ring	205
CICS for Windows NT V2	TCP/IP for Windows NT PC/TCP V3.0 from FTP Software	Windows	Token-ring	205
CICS for Windows NT V2	TCP/IP for Windows NT Novell's LAN Workplace	DOS	Token-ring	215
CICS for Windows NT V2	TCP/IP for Windows NT Novell's LAN Workplace	Windows	Token-ring	215

NetBIOS Configurations

Table 4 lists the sample NetBIOS configurations.

Table 4. NetBIOS Configurations

Server	Product	Client	Network	Page
CICS for OS/2 V2.0.1	NTS/2	OS/2	Token-ring	225
CICS for OS/2 V2.0.1	NTS/2 LAN Support Program	DOS	Token-ring	233
CICS for OS/2 V2.0.1	NTS/2 LAN Support Program	Windows	Token-ring	233

Printer Configurations

Table 5 lists the sample printer configurations.

Table 5. Printer Configurations

Server	Product	Client	Network	Page
CICS for OS/2 V2.0.1	NTS/2	OS/2	Token-ring	245
CICS/6000 V1.2	NTS/2	OS/2	Token-ring	245

3

CICS/ESA • CICS Client for OS/2 Using CM/2

― This chapter covers the following topics: ―
- "Software Checklist" on page 30
- "Definitions Checklist" on page 31
- "Matching Definitions" on page 32
- "Sample Definitions" on page 32
  - ➢ VTAM
  - ➢ CICS/ESA
  - ➢ CM/2
    (detailed step-by-step example)
  - ➢ IBM CICS Client for OS/2
- "Testing Your Configuration" on page 47

This sample configuration (see Figure 13 on page 30) consists of an IBM CICS Client for OS/2 V1.0[1] connecting to a CICS mainframe through SNA LU6.2 (APPC) communication, provided by CM/2 on the client workstation and VTAM on the mainframe server.

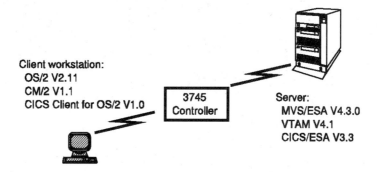

Figure 13. SNA Configuration Using CM/2

Although the sample configuration uses CICS/ESA V3.3 as the mainframe server, you could also use CICS/MVS V2.1.2, CICS/ESA V4.1 (or later), or CICS/VSE V2.2 (or later).

We used a token-ring network for this configuration, but you can use other physical links, for example, SDLC or coaxial connections.

Software Checklist

The levels of software used in the sample configuration are not necessarily the latest levels available. You should check the relevant products for levels of compatible software.

The software required on the server is:

- ❑ MVS/ESA operating system V4.3.0
- ❑ VTAM V4.1
- ❑ CICS/ESA V3.3

The software required on the client workstation is:

- ❑ OS/2 V2.11 operating system
- ❑ CM/2 V1.1
- ❑ IBM CICS Client for OS/2 V1.0

---

[1] Hereafter referred to as CICS Client for OS/2.

Definitions Checklist

Before you configure the products, we recommend that you acquire definitions for the parameters listed below. Reference keys are assigned to definitions that must contain the same value in more than one product. For example, XID has the reference key **1**. These reference keys are used in later sections of this chapter.

- VTAM
    - XID (IDBLK+IDNUM) **1**
    - PU
    - LU **2**
    - Logmode **3**
    - APPL **4**
    - NETID **5**
- CICS/ESA
    - ISC SIT override
    - DFHISC group
    - Applid **4**
    - Netname in the LU6.2 connection definition **2**
    - Modename in the LU6.2 sessions definition **3**
- CM/2
    - Network ID **5**
    - Local node name
    - Local node ID **1**
    - LAN Destination Address
    - Local LU **2**
    - Partner LU **4**
    - Mode name **3**
    - Transaction program (CRSR)
    - CNOS (session establishment, optional)
- Workstation definitions. These entries are defined in the CICSCLI.INI initialization file, generally found in the \CICSCLI\BIN subdirectory.
    - Server
    - Network.Netname **5**.**4**
    - Protocol
    - LocalLUName **2**

➢ Modename **3**
➢ Driver
➢ DriverName

Matching Definitions

In the sample configuration a number of definitions must match. Table 6 shows the definitions that must be the same. The last column (Example) shows the values we used in our configuration (see "Sample Definitions" on page 32).

Table 6. Matching Definitions: CICS/ESA-CICS Client for OS/2 Using CM/2

	VTAM	CICS/ESA V3.3	CM/2	CICSCLI.INI	Example
1	XID	-	Local node ID	-	05DA2072
2	LU	Netname	Local LU	LocalLUName	SJA2072I
3	Logmode	Modename	Mode name	Modename	LU62APPB
4	APPL	Applid	Partner LU	Netname	SCMCICSA
5	NETID	-	Network ID	Network	USIBMSC

Sample Definitions

This section presents examples of each of the definitions mentioned in "Definitions Checklist" on page 31. The values highlighted in the figures refer to the Example column of Table 6.

VTAM

In this section we present the VTAM definitions for the server.

XID, PU, and LU

Figure 14 on page 33 shows the VTAM XID **1**, PU, and LU **2** definitions we used in the sample configuration.

```
*     ...
*
SJA2072    PU    ADDR=01,
                 IDBLK=05D,IDNUM=A2072,
                 ANS=CONT,DISCNT=NO,
                 IRETRY=NO,ISTATUS=ACTIVE,
                 MAXDATA=265,MAXOUT=1,
                 MAXPATH=1,
                 PUTYPE=2,SECNET=NO,
                 MODETAB=POKMODE,DLOGMOD=DYNRMT,
                 USSTAB=USSRDYN,LOGAPPL=SCGVAMP,
                 PACING=1,VPACING=2
*
SJA2072I   LU    LOCADDR=0,DLOGMOD=LU62APPB
SJA2072J   LU    LOCADDR=0,DLOGMOD=LU62APPB
SJA2072K   LU    LOCADDR=0,DLOGMOD=LU62APPA
SJA2072L   LU    LOCADDR=0,DLOGMOD=LU62APPA
       ...
```

Figure 14. VTAM XID, PU, and LU Definitions: CICS/ESA-CICS Client for OS/2 Using CM/2

Note how the XID **1** is split into two parts: IDBLK and IDNUM.

The LU, SJA2072I **2**, is defined as an independent LU.

Logmode

Figure 15 shows the VTAM LOGMODE **3** required for the user sessions.

```
LU62APPB    MODEENT LOGMODE=LU62APPB,
                FMPROF=X'13',TSPROF=X'07',
                PRIPROT=X'B0',SECPROT=X'B0',
                COMPROT=X'50B5',RUSIZES=X'8585',
                PSERVIC=X'0602000000000000000002F00',
                TYPE=X'00'
```

Figure 15. VTAM Logmode Definition: CICS/ESA-CICS Client for OS/2 Using CM/2

APPL

Figure 16 on page 34 shows the VTAM APPL **4** definition required for the sample configuration.

Sample Definitions

```
         ...
SCMACICS  VBUILD  TYPE=APPL
SCMCICSA  APPL    AUTH=(ACQ),EAS=1200,ACBNAME=SCMCICSA,PARSESS=YES,
                  MODETAB=SCMODIMS
         ...
```

Figure 16. VTAM APPL Definition: CICS/ESA-CICS Client for OS/2 Using CM/2

Generally, LU6.2 parallel rather than single sessions are used, in which case you must set PARSESS to YES to allow LU6.2 parallel sessions.

NETID

You specify the NETID **5** for VTAM in your VTAM startup procedure. For the sample configuration, this takes the form:

```
    :::
  NETID=USIBMSC,
    :::
```

CICS/ESA

In this section we present the CICS/ESA definitions for the server.

System Initialization Table Parameters

Figure 17 shows the SIT parameters to enable intersystem communication (ISC).

```
      ...
   ISC=YES,
   APPLID=SCMCICSA
      ...
```

Figure 17. System Initialization Table Definitions: CICS/ESA-CICS Client for OS/2 Using CM/2

DFHISC Group

To enable ISC on CICS/ESA, you must install the DFHISC group (see Figure 18 on page 35).

Sample Definitions

```
Either:     CEDA INSTALL GROUP(DFHISC)
And/or:     CEDA ADD LIST(grplist) GROUP(DFHISC)
            where 'grplist' is the list of groups
            CICS installs during start-up.
```

Figure 18. Install DFHISC: CICS/ESA-CICS Client for OS/2 Using CM/2

LU6.2 Connection

Figure 19 shows the LU6.2 connection definition that we installed on CICS/ESA by using resource definition online (RDO).

```
 OBJECT CHARACTERISTICS                              CICS RELEASE = 0330    CEDA  View
    Connection     : C272
    Group          : CICSRES1
    DEscription    : CONNECTION TO WORKSTATION SJA2072I
 CONNECTION IDENTIFIERS
    Netname        : SJA2072I
    INDsys         :
 REMOTE ATTRIBUTES
    REMOTESystem   :
    REMOTEName     :
 CONNECTION PROPERTIES
    ACcessmethod   : Vtam            Vtam ] IRc ] INdirect ] Xm
    Protocol       : Appc            Appc ] Lu61
    SInglesess     : No              No ] Yes
    DAtastream     : User            User ] 3270 ] SCs ] STrfield ] Lms
    RECordformat   : U               U ] Vb
 OPERATIONAL PROPERTIES
 +  AUtoconnect    : Yes             No ] Yes ] All
                                                                APPLID=SCMCICSA
 PF 1 HELP 2 COM 3 END            6 CRSR 7 SBH 8 SFH 9 MSG 10 SB 11 SF 12 CNCL
```

Figure 19. LU6.2 Connection Definition: CICS/ESA-CICS Client for OS/2 Using CM/2

Note: The LU6.2 connection definition and the LU6.2 sessions definition must reside in the same group and be installed simultaneously.

LU6.2 Sessions

Figure 20 on page 36 shows the LU6.2 sessions definition that we installed on CICS/ESA by using RDO.

Sample Definitions

```
  OBJECT CHARACTERISTICS                           CICS RELEASE = 0330   CEDA  View
     Sessions         : S2072
     Group            : CICSRES1
     DEscription      : SESSION FOR SJA2072I
  SESSION IDENTIFIERS
     Connection       : C272
     SESSName         :
     NETnameq         :
     MOdename         : LU62APPB
  SESSION PROPERTIES
     Protocol         : Appc                Appc ] Lu61
     MAximum          : 008 , 004           0-999
     RECEIVEPfx       :
     RECEIVECount     :                     1-999
     SENDPfx          :
     SENDCount        :                     1-999
     SENDSize         : 00256               1-30720
  +  RECEIVESize      : 00256               1-30720
                                                                APPLID=SCMCICSA
  PF 1 HELP 2 COM 3 END            6 CRSR 7 SBH 8 SFH 9 MSG 10 SB 11 SF 12 CNCL
```

Figure 20. LU6.2 Sessions Definition: CICS/ESA-CICS Client for OS/2 Using CM/2

Note: The LU6.2 connection definition and the LU6.2 sessions definition must reside in the same group and be installed simultaneously.

Communications Manager/2

In this section we explain in detail how to define your values to CM/2.

We recommend that you use a new configuration file because adding values to an existing configuration file may cause conflicts with existing values.

To configure CM/2 as in our example, follow these steps:

1. Run Communications Manager Setup from the Communications Manager/2 folder on the OS/2 desktop.
2. Follow through the windows to display the Communications Manager Configuration Definition window (see Figure 21 on page 37).
3. Click on the **Token-ring or other LAN types** option in the Workstation Connection Type list box.
4. Click on the **APPC APIs** in the Feature or Application list box.

5. Click on **Configure...** to get to the Communications Manager Profile List (see Figure 22 on page 38).

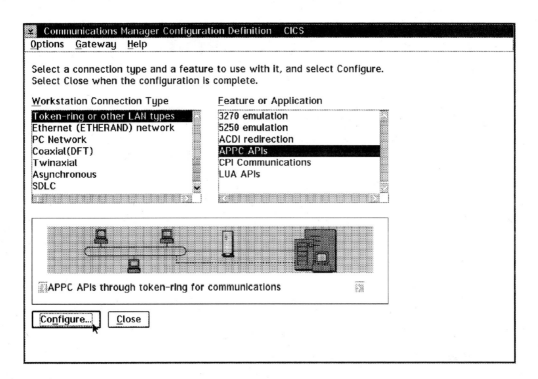

Figure 21. Communications Manager Configuration Definition: CICS/ESA-CICS Client for OS/2 Using CM/2

Figure 22 on page 38 shows the Communications Manager Profile List. For our sample configuration all four profiles must be configured. To configure the DLC - Token-ring or other LAN types profile, follow these steps:

1. Click on **DLC - Token-ring or other LAN types**, then on **Configure...** .

2. On the DLC - Token-ring or other LAN types window (not shown), the only field that requires an entry for our sample configuration is C&SM LAN ID. You can enter the value ANYTHING in this field.

3. After completing the DLC - Token-ring or other LAN types window, return to the Communications Manager Profile List (Figure 22 on page 38).

4. Double-click on **SNA local node characteristics**.

Sample Definitions

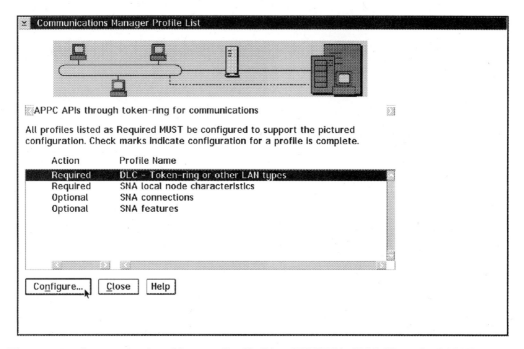

Figure 22. Communications Manager Profile List: CICS/ESA-CICS Client for OS/2 Using CM/2

Local Node Characteristics

Figure 23 on page 39 shows the Local Node Characteristics configuration on CM/2. This window contains definitions for the:

- Network ID **5**
- Local node name
- Local node ID **1**

Sample Definitions

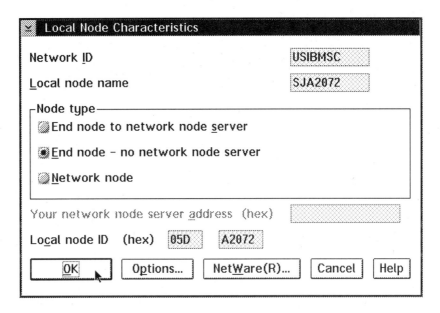

Figure 23. Local Node Characteristics: CICS/ESA-CICS Client for OS/2 Using CM/2

The Local node name must be a unique name. It is the name other nodes in your network use to address your node, for example, in an Advanced Peer-to-Peer Network (APPN). For the sample configuration the name is unimportant, but you can enter a value meaningful to the end user, for example, the name of the VTAM PU.

After entering your local node characteristics, return to the Communications Manager Profile List window (Figure 22 on page 38):

1. Double-click on **SNA connections**.
2. On the Connections List window (not shown), click on the **To Host** radio button.
3. Click on **Create...** .
4. On the Adapter List window (not shown), **Token ring or other LAN types** will be highlighted. Click on **Continue...** to display the Connection to a Host window (Figure 24 on page 40).

On the Connection to a Host window:

- Link name must be unique within CM/2. You can make this value meaningful to the end user.
- Local PU name will contain your Local node name. This field is not required and will be shaded out.
- Node ID **1** will already be entered for you.

Chapter 3. CICS/ESA • CICS Client for OS/2 Using CM/2   39

Sample Definitions

- ❑ Enter your LAN destination address. In the sample configuration the LAN destination address is the token-ring address of the 3745 network controller.
- ❑ Partner network ID in the sample configuration is our Network ID **5**.
- ❑ Partner node name is required in an APPN. For the sample configuration you can enter a value that is meaningful to the end user, for example, the Partner LU **4**.

```
Connection to a Host

Link name              CICSESA         ☑ Activate at startup
Local PU name          SJA2072         ☐ APPN support
Node ID   (hex)   05D    A2072
LAN destination address (hex)   Address format        Remote SAP (hex)
400008210200                    Token Ring            04
Adjacent node ID  (hex)
Partner network ID              USIBMSC
                                                (Required for partner
Partner node name               SCMCICSA         LU definition)
☑ Use this host connection as your focal point support
Optional comment
Token Ring connection via 3745 network controller
[OK]   [Define Partner LUs...]   [Cancel]   [Help]
```

Figure 24. Connection to a Host: CICS/ESA-CICS Client for OS/2 Using CM/2

Click on **Define Partner LUs...** to get the Partner LUs window (Figure 25 on page 41).

Enter the Network ID **5** and LU name **4** of your partner.

Note: Be careful when using aliases for LU names, as they can often cause confusion when configuring your setup for the first time. If you are unsure whether or not to use an alias, use the same value for the LU name and its alias.

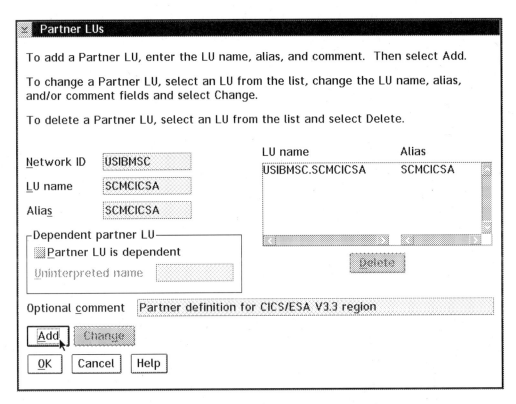

Figure 25. Partner LUs: CICS/ESA-CICS Client for OS/2 Using CM/2

After adding the LU name of your Partner LU, return to the Communications Manager Profile List (Figure 22 on page 38) and select **SNA features**.

SNA Features

The SNA Features List (not shown) enables you to define the Local LU, Modename, and Transaction Program required for the sample configuration.

Local LU

To define your Local LU click on **Local LUs** and then **Configure...**.

Enter your Local LU as shown in Figure 26 on page 42.

Note: Be careful when using aliases for LU names, as they can often cause confusion when configuring your setup for the first time. If you are unsure whether or not to use an alias, use the same value for the LU name and its alias.

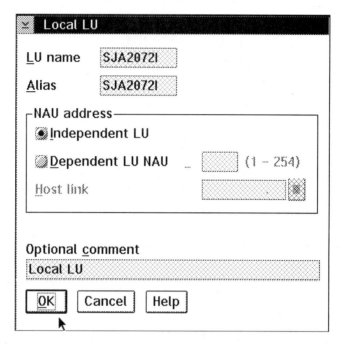

Figure 26. Local LU Name Definition: CICS/ESA-CICS Client for OS/2 Using CM/2

Partner LU

You have already entered the Partner LU in the Partner LUs window (see Figure 25 on page 41).

> **Warning**
>
> For the sample configuration be sure to enter the Partner LU from the Partner LUs window rather than from the SNA features list. If you use the SNA features list, you will not be able to associate the Partner LU with the link name, an association that is required (see Figure 24 on page 40).

Mode Name

To define the Mode name click on **Modes** from the SNA features list and then **Configure...**.

Enter your Mode name as shown in Figure 27 on page 43. We recommend using #CONNECT as the Class of service.

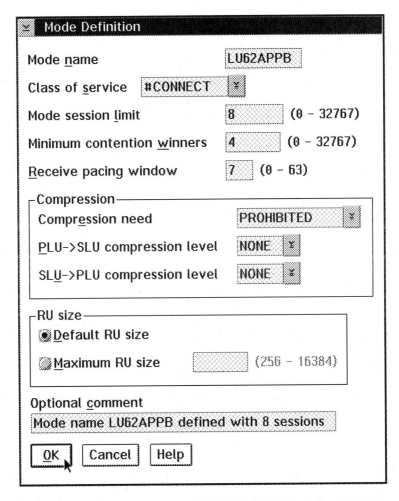

Figure 27. Mode Name Definition: CICS/ESA-CICS Client for OS/2 Using CM/2

CRSR Transaction Program

Figure 28 on page 44 shows the Transaction Program Definition window and the transaction program, CRSR.

CRSR is required if the CICS server supports terminal emulation. It is used to perform automatic transaction initiation (ATI) against the CICS client terminals.

Sample Definitions

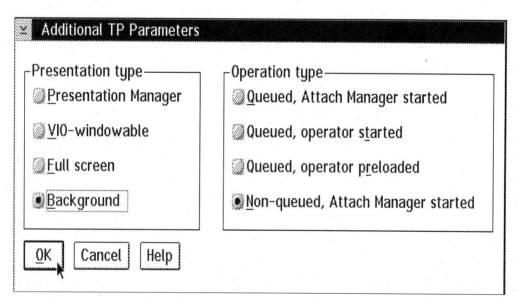

Figure 28. Transaction Program Definition: CICS/ESA-CICS Client for OS/2 Using CM/2

After you have entered all of your CM/2 definitions, select **Close** on each window to exit CM/2. Your values will then be verified by CM/2. Any errors in your configuration will be reported in a pop-up window.

Change Number of Sessions

With CM/2, before the client connection to the server can be started, the sessions between the client and the server must be started by adding change number of sessions (CNOS) statements to the node definition file (.NDF).

To add CNOS statements:

1. Note the name of the CM/2 configuration containing your SNA definitions.
2. Stop CM/2.
3. Locate your .NDF file. This file is usually found in the CMLIB directory.
4. Using an ASCII editor, add CNOS statements to the bottom of your .NDF file similar to those shown in Figure 29 on page 46.
5. Ensure that:
    - LOCAL_LU_ALIAS matches the alias entered on the Local LU window (Figure 26 on page 42)
    - FQ_PARTNER_LU_NAME matches your Network ID 5 and Partner LU name 4 (separated by a period)
    - MODE_NAME matches the Mode name 3
    - PLU_MODE_SESSION_LIMIT matches the Mode session limit (see Figure 27 on page 43)
    - AUTO_ACTIVATE is not greater than PLU_MODE_SESSION_LIMIT (but it must be greater than zero to establish at least one user session).
6. Run CMVERIFY to produce a .CF2 file. (The .CF2 file is a binary translation of the .NDF file and is used to initialize the SNA definitions when APPC is started.)

Sample Definitions

```
   :::

   START_ATTACH_MANAGER;

   :::

   CNOS  LOCAL_LU_ALIAS(SJA2072I)
         FQ_PARTNER_LU_NAME(USIBMSC.SCMCICSA)
         MODE_NAME(LU62APPB)
         SET_NEGOTIABLE(NO)
         PLU_MODE_SESSION_LIMIT(8)
         MIN_CONWINNERS_SOURCE(4)
         MIN_CONWINNERS_TARGET(4)
         AUTO_ACTIVATE(4);
```

Figure 29. Sample CNOS Statements: CICS/ESA-CICS Client for OS/2 Using CM/2

CICSCLI.INI

The CICSCLI.INI file is found in the CICS Client for OS/2 \CICS-CLI\BIN subdirectory. Figure 30 shows the definitions required for the sample configuration.

```
   :::

   Server         = CICSESA
   Netname        = USIBMSC.SCMCICSA    5 4
   Protocol       = SNA
   LocalLUName    = SJA2072I            2
   ModeName       = LU62APPB            3

   :::

   Driver         = SNA
   DriverName     = CCLIBMSN
```

Figure 30. CICSCLI.INI Definitions: CICS/ESA-CICS Client for OS/2 Using CM/2

Notes:

1. A separate **Server** definition is required for each server to which the client needs to connect. You can make this value meaningful to the end user, for example, CICSESA.

2. The **Netname** is the fully qualified Applid of the server.

3. The value for **Protocol** identifies the communication protocol to be used to communicate between the client and the server. This value must match the value you have assigned to **Driver**. You can make this value meaningful to the end user, for example, SNA or APPC.

4. The **LocalLUName** is the name of the local LU to be used when connecting to the server. The same LU can be used for all server connections.

5. The **ModeName** specifies the user mode name to be used when connecting to the server. If you choose to use a blank mode name, you can specify a value of * (asterisk).

6. **Driver** must be the same as **Protocol**.

7. The device driver used by CM/2 in the sample configuration is **CCLIBMSN**.

Testing Your Configuration

After you have installed and configured all relevant products for this sample configuration, we recommend that you do the following:

Step 1. Start the CICS server.

Step 2. Start CM/2 on the client workstation.

Step 3. Activate the connection between CM/2 and the CICS mainframe.
→ See "Establishing a Connection Between CM/2 and CICS Mainframe" on page 316.

Step 4. Start the CICS Client for OS/2.
Issue **CICSCLI /S=CICSESA**.
→ See "Starting and Stopping Your CICS Client" on page 321.

Step 5. Check the status of the CICS Client for OS/2.
Issue **CICSCLI /L**.
→ See "Checking the Status of Your CICS Client" on page 322.

Step 6. Prepare for data conversion.
→ See "Data Conversion: ASCII to EBCDIC" on page 326.

Step 7. Run a simple ECI application.
→ See "Sample Implementation" on page 277.

Step 8. Problems?
→ See Chapter 21, "Problem Determination," on page 293.
→ See Appendix C, "Common Problems: Symptoms and Solutions," on page 339.
→ See Appendix F, "CM/2 .NDF and APPC NS/Windows NSD.INI Files," on page 367.

Step 9. Need further information?
→ See Appendix B, "Frequently Asked Questions," on page 331.

4

CICS/ESA • Token-Ring • Client Using APPC NS/Windows

This chapter covers the following topics:

- "Software Checklist" on page 50
- "Definitions Checklist" on page 51
- "Matching Definitions" on page 52
- "Sample Definitions" on page 53
    - VTAM
    - CICS/ESA
    - APPC Networking Services for Windows V1.0 (detailed step-by-step example)
    - IBM CICS Client for Windows
- "Testing Your Configuration" on page 63

This sample configuration (see Figure 31) consists of an IBM CICS Client for Windows[1] connecting to a CICS mainframe through SNA LU6.2 (APPC) communication provided by APPC Networking Services for Windows V1.0[2] on the client workstation and VTAM on the mainframe server.

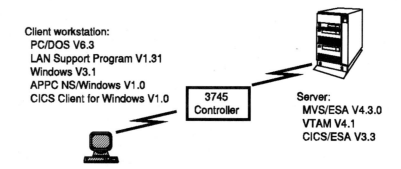

Figure 31. SNA Configuration Using APPC NS/Windows

Although the sample configuration uses CICS/ESA V3.3 as the mainframe server, you could use CICS/MVS V2.1.2, CICS/ESA V4.1 (or later), or CICS/VSE V2.2 (or later).

We used a token-ring network for this configuration, but you can use other physical links, for example, SDLC or coaxial connections.

Software Checklist

The levels of software used in the sample configuration are not necessarily the latest levels available. You should check the relevant products for levels of compatible software.

The software required on the server is:

- ❏ MVS/ESA operating system V4.3.0
- ❏ VTAM V4.1
- ❏ CICS/ESA V3.3

The software required on the client workstation is:

- ❏ PC DOS V6.3 operating system
- ❏ LAN Support Program V1.31

---

[1] Hereafter referred to as CICS Client for Windows.
[2] Hereafter referred to as APPC NS/Windows.

- ❏ Windows V3.1
- ❏ APPC NS/Windows
- ❏ IBM CICS Client for Windows V1.0

Note: When installing the LAN Support Program on the client workstation you must select the **802.2 interface support** option (see "LAN Support Program" on page 238). If you attempt to run APPC NS/Windows without the 802.2 interface support, you receive the error message: Adapter not present.

Definitions Checklist

Before you configure the products, we recommend that you acquire definitions for the parameters listed below. Reference keys are assigned to definitions that must contain the same value in more than one product. For example, XID has the reference key **1**. These reference keys are used in later sections of this chapter.

- ❏ VTAM
  - ➢ XID (IDBLK+IDNUM) **1**
  - ➢ PU
  - ➢ LU **2**
  - ➢ Logmode **3**
  - ➢ APPL **4**
  - ➢ NETID **5**

  Note: APPC NS/Windows V1.0 only supports independent logical units (ILUs). Therefore, your LU **2** must be defined as an ILU and not as a dependent LU (DLU).

- ❏ CICS/ESA
  - ➢ ISC SIT override
  - ➢ DFHISC group
  - ➢ Applid **4**
  - ➢ Netname in the LU6.2 connection definition **2**
  - ➢ Modename in the LU6.2 sessions definition **3**

- ❏ APPC NS/Windows
  - ➢ Network ID **5**
  - ➢ Local LU **2**
  - ➢ Connection Type
  - ➢ Link Name

- LAN Destination Address
- Mode name **3**
- Transaction program (CRSR)
- Node ID (in NSD.INI file) **1**
- CNOS (session establishment, optional)

Note: APPC NS/Windows dynamically creates a partner LU definition when the first session with a partner LU is activated. The CICS Client for Windows automatically issues an allocate (CMALLC) request for a partner LU that is not defined to establish this connection. Alternatively, you can manually establish the connection by using the **Advanced Operations** program to request activation of sessions with a partner LU that is not yet defined. (See "Testing Your Configuration" on page 63 to see how this is done.)

❏ Workstation definitions. These entries are defined in the CICS-CLI.INI initialization file, generally found in the \CICSCLI\BIN subdirectory:

- Server
- Network.Netname **5**.**4**
- Protocol
- LocalLUName **2**
- Modename **3**
- Driver
- DriverName

Matching Definitions

In the sample configuration a number of definitions must match. Table 7 shows the definitions that must be the same. The last column (Example) shows the values we used in our configuration (see "Sample Definitions" on page 53).

Table 7.	Matching Definitions: CICS/ESA-Token-Ring-Client Using APPC NS/Windows				
	VTAM	**CICS/ESA V3.3**	**APPC NS/Windows**	**CICSCLI.INI**	**Example**
1	XID	-	Node ID	-	05DA2072
2	LU	Netname	Local LU	LocalLUName	SJA2072I
3	Logmode	Modename	Mode name	Modename	LU62APPB
4	APPL	Applid	-	Netname	SCMCICSA
5	NETID	-	Network ID	Network	USIBMSC

Sample Definitions

This section presents examples of each of the definitions mentioned in "Definitions Checklist" on page 51. The values highlighted in the figures refer to the Example column of Table 7.

VTAM

In this section we present the VTAM definitions for the server.

XID, PU, and LU

Figure 32 on page 53 shows the VTAM XID **1**, PU, and LU **2** definitions we used in the sample configuration.

```
*
         ...
*
SJA2072    PU     ADDR=01,
                  IDBLK=05D,IDNUM=A2072,
                  ANS=CONT,DISCNT=NO,
                  IRETRY=NO,ISTATUS=ACTIVE,
                  MAXDATA=265,MAXOUT=1,
                  MAXPATH=1,
                  PUTYPE=2,SECNET=NO,
                  MODETAB=POKMODE,DLOGMOD=DYNRMT,
                  USSTAB=USSRDYN,LOGAPPL=SCGVAMP,
                  PACING=1,VPACING=2
*
SJA2072I   LU     LOCADDR=0,DLOGMOD=LU62APPB
SJA2072J   LU     LOCADDR=0,DLOGMOD=LU62APPB
SJA2072K   LU     LOCADDR=0,DLOGMOD=LU62APPA
SJA2072L   LU     LOCADDR=0,DLOGMOD=LU62APPA
         ...
```

Figure 32. VTAM XID, PU, and LU Definitions: CICS/ESA-Token-Ring-Client Using APPC NS/Windows

Note how the XID **1** is split into two parts: IDBLK and IDNUM.

The LU, SJA2072I **2**, is defined as an independent LU.

Logmode

Figure 33 shows the VTAM LOGMODE **3** required for the user sessions.

Sample Definitions

```
LU62APPB   MODEENT LOGMODE=LU62APPB,
               FMPROF=X'13',TSPROF=X'07',
               PRIPROT=X'B0',SECPROT=X'B0',
               COMPROT=X'50B5',RUSIZES=X'8585',
               PSERVIC=X'060200000000000000002F00',
               TYPE=X'00'
```

Figure 33. VTAM Logmode Definition: CICS/ESA-Token-Ring-Client Using APPC NS/Windows

APPL

Figure 34 on page 54 shows the VTAM APPL 4 definition required for the sample configuration.

```
     ...
SCMACICS   VBUILD TYPE=APPL
SCMCICSA   APPL   AUTH=(ACQ),EAS=1200,ACBNAME=SCMCICSA,PARSESS=YES,
               MODETAB=SCMODIMS
     ...
```

Figure 34. VTAM APPL Definition: CICS/ESA-Token-Ring-Client Using APPC NS/Windows

Generally, LU6.2 parallel rather than single sessions are used, in which case you must set PARSESS to YES to allow LU6.2 parallel sessions.

NETID

You specify the NETID 5 for VTAM in your VTAM startup procedure. For the sample configuration, this takes the form:

```
     :::
   NETID=USIBMSC,
     :::
```

CICS/ESA

In this section we present the CICS/ESA definitions for the server.

System Initialization Table Parameters

Figure 35 shows the SIT parameters to enable ISC.

```
    ...
ISC=YES,
APPLID=SCMCICSA
    ...
```

Figure 35. System Initialization Table Definitions: CICS/ESA-Token-Ring-Client Using APPC NS/Windows

DFHISC Group

To enable ISC on CICS/ESA, you must install the DFHISC group (see Figure 36 on page 55).

```
Either:     CEDA INSTALL GROUP(DFHISC)
And/or:     CEDA ADD LIST(grplist) GROUP(DFHISC)
            where 'grplist' is the list of groups
            CICS installs during start-up.
```

Figure 36. Install DFHISC: CICS/ESA-Token-Ring-Client Using APPC NS/Windows

LU6.2 Connection

Figure 37 shows the LU6.2 connection definition that we installed on CICS/ESA by using RDO.

```
 OBJECT CHARACTERISTICS                       CICS RELEASE = 0330    CEDA  View
    Connection     : C272
    Group          : CICSRES1
    DEscription    : CONNECTION TO WORKSTATION SJA2072I
 CONNECTION IDENTIFIERS
    Netname        : SJA2072I
    INDsys         :
 REMOTE ATTRIBUTES
    REMOTESystem   :
    REMOTEName     :
 CONNECTION PROPERTIES
    ACcessmethod   : Vtam              Vtam ] IRc ] INdirect ] Xm
    Protocol       : Appc              Appc ] Lu61
    SInglesess     : No                No ] Yes
    DAtastream     : User              User ] 3270 ] SCs ] STrfield ] Lms
    RECordformat   : U                 U ] Vb
 OPERATIONAL PROPERTIES
  + AUtoconnect    : Yes               No ] Yes ] All
                                                          APPLID=SCMCICSA
 PF 1 HELP 2 COM 3 END          6 CRSR 7 SBH 8 SFH 9 MSG 10 SB 11 SF 12 CNCL
```

Figure 37. LU6.2 Connection Definition: CICS/ESA-Token-Ring-Client Using APPC NS/Windows

Sample Definitions

Note: The LU6.2 connection definition and the LU6.2 sessions definition must reside in the same group and be installed simultaneously.

LU6.2 Sessions

Figure 38 on page 56 shows the LU6.2 sessions definition that we installed on CICS/ESA by using RDO.

```
  OBJECT CHARACTERISTICS                            CICS RELEASE = 0330    CEDA  View
     Sessions       : S2072
     Group          : CICSRES1
     DEscription    : SESSION FOR SJA2072I
  SESSION IDENTIFIERS
     Connection     : C272
     SESSName       :
     NETnameq       :
     MOdename       : LU62APPB
  SESSION PROPERTIES
     Protocol       : Appc              Appc ] Lu61
     MAximum        : 008 , 004         0-999
     RECEIVEPfx     :
     RECEIVECount   :                   1-999
     SENDPfx        :
     SENDCount      :                   1-999
     SENDSize       : 00256             1-30720
  +  RECEIVESize    : 00256             1-30720
                                                              APPLID=SCMCICSA
  PF 1 HELP 2 COM 3 END              6 CRSR 7 SBH 8 SFH 9 MSG 10 SB 11 SF 12 CNCL
```

Figure 38. LU6.2 Sessions Definition: CICS/ESA-Token-Ring-Client Using APPC NS/Windows

Note: The LU6.2 connection definition and the LU6.2 sessions definition must reside in the same group and be installed simultaneously.

APPC NS/Windows

In this section we explain in detail how to define your values to APPC NS/Windows.

For the sample configuration you must install the following APPC NS/Windows components:

BASE   required for networking modules

LAN enables connections to token-ring, Ethernet, PC Network, and mobile LANs.

During installation of APPC NS/Windows you are asked the following question:

```
Do you wish to run configuration at this time?
```

Select **Yes**.

Note: If you have already installed the product, you can run the configuration utility by clicking on the **Configure** icon from the IBM APPC Networking Services application group.

After the BASE and LAN components have been installed, you are presented with the Networking Services Configuration window (see Figure 39).

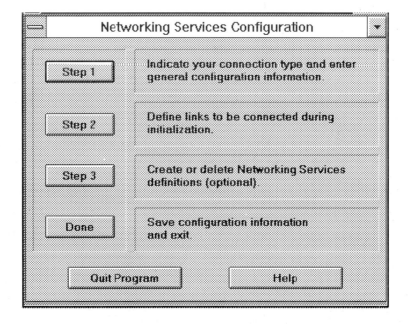

Figure 39. Networking Services Configuration Window

Select **Step 1** to get to the General Configuration window.

General Configuration Window

On the General Configuration window (Figure 40):

Sample Definitions

1. Specify your fully qualified local LU name, which is your Network ID 5 and Local LU 2 separated by a period.
2. Select the connection type to be used by Networking Services. For the sample configuration you should select **Local Area Network (LAN)** for a token-ring network.
3. Select **OK** to return to the Networking Services Configuration window (Figure 39).

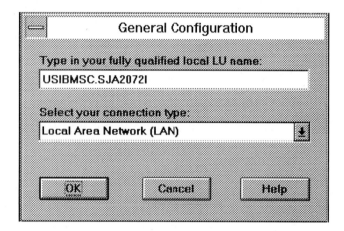

Figure 40. General Configuration Window

On the Networking Services Configuration window select **Step 2** to get to the LAN Configuration window.

LAN Configuration Window

On the LAN Configuration window (Figure 41 on page 59):

1. Specify a name (that will only be used by your workstation) to refer to the link between your workstation and the server system. You can make this name meaningful to the end user, for example, CICSESA.
2. Specify the LAN address of the remote system. In our sample configuration this is the token-ring address of the 3745 network controller.
3. Select **OK** to return to the Networking Services Configuration window (Figure 39 on page 57).

Sample Definitions

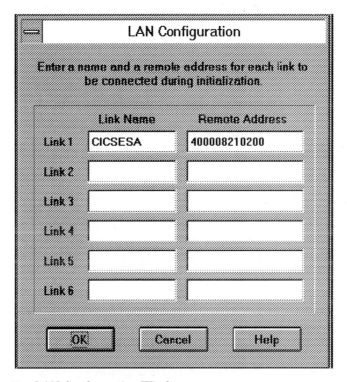

Figure 41. LAN Configuration Window

Defining the Mode and CRSR Transaction Program

To define the mode for your LU6.2 user sessions, follow these steps:

1. From the Networking Services Configuration window select **Step 3** to get to the Definitions window (not shown).

2. Select the **Modes** radio button and then **Define** to get to the Define Mode window (see Figure 42 on page 60).

3. Enter your mode name details.

4. Select **OK** to return to the Definitions window.

Note: As with most other products supporting LU6.2 parallel sessions, APPC NS/Windows predefines the SNASVCMG sessions for you.

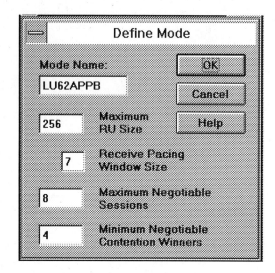

Figure 42. Define Mode Window: CICS/ESA-Token-Ring-Client Using APPC NS/Windows

To define the CRSR transaction program, [1] follow these steps:

1. On the Definitions window select the **Transaction Programs** radio button and then **Define** to get to the Define Transaction Program window.
2. Enter your transaction program definition for CRSR as shown in Figure 43 on page 61.
3. Select **OK** to return to the Definitions Window.
4. Select **Close** to return to the Networking Services Configuration window (Figure 39 on page 57).

On the Networking Services Configuration window select **Done** to complete your configuration.

---

[1] CRSR is required if the CICS server supports terminal emulation (see Table 1 on page 8). It is used to perform ATI against the CICS client terminals.

Sample Definitions

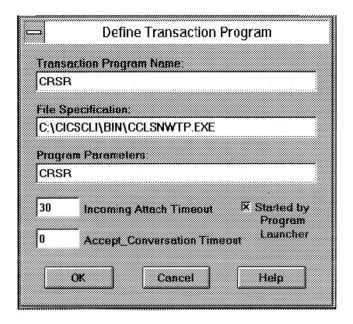

Figure 43. Define Transaction Program Window: CICS/ESA-Token-Ring-Client Using APPC NS/Windows

Node ID Definition

For the sample configuration you must specify the correct Node ID ■ of your workstation in the NSD.INI file. The Node ID must match the Node ID configured in VTAM; otherwise your workstation may be unresponsive after it attempts to connect to the server system.

The NSD.INI file is found in your WINDOWS directory. Using an ASCII editor, edit the NSD.INI file and enter your Node ID on the NODEID= statement within the [Configuration] section. For example:

```
[Configuration]
DLCTYPE=LAN
  :::        :::
LOCALLUNAME=USIBMSC.SJA2072I
NODEID=05DA2072 ■
  :::        :::
```

CICSCLI.INI

The CICSCLI.INI file is found in the CICS Client for Windows BIN subdirectory. Figure 44 shows the definitions required for the sample configuration.

```
  :::
     Server              = CICSESA
     Network.Netname     = USIBMSC.SCMCICSA    5 4
     Protocol            = SNA
     LocalLUName         = SJA2072I            2
     ModeName            = LU62APPB            3

  :::

     Driver              = SNA
     DriverName          = CCLIBMSN
```

Figure 44. CICSCLI.INI Definitions: CICS/ESA-Token-Ring-Client Using APPC NS/Windows

Notes:

1. A separate **Server** definition is required for each server to which the client needs to connect. You can make this value meaningful to the end user, for example, CICSESA.

2. The **Netname** is the fully qualified applid of the server, that is, your Network ID and Local LU separated by a period.

3. The value of **Protocol** identifies the communication protocol to be used between the client and the server. This value must match the value you have assigned to **Driver**. You can make this value meaningful to the end user, for example, SNA or APPC.

4. The **LocalLUName** is the local LU to be used when connecting to the server. The same LU can be used for all server connections.

5. The **ModeName** specifies the user mode name to be used when connecting to the server. If you choose to use a blank mode name, you can specify a value of * (asterisk).

6. **Driver** must be the same as **Protocol**.

7. The device driver used by APPC NS/Windows in the sample configuration is **CCLIBMSN**.

Testing Your Configuration

After you have installed and configured all relevant products for this sample configuration, we recommend that you do the following:

Step 1. Start the CICS server.

Step 2. Start APPC NS/Windows on the client workstation.

Step 3. Activate the connection between APPC NS/Windows and the CICS mainframe.
→ See "Establishing a Connection Using APPC NS/Windows" on page 317.

Step 4. Start the CICS Client for Windows.
Issue **CICSCLI /S=CICSESA**.
→ See "Starting and Stopping Your CICS Client" on page 321.

Step 5. Check the status of the CICS Client for Windows.
Issue **CICSCLI /L**.
→ See "Checking the Status of Your CICS Client" on page 322.

Step 6. Prepare for data conversion.
→ See "Data Conversion: ASCII to EBCDIC" on page 326.

Step 7. Run a simple ECI application.
→ See "Sample Implementation" on page 277.

Step 8. Problems?
→ See Chapter 21, "Problem Determination," on page 293.
→ See Appendix C, "Common Problems: Symptoms and Solutions," on page 339.
→ See Appendix F, "CM/2 .NDF and APPC NS/Windows NSD.INI Files," on page 367.

Step 9. Need further information?
→ See Appendix B, "Frequently Asked Questions," on page 331.

Testing Your Configuration

5

CICS/ESA • NetWare for SAA Gateway • CICS Clients

This chapter covers the following topics:
- "Definitions Checklist" on page 67
- "Matching Definitions" on page 68
- "Sample Definitions" on page 68
    - VTAM
    - CICS/ESA
    - NetWare for SAA on the gateway
    - DOS client definitions
    - Windows client definitions
    - IBM CICS Client for DOS/Windows
- "Testing Your Configuration" on page 75

This sample configuration consists of an IBM CICS Client for Windows [1] and an IBM CICS Client for DOS [2] connecting to a CICS mainframe through SNA LU6.2 (APPC) communication provided by a Novell NetWare for SAA gateway workstation and VTAM on the mainframe server.

Although the sample configuration uses CICS/ESA V3.3 as the mainframe server, you could use CICS/MVS V2.1.2, CICS/VSE V2.2, or CICS/ESA V4.1 (or later).

The levels of software used in the sample configuration are not necessarily the latest levels available. You should check the relevant products for levels of compatible software.

The software required on the server is:
- MVS/ESA operating system V4.3.0
- VTAM V4.1
- CICS/ESA V3.3

The NetWare software required on the gateway workstation is either:
- NetWare Communications Executive (COMMEXEC) V1.3.46 (or later)
- NetWare for SAA V1.3.58 (or later)

or
- NetWare Communications Executive (COMMEXEC) V2 (or later)
- NetWare for SAA V2.0.19 (or later)

If you are using NetWare for SAA V1.3, Attachmate 3270 LAN Workstation for DOS V3.0 is required on the DOS client workstation. If you are using NetWare for SAA V2.0 all required code is packaged with the NetWare for SAA V2.0 server.

For the Windows client all required code is packaged with the NetWare for SAA V1.3 and 2.0 servers.

---

[1] Hereafter referred to as CICS Client for Windows.
[2] Hereafter referred to as CICS Client for DOS.

Definitions Checklist

Before you configure the products, we recommend that you acquire definitions for the parameters listed below. Reference keys are assigned to definitions that must contain the same value in more than one product. For example, NETID has the reference key **1**. These reference keys are used in later sections of this chapter.

- ❏ VTAM
    - ➤ NETID **1**
    - ➤ LU **2**
    - ➤ APPL **3**
    - ➤ Logmode **4**
    - ➤ XID **5**
- ❏ CICS/ESA V3.3
    - ➤ ISC SIT override
    - ➤ DFHISC group
    - ➤ Netname in the LU6.2 connection definition **2**
    - ➤ Applid **3**
    - ➤ Modename **4**
- ❏ NetWare for SAA definitions on the gateway
    - ➤ SNA Network ID **1**
    - ➤ BlockID/PUID **5**
- ❏ CICS Client definitions on the workstation. These entries are defined in the CICSCLI.INI initialization file, generally found in the \CICSCLI\BIN subdirectory:
    - ➤ Server
    - ➤ Netname **3**
    - ➤ Protocol
    - ➤ LocalLUName **2**
    - ➤ Modename **4**
    - ➤ Driver
    - ➤ DriverName

Matching Definitions

In the sample configuration a number of definitions must match. Table 8 shows the definitions that must be the same. The last column (Example) shows the values we used in our configuration (see "Sample Definitions" on page 68).

Table 8. Matching Definitions: CICS/ESA-NetWare for SAA Gateway-CICS Clients

	VTAM	CICS/ESA	NWSAA	CICSCLI.INI	Example
1	NETID	-	SNA Network ID	-	USIBMSC
2	LU	Netname	-	LocalLUName	SJA2072I
3	APPL	Applid	-	Netname	SCMCICSA
4	Logmode	Modename	-	Modename	LU62APPB
5	XID	-	BlockID/PUID	-	05DA2072

Sample Definitions

This section presents the values of each of the definitions listed in "Definitions Checklist" on page 67. The values highlighted in the figures refer to the Example column of Table 8.

VTAM

In this section we present the VTAM definitions required by the server.

XID, PU, and LU

Figure 45 on page 69 shows the VTAM XID **5**, PU, and LU **2** definitions we used in the sample configuration.

```
*                ...
 SJA2072   PU    ADDR=01,
                 IDBLK=05D,IDNUM=A2072,
                 ANS=CONT,DISCNT=NO,
                 IRETRY=NO,ISTATUS=ACTIVE,
                 MAXDATA=2057,MAXOUT=1,
                 MAXPATH=1,
                 PUTYPE=2,SECNET=NO,
                 MODETAB=POKMODE,DLOGMOD=DYNRMT,
                 USSTAB=USSRDYN,LOGAPPL=SCGVAMP,
                 PACING=1,VPACING=2
*
 SJA2072I LU     LOCADDR=0,DLOGMOD=LU62APPB
 SJA2072J LU     LOCADDR=0,DLOGMOD=LU62APPB
 SJA2072K LU     LOCADDR=0,DLOGMOD=LU62APPA
 SJA2072L LU     LOCADDR=0,DLOGMOD=LU62APPA
                ...
```

Figure 45. VTAM XID, PU, and LU Definitions: CICS/ESA-NetWare for SAA Gateway-CICS Clients

Note how the XID **5** is split into two parts: IDBLK and IDNUM.

The LU, SJA2072I **2**, is defined as an independent LU.

Logmode

Figure 46 shows the VTAM LOGMODE **4** required for the user sessions.

```
LU62APPB   MODEENT LOGMODE=LU62APPB,
                   FMPROF=X'13',TSPROF=X'07',
                   PRIPROT=X'B0',SECPROT=X'B0',
                   COMPROT=X'50B5',RUSIZES=X'8888',
                   PSERVIC=X'060200000000000000002F00',
                   TYPE=X'00'
```

Figure 46. VTAM Logmode Definition: CICS/ESA-NetWare for SAA Gateway-CICS Clients

APPL

Figure 47 on page 70 shows the VTAM APPL **3** definition required for the sample configuration.

Sample Definitions

```
      ...
SCMACICS   VBUILD TYPE=APPL
SCMCICSA   APPL   AUTH=(ACQ),EAS=1200,ACBNAME=SCMCICSA,PARSESS=YES,
                  MODETAB=SCMODIMS
      ...
```

Figure 47. VTAM APPL Definition: CICS/ESA-NetWare for SAA Gateway-CICS Clients

Generally, LU6.2 parallel rather than single sessions are used, in which case you must set PARSESS to YES to allow LU6.2 parallel sessions.

NETID

You specify the NETID **1** for VTAM in your VTAM startup procedure. For the sample configuration, this will take the form:

```
   :::
 NETID=USIBMSC,
   :::
```

CICS/ESA

In this section we present the CICS/ESA definitions for the server.

System Initialization Table Parameters

Figure 48 shows the SIT parameters to enable ISC.

```
      ...
   ISC=YES,
   APPLID=SCMCICSA
      ...
```

Figure 48. System Initialization Table Definitions: CICS/ESA-NetWare for SAA Gateway-CICS Clients

DFHISC Group

To enable ISC on CICS/ESA, you must install the DFHISC group (see Figure 49 on page 71).

Sample Definitions

```
Either:      CEDA INSTALL GROUP(DFHISC)
And/or:      CEDA ADD LIST(grplist) GROUP(DFHISC)
             where 'grplist' is the list of groups
             CICS installs during start-up.
```

Figure 49. Install DFHISC: CICS/ESA-NetWare for SAA Gateway-CICS Clients

LU6.2 Connection

Figure 50 shows the LU6.2 connection definition that we installed on CICS/ESA by using RDO.

```
 OBJECT CHARACTERISTICS                         CICS RELEASE = 0330    CEDA  View
    Connection     : C272
    Group          : CICSRES1
    DEscription    : CONNECTION TO WORKSTATION SJA2072I
  CONNECTION IDENTIFIERS
    Netname        : SJA2072I
    INDsys         :
  REMOTE ATTRIBUTES
    REMOTESystem   :
    REMOTEName     :
  CONNECTION PROPERTIES
    ACcessmethod   : Vtam              Vtam ] IRc ] INdirect ] Xm
    Protocol       : Appc              Appc ] Lu61
    SInglesess     : No                No ] Yes
    DAtastream     : User              User ] 3270 ] SCs ] STrfield ] Lms
    RECordformat   : U                 U ] Vb
  OPERATIONAL PROPERTIES
+   AUtoconnect    : Yes               No ] Yes ] All
                                                              APPLID=SCMCICSA
 PF 1 HELP 2 COM 3 END         6 CRSR 7 SBH 8 SFH 9 MSG 10 SB 11 SF 12 CNCL
```

Figure 50. LU6.2 Connection Definition: CICS/ESA-NetWare for SAA Gateway-CICS Clients

Note: The LU6.2 connection definition and the LU6.2 sessions definition must reside in the same group and be installed simultaneously.

LU6.2 Sessions

Figure 51 on page 72 shows the LU6.2 sessions definition that we installed on CICS/ESA by using RDO.

Sample Definitions

```
  OBJECT CHARACTERISTICS                          CICS RELEASE = 0330    CEDA  View
    Sessions         : S2072
    Group            : CICSRES1
    DEscription      : SESSION FOR SJA2072I
  SESSION IDENTIFIERS
    Connection       : C272
    SESSName         :
    NETnameq         :
    MOdename         : LU62APPB
  SESSION PROPERTIES
    Protocol         : Appc                Appc ] Lu61
    MAximum          : 008 , 004           0-999
    RECEIVEPfx       :
    RECEIVECount     :                     1-999
    SENDPfx          :
    SENDCount        :                     1-999
    SENDSize         : 00256               1-30720
  + RECEIVESize      : 00256               1-30720
                                                               APPLID=SCMCICSA
  PF 1 HELP 2 COM 3 END        6 CRSR 7 SBH 8 SFH 9 MSG 10 SB 11 SF 12 CNCL
```

Figure 51. LU6.2 Sessions Definition: CICS/ESA-NetWare for SAA Gateway-CICS Clients

Note: The LU6.2 connection definition and the LU6.2 sessions definition must reside in the same group and be installed simultaneously.

NetWare for SAA Gateway

To define the NetWare for SAA gateway:

- ❏ Configure the server using the CSCON utility provided with NetWare for SAA.
- ❏ Use the CSSTATUS utility to review your definitions.
- ❏ Create an SNA Service Profile and assign a name to it, for example, ESA_21 (Node Type 2.1). If you are using dependent sessions, rather than independent sessions, your Service Profile should specify Node Type 2.0.
- ❏ Specify the command:

    csload ESA_21

  to start the SNA Service Profile in the AUTOEXEC.NCF file.
- ❏ For the host connection define the following:

  Parameter   **Example**

SNA Network ID	USIBMSC
Node Control Point Name	CPNAME
Number of independent sessions	8
Host attachment	token-ring

❑ For the SNA token-ring define the following:

Parameter	Example
TR Source Service Access Point	04 hex.
TR Adapter Type	Primary
Block ID	05D hex.
PUID for TR connection	A2072
Logical Adapter Name	ADAPT1

DOS Client

To define the DOS client:

❑ Enter:

   WSCONFIG name.CFG

to get to the configuration panel

❑ In the Connection section specify:

➢ LAN Interface

➢ APPC Support

➢ Select APPC (LU6.2) support

➢ Server Name [CICSNET ...]

➢ Service Name [ESA_21].

Windows Client

For the Windows client the configuration information is in the WS.CFG file in the WINDOWS directory. Define the following:

```
[LU62]
TRANS_FILE = TABLE.DAT
LU_TYPE = 6
NETWARE_SAA_SERVER        = CICSNET
NETWARE_SAA_USER_NAME     = SUPERVISOR
```

Sample Definitions

```
NETWARE_SAA_SERVICE_NAME = ESA_21
TRAN_SPX_READ_DOS_MEMORY = 8192
TRAN_SPX_GLOBAL_MEMORY   = 64000
```

If you do not specify the values highlighted in the example above, the user will be prompted at run time to specify them.

CICSCLI.INI

The CICSCLI.INI file is found in the CICS Client for DOS/Windows BIN subdirectory. Figure 52 shows the definitions required for the sample configuration.

```
    :::
   Server             = CICSESA
   Netname            = SCMCICSA
   Protocol           = NW-APPC
   LocalLUName        = SJA2072I
   ModeName           = LU62APPB
   SnaLocalLUAddr     = 00
   SnaSessionLimit    = 8
   SnaDLCName         = ITRN
   SnaPLUAdapterAddr  = 400008210200
   SnaMaxRUSize       = 2048
   SnaPacingSize      = 7
    :::
   Driver             = NW-APPC
   DriverName         = CCLNOVSN
```

Figure 52. CICSCLI.INI Definitions: CICS/ESA-NetWare for SAA Gateway-CICS Clients

Notes:

1. A separate **Server** definition is required for each server to which the client needs to connect. You can make this value meaningful to the end user, for example, CICSESA.

2. The **Netname** is normally the fully qualified Applid of the server. However, when using the NetWare for SAA gateway, do not specify the Network ID.

3. The value for **Protocol** identifies the communication protocol to be used to communicate between the client and the server. This value must match the value you have assigned to **Driver**. You can make this value meaningful to the end user, for example, NW-APPC.

4. The **LocalLUName** is the name of the local LU to be used when connecting to the server. The same LU can be used for all server connections.

5. The **ModeName** specifies the user mode name to be used when connecting to the server.

6. NetWare for SAA parameters:

SnaLocalLUAddr	logical session number for the local LU
SnaSessionLimit	number of LU6.2 sessions
SnaDLCName	ITRN is for a token-ring network
SnaPLUAdapterAddr	network adapter address of PU
SnaMaxRUSize	maximum request unit size
SnaPacingSize	pacing response value

7. **Driver** must be the same as **Protocol**.

8. The device driver used by Netware clients in the sample configuration is **CCLNOVSN**.

Testing Your Configuration

After you have installed and configured all relevant products for this sample configuration, we recommend that you do the following:

Step 1. Start the CICS server.

Step 2. Start NetWare for SAA gateway server.

Step 3. Start the CICS Client for DOS/Windows.
Issue **CICSCLI /S=CICSESA**.
→ See "Starting and Stopping Your CICS Client" on page 321.

Step 4. Check the status of the CICS Client for DOS/Windows.
Issue **CICSCLI /L**.
→ See "Checking the Status of Your CICS Client" on page 322.

Step 5. Prepare for data conversion.
→ See "Data Conversion: ASCII to EBCDIC" on page 326.

Step 6. Run a simple ECI application.
→ See "Sample Implementation" on page 277.

Step 7. Problems?
→ See Chapter 21, "Problem Determination," on page 293.
→ See Appendix C, "Common Problems: Symptoms and Solutions," on page 339.

Step 8. Need further information?
→ See Appendix B, "Frequently Asked Questions," on page 331.

6

CICS/VSE • SDLC • CICS Client for OS/2 Using CM/2

This chapter covers the following topics:
- "Software Checklist" on page 78
- "Definitions Checklist" on page 79
- "Matching Definitions" on page 80
- "Sample Definitions" on page 80
    - VTAM
    - CICS/VSE
    - Communications Manager/2 (detailed step-by-step example)
    - IBM CICS Client for OS/2
- "Testing Your Configuration" on page 93

Software Checklist

This sample configuration (see Figure 53 on page 78) consists of an IBM CICS Client for OS/2[1] connecting to a CICS mainframe using SNA LU6.2 (APPC) communication provided by CM/2 on the client workstation and VTAM on the mainframe server.

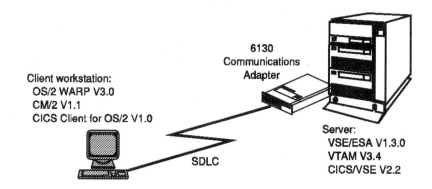

Figure 53. SDLC Configuration: CICS/VSE-SDLC-CICS Client for OS/2 Using CM/2

Although the sample configuration uses CICS/VSE V2.2 as the mainframe server, you could use CICS/MVS V2.1.2, CICS/ESA V3.3, or CICS/ESA V4.1 (or later).

We used an SDLC connection for this configuration, but you can use other physical links, for example, token-ring or Ethernet.

Software Checklist

The levels of software used in the sample configuration are not necessarily the latest levels available. You should check the relevant products for levels of compatible software.

The software required on the server is:

- ❑ VSE/ESA operating system V1.3.0
- ❑ VTAM V3.4
- ❑ CICS/VSE V2.2 + PTF UN63772

The software required on the client workstation is:

- ❑ OS/2 WARP V3.0 operating system

---

[1] Hereafter referred to as CICS Client for OS/2.

- CM/2 V1.1
- IBM CICS Client for OS/2 V1.0

Definitions Checklist

Before you configure the products, we recommend that you acquire definitions for the parameters listed in the tables that follow. Reference keys are assigned to definitions that must contain the same value in more than one product. For example, ADDR has the reference key **1**. These reference keys are used in later sections of this chapter.

- VTAM
  - ADDR **1**
  - PU
  - LU **2**
  - APPL **3**
  - NETID **4**
- CICS/VSE V2.2
  - ISC SIT override
  - DFHISC group
  - Applid **3**
  - Netname in the LU6.2 connection definition **2**
- CM/2
  - Local station address **1**
  - Network ID **4**
  - Local node name
  - Local LU **2**
  - Partner LU **3**
  - Transaction program (CRSR)
  - CNOS (session establishment, optional)
- Workstation definitions. These entries are defined in the CICSCLI.INI initialization file, generally found in the \CICSCLI\BIN subdirectory:
  - Server
  - Network.Netname **4**.**3**
  - Protocol
  - LocalLUName **2**

➢ Driver
➢ DriverName

Matching Definitions

In the sample configuration a number of definitions must match. Table 9 shows the definitions that must be the same. The last column (Example) shows the values we used in our configuration (see "Sample Definitions" on page 80).

Table 9. Matching Definitions: CICS/VSE-SDLC-CICS Client for OS/2 Using CM/2

	VTAM	CICS/VSE V2.2	CM/2	CICSCLI.INI	Example
1	ADDR	-	Local Station Address	-	C1
2	LU	Netname	Local LU	LocalLUName	CCLICALU
3	APPL	Applid	Partner LU	Netname	CICSSA22
4	NETID	-	Network ID	Network	DEIBMIPF

Sample Definitions

This section presents examples of each of the definitions mentioned in "Definitions Checklist" on page 79. The values highlighted in the figures refer to the Example column of Table 9.

VTAM

In this section we present the VTAM definitions required by the server.

NETID

You specify the NETID **4** for VTAM in the VTAM startup procedure. Figure 54 on page 81 shows the VTAM startup procedure (ATCSTR04.B) that we used in the sample configuration.

```
* $$ JOB JNM=BOESTR04,DISP=D,PRI=3,                              C
* $$ NTFY=YES                                                    C
* $$ LDEST=*,                                                    C
* $$ CLASS=0
// JOB BOESTR04 CATALOG VTAM START OPTION LIST
// EXEC LIBR,PARM='MSHP'
ACCESS SUBLIB=PRD2.CONFIG
CATALOG    ATCSTR04.B    REPLACE=YES
SSCPID=22,                                                       *
HOSTSA=22,                                                       *
SSCPNAME=IPFV2B,                                                 *
HOSTPU=IPFVM22,                                                  *
NETID=DEIBMIPF,                                                  *
MAXSUBA=255,                                                     *
CONFIG=04,                                                       *
IOINT=0,                                                         *
SGALIMIT=1M,                                                     *
BSBUF=(28,,,1),                                                  *
CRPLBUF=(60,,,1),                                                *
LFBUF=(300,288,,20),                                             *
LPBUF=(12,,,6),                                                  *
SFBUF=(20,,,20),                                                 *
SPBUF=(210,,,32),                                                *
VFBUF=204800,                                                    *
VPBUF=528384,                                                    *
XDBUF=(6,,,1)
/+
/*
/&
* $$ EOJ
```

Figure 54. VTAM Startup Procedure ATCSTR04.B

PU, ADDR, and LU

Figure 55 on page 82 shows the VTAM PU, ADDR **1**, and LU **2** definitions we used in the sample configuration.

Sample Definitions

```
CCLICA    VBUILD TYPE=CA
CCLICAGR  GROUP  LNCTL=SDLC,
                 DIAL=NO,
                 ISTATUS=INACTIVE
CCLICALI  LINE   ADDRESS=B40,
                 CORNUM=(1,2),
                 MAXBFRU=(2,8),
                 PORT=A
CCLICAPU  PU     ADDR=C1,
                 XID=YES,
                 PUTYPE=2,MAXDATA=265
CCLICALU  LU     LOCADDR=0,
                 ISTATUS=ACTIVE,MODETAB=IESINCLM
          ...
```

Figure 55. PU, ADDR, and LU Definitions in VTAM CA Major Node

Notes:

- You must specify XID=YES for PU Type 2.1 nodes to enable parallel sessions communication.
- The LU, CCLICALU **2**, is defined as an independent LU, specifying **0** in the LOCADDR parameter.

APPL

Figure 56 shows the VTAM APPL **3** definition required for the sample configuration.

```
          ...
BOEAPPL     VBUILD TYPE=APPL
CICSSA22 APPL  AUTH=(PASS,ACQ,VPACE),ACBNAME=CICSSA22,
               EAS=4000,APPC=NO,PARSESS=YES,
               SONSCIP=YES,VPACING=3
```

Figure 56. VTAM APPL Major Node Definition: CICS/VSE-SDLC-CICS Client for OS/2 Using CM/2

Generally, LU6.2 parallel rather than single sessions are used, in which case you must set PARSESS to YES to allow LU 6.2 parallel sessions.

Although the communication between the client and the server uses APPC, you must specify **APPC=NO** in the APPL definition.

APPC=YES indicates that the application uses the ACF/VTAM APPC-CMD programming interface. CICS does not use this VTAM function. Instead it has implemented its support of APPC through the traditional VTAM macro interface. Coding APPC=YES not only indicates that the application will use the new interface, but also causes VTAM not to allow the application to use the traditional macros to manipulate an LU6.2 APPC session. So, not only is APPC=YES not needed for CICS coding, it also stops the existing CICS support from working.

CICS/VSE

In this section we present the CICS/VSE definitions for the server.

System Initialization Table Parameters

Figure 57 shows the SIT parameters to enable ISC.

```
    ...
    ISC=YES,
    APPLID=CICSSA22
    ...
```

Figure 57. System Initialization Table Definitions: CICS/VSE-SDLC-CICS Client for OS/2 Using CM/2

DFHISC Group

To enable ISC on CICS/VSE, you must install the DFHISC group (see Figure 58).

```
Either:      CEDA INSTALL GROUP(DFHISC)
And/or:      CEDA ADD LIST(grplist) GROUP(DFHISC)
             where 'grplist' is the list of groups
             CICS installs during start-up.
```

Figure 58. Install DFHISC: CICS/VSE-SDLC-CICS Client for OS/2 Using CM/2

LU6.2 Connection

Figure 59 on page 84 shows the LU6.2 connection definition we installed on CICS/VSE by using RDO.

Sample Definitions

```
      OBJECT CHARACTERISTICS
       CEDA  View
         Connection    : CCLS
         Group         : CCLSDLC
       CONNECTION IDENTIFIERS
         Netname       : CCLICALU
         INDsys        :
       REMOTE ATTRIBUTES
         REMOTESystem  :
         REMOTEName    :
       CONNECTION PROPERTIES
         ACcessmethod  : Vtam             Vtam ] IRc ] INdirect
         Protocol      : Appc             Appc ] Lu61
         SInglesess    : No               No ] Yes
         Datastream    : User             User ] 3270 ] SCs ] STrfield ] Lm
    s
         RECordformat  : U                U ] Vb
       OPERATIONAL PROPERTIES
         AUtoconnect   : Yes              No ] Yes ] All
    +    INService     : Yes              Yes ] No
```

Figure 59. LU6.2 Connection Definition: CICS/VSE-SDLC-CICS Client for OS/2 Using CM/2

Note: The LU6.2 connection definition and the LU6.2 sessions definition must reside in the same group and be installed simultaneously.

LU6.2 Sessions

Figure 60 on page 85 shows the LU6.2 sessions definition we installed on CICS/VSE by using RDO.

```
OBJECT CHARACTERISTICS
 CEDA  View
   Sessions          : CCLS
   Group             : CCLSDLC
 SESSION IDENTIFIERS
   Connection        : CCLS
   SESSName          :
   NETnameq          :
   MOdename          :
 SESSION PROPERTIES
   Protocol          : Appc            Appc ] Lu61
   MAximum           : 00012 , 00004   0-32767
   RECEIVEPfx        :
   RECEIVECount      : No              No ] 1-999
   SENDPfx           :
   SENDCount         : No              No ] 1-999
   SENDSize          : 04096           1-30720
   RECEIVESize       : 04096           1-30720
+ OPERATOR DEFAULTS
```

Figure 60. LU6.2 Sessions Definition: CICS/VSE-SDLC-CICS Client for OS/2 using CM/2

Note: The LU6.2 connection definition and the LU6.2 sessions definition must reside in the same group and be installed simultaneously.

Communications Manager/2

In this section we explain in detail how to define your values to CM/2.

We recommend that you use a new configuration file because adding values to an existing configuration file may cause conflicts with existing values.

To configure CM/2 as in our example, follow these steps:

1. Run Communications Manager Setup from the Communications Manager/2 folder on the OS/2 desktop.
2. Follow through the windows to display the Communications Manager Configuration Definition window (see Figure 61 on page 86).
3. Click on the **SDLC** option in the Workstation Connection Type list box.
4. Click on the **APPC APIs** in the Feature or Application list box.
5. Click on **Configure...** to get to the Communications Manager Profile List window (see Figure 62).

Sample Definitions

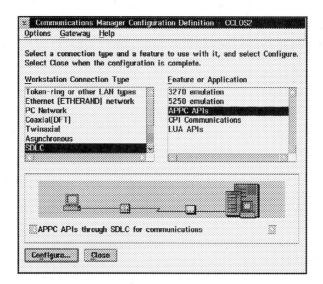

Figure 61. Communications Manager Configuration Definition Window

Figure 62 shows the Communications Manager Profile List window. For our sample configuration all four profiles must be configured. To configure the DLC-SDLC profile, follow these steps:

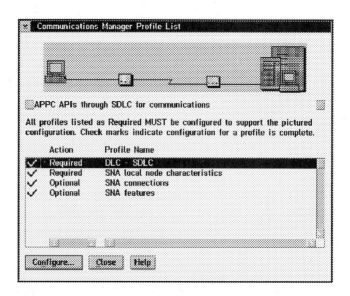

Figure 62. Communications Manager Profile List Window

1. Click on **DLC - SDLC**, then on **Configure...**

2. On the SDLC DLC Adapter Parameters window (Figure 63) select:
   - Adapter **0**
   - Line type as **Non-switched**
   - Link station role as **Secondary**.

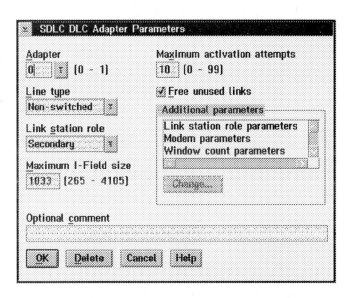

Figure 63. SDLC DLC Adapter Parameters Window

3. Click on **Link station role parameters** in the Additional parameters list.
4. Click on **Change** to get the Link Station Role Parameters window (not shown). The only field that requires an entry for our sample configuration is Local station address ◨.
5. Return to the Communications Manager Profile List window (Figure 62 on page 86).
6. Double-click on **SNA local node characteristics**.

Local Node Characteristics

Figure 64 on page 88 shows the Local Node Characteristics configuration on CM/2. This window contains definitions for the:

- ❑ Network ID ◨
- ❑ Local node name
- ❑ Local node ID

Sample Definitions

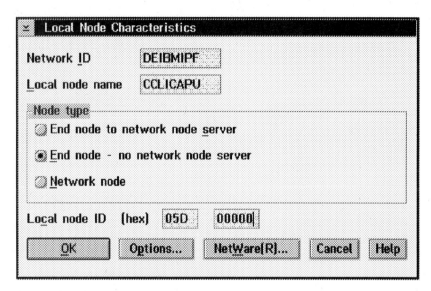

Figure 64. Local Node Characteristics Window

The Network ID must match the NETID specified at VTAM startup (see Figure 54 on page 81).

The Local node name must be a unique name. It is the name other nodes in your network use to address your node, for example, in an APPN. For the sample configuration the name is unimportant, but you can enter a value meaningful to the end user, for example, the name of the VTAM PU.

In a leased SDLC connection, a value for Local node ID is not required. You can accept the default value supplied by the configuration program.

After entering your local node characteristics, return to the Communications Manager Profile List window (Figure 62 on page 86):

1. Double-click on **SNA connections**.
2. On the Connections List window (not shown), click on the **To Host** radio button.
3. Click on **Create**.
4. On the Adapter List window (not shown), **SDLC Adapter 0, 1 Regular...** is highlighted.
   Click on **Continue...** to display the Connection to a Host window (Figure 65 on page 89).

On the Connection to a Host window:

- Link name must be unique within CM/2. You can make this value meaningful to the end user.
- Local PU name will contain your Local node name. This field is not required and will be shaded out.
- Partner network ID in the sample configuration is our Network ID 4.
- Partner node name is required in an APPN. In our sample configuration we used the SSCPNAME (IPFV2B) as specified in our VTAM definitions (see Figure 54 on page 81).

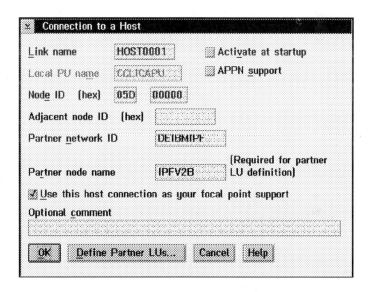

Figure 65. Connection to a Host Window

Click on **Define Partner LUs...** to get to Partner LUs window (Figure 66 on page 90).

Enter the Network ID 4 and LU name 2 of your partner.

Note: Be careful when using aliases for LU names, as they can cause confusion when configuring your setup for the first time. If you are unsure whether or not to use an alias, use the same value for the LU name and its alias.

Sample Definitions

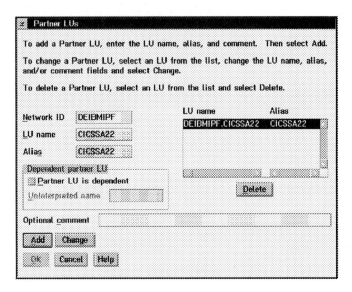

Figure 66. Partner LUs Window

Communications Manager Profile List (Figure 62 on page 86) and select **SNA features**.

SNA Features

The SNA Features list (not shown) enables you to define the Local LU and Transaction Program required for the sample configuration.

Local LU

To define your Local LU click on **Local LUs** and then **Configure...**

Enter your Local LU as shown in Figure 67 on page 91.

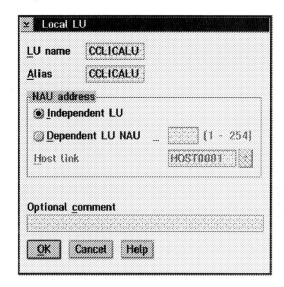

Figure 67. Local LU Name Definition Window

Partner LU

You have already entered the Partner LU in the Partner LUs window (see Figure 66 on page 90).

Warning: For the sample configuration be sure to enter the Partner LU from the Partner LUs window rather than from the SNA feature list. If you use the SNA feature list, you will not be able to associate the Partner LU with the link name, an association that is required (see Figure 65 on page 89).

CRSR Transaction Program

The CRSR transaction program is required if the CICS server supports CICS 3270 terminal emulation. It is used to perform ATI against the CICS client terminals. CICS/VSE V2.2 does not support CICS 3270 terminal emulation, so for this sample configuration you do not need to define the CRSR transaction to CM/2.

For those CICS servers that support CICS 3270 terminal emulation, see "CRSR Transaction Program" on page 43 for details on how to define the CRSR transaction to CM/2 or "Defining the Mode and CRSR Transaction Program" on page 59 for details on how to define the CRSR transaction to APPC Networking Services V1.0.

Change Number of Sessions

With CM/2, before the client connection to the server can be started, the sessions between the client and the server must be started by adding CNOS statements to the .NDF file.

To add CNOS statements:

1. Note the name of the CM/2 configuration containing your SNA definitions.
2. Stop CM/2.
3. Locate your .NDF file. This file is usually in the CMLIB directory.
4. Using an ASCII editor add CNOS statements to the bottom of your .NDF file similar to the statements shown in Figure 68.
5. Ensure that:

    - LOCAL_LU_ALIAS matches the alias entered on the Local LU window (Figure 67 on page 91)
    - FQ_PARTNER_LU_NAME matches your Network ID 4 and Partner LU name 3 (separated by a period)
    - AUTO_ACTIVATE is not greater than PLU_MODE_SESSION_LIMIT

6. Run CMVERIFY to produce a .CF2 file. (The .CF2 file is a binary translation of the .NDF file and is used to initialize the SNA definitions when APPC is started.)

```
CNOS  LOCAL_LU_ALIAS(CCLICALU)
      FQ_PARTNER_LU_NAME(DEIBMIPF.CICSSA22)
      MODE_NAME(BLANK)
      SET_NEGOTIABLE(NO)
      PLU_MODE_SESSION_LIMIT(8)
      MIN_CONWINNERS_SOURCE(4)
      MIN_CONWINNERS_TARGET(4)
      AUTO_ACTIVATE(4);
```

Figure 68. Sample CNOS Statements: CICS/VSE-SDLC-CICS Client for OS/2 Using CM/2

Warning: Be sure that you have applied PTF UN63772 to your CICS/VSE. Without that PTF, CM/2 cannot start the sessions between the client and the server.

CICSCLI.INI

The CICSCLI.INI file is found in the CICS Client for OS/2 BIN subdirectory. Figure 69 on page 93 shows the definitions required for the sample configuration.

```
   :::
   Server              = CICSVSE
   Netname             = DEIBMIPF.CICSSA22      4.3
   Protocol            = SNA
   LocalLUName         = CCLICALU               2
   ModeName            = *

   :::

   Driver              = SNA
   DriverName          = CCLIBMSN
```

Figure 69. CICSCLI.INI Definitions: CICS/VSE-SDLC-CICS Client for OS/2 Using CM/2

Notes:

1. A separate **Server** definition is required for each server to which the client needs to connect. You can make this value meaningful to the end user, for example, CICSVSE.

2. The **Netname** is the fully qualified applid of the server, that is, your Network ID and Local LU separated by a period.

3. The value of **Protocol** identifies the communication protocol to be used between the client and the server. This value must match the value you have assigned to **Driver**. You can make this value meaningful to the end user, for example, SNA or APPC.

4. The **LocalLUName** is the local LU to be used when connecting to the server. The same LU can be used for all server connections.

5. The **ModeName** in the sample configuration has a value of * (asterisk). This value indicates that a blank modename is to be used.

6. **Driver** must be the same as **Protocol**.

7. The device driver used by CM/2 in the sample configuration is **CCLIBMSN**.

Testing Your Configuration

After you have installed and configured all relevant products for this sample configuration, we recommend that you do the following:

Step 1. Start the CICS server.

Step 2. Start CM/2 on the client workstation.

Testing Your Configuration

Step 3. Activate the connection between CM/2 and the CICS mainframe.
→ See "Establishing a Connection Between CM/2 and CICS Mainframe" on page 316.

Step 4. Start the CICS Client for OS/2.
Issue **CICSCLI /S=CICSVSE**.
→ See "Starting and Stopping Your CICS Client" on page 321.

Step 5. Check the status of the CICS Client for OS/2.
Issue **CICSCLI /L**.
→ See "Checking the Status of Your CICS Client" on page 322.

Step 6. Prepare for data conversion.
→ See "Data Conversion: ASCII to EBCDIC" on page 326.

Step 7. Run a simple ECI application.
→ See "Sample Implementation" on page 277.

Step 8. Problems?
→ See Chapter 21, "Problem Determination," on page 293.
→ See Appendix C, "Common Problems: Symptoms and Solutions," on page 339.
→ See Appendix F, "CM/2 .NDF and APPC NS/Windows NSD.INI Files," on page 367.

Step 9. Need further information?
→ See Appendix B, "Frequently Asked Questions," on page 331.

7

CICS/VSE • SDLC • Client Using APPC NS/Windows

This chapter covers the following topics:
- "Software Checklist" on page 96
- "Definitions Checklist" on page 97
- "Matching Definitions" on page 98
- "Sample Definitions" on page 98
  - VTAM
  - CICS/VSE
  - APPC Networking Services for Windows V1.0 (detailed step-by-step example)
  - IBM CICS Client for Windows
- "Testing Your Configuration" on page 109

Software Checklist

This sample configuration (see Figure 70) consists of an IBM CICS Client for Windows[1] connecting to a CICS mainframe using SNA LU6.2 (APPC) communication provided by APPC Networking Services for Windows V1.0[2] on the client workstation and VTAM on the mainframe server.

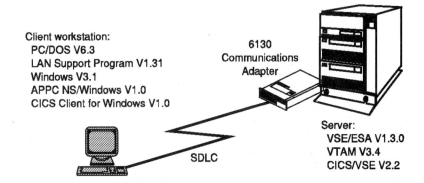

Figure 70. SDLC Configuration Using APPC NS/Windows

Although the sample configuration uses CICS/VSE V2.2 as the mainframe server, you could use CICS/MVS V2.1.2, CICS/ESA V3.3, or CICS/ESA V4.1 (or later).

We used an SDLC connection for this configuration, but you can use other physical links, for example, token-ring or Ethernet.

Software Checklist

The levels of software used in the sample configuration are not necessarily the latest levels available. You should check the relevant products for levels of compatible software.

The software required on the server is:

❑ VSE/ESA operating system V1.3.0

❑ VTAM V3.4

❑ CICS/VSE V2.2

The software required on the client workstation is:

❑ PC DOS V6.3 operating system

---

[1] Hereafter referred to as CICS Client for Windows.
[2] Hereafter referred to as APPC NS/Windows.

- Windows V3.1
- APPC NS/Windows V1.0
- IBM CICS Client for Windows V1.0

Definitions Checklist

Before you configure the products, we recommend that you acquire definitions for the parameters listed below. Reference keys are assigned to definitions that must contain the same value in more than one product. For example, ADDR has the reference key **1**. These reference keys are used in later sections of this chapter.

- VTAM
    - ADDR **1**
    - PU
    - LU **2**
    - APPL **3**
    - NETID **4**
- CICS/VSE
    - ISC SIT override
    - DFHISC group
    - Applid **3**
    - Netname in the LU6.2 connection definition **2**
- APPC NS/Windows
    - Network ID **4**
    - Local LU name **2**
    - Connection type
    - Link name
    - Local station address **1**
    - Transaction program (CRSR)

Note: APPC NS/Windows dynamically creates a partner LU definition when the first session with a partner LU is activated. The CICS Client for Windows automatically issues an allocate (CMALLC) request for a partner LU that is not defined to establish this connection. Alternatively, you can manually establish the connection by using the **Advanced Operations** program to request activation of sessions with a partner LU that is not yet defined. (See Appendix A, "Hints and Tips," on page 315 to see how this is done.)

Matching Definitions

- Workstation definitions. These entries are defined in the CICS-CLI.INI initialization file, generally found in the \CICSCLI\BIN subdirectory:
  - Server
  - Network.Netname **4**.**3**
  - Protocol
  - LocalLUName **2**
  - Driver
  - DriverName

Matching Definitions

In the sample configuration a number of definitions must match. Table 10 shows the definitions that must be the same. The last column (Example) shows the values we used in our configuration (see "Sample Definitions" on page 98).

Table 10. Matching Definitions: CICS/VSE-SDLC-Client Using APPC NS/Windows

	VTAM	CICS/VSE V2.2	APPC NS/Windows	CICSCLI.INI	Example
1	ADDR	-	Local station address	-	C1
2	LU	Netname	Local LU name	LocalLUName	CCLICALU
3	APPL	Applid	-	Netname	CICSSA22
4	NETID	-	Network ID	Network	DEIBMIPF

Sample Definitions

This section presents the values of each of the definitions mentioned in "Definitions Checklist" on page 97. The values highlighted in the figures refer to the Example column of Table 10.

VTAM

In this section we present the VTAM definitions for the server.

NETID

You specify the NETID **4** for VTAM in the VTAM startup procedure. Figure 71 shows the VTAM startup procedure, ATCSTR04.B, that we used in the sample configuration.

```
* $$ JOB JNM=BOESTR04,DISP=D,PRI=3,                              C
* $$ NTFY=YES                                                    C
* $$ LDEST=*,                                                    C
* $$ CLASS=0
// JOB BOESTR04 CATALOG VTAM START OPTION LIST
// EXEC LIBR,PARM='MSHP'
ACCESS SUBLIB=PRD2.CONFIG
CATALOG    ATCSTR04.B    REPLACE=YES
SSCPID=22,                                                       *
HOSTSA=22,                                                       *
SSCPNAME=IPFV2B,                                                 *
HOSTPU=IPFVM22,                                                  *
NETID=DEIBMIPF,                                                  *
MAXSUBA=255,                                                     *
CONFIG=04,                                                       *
IOINT=0,                                                         *
SGALIMIT=1M,                                                     *
BSBUF=(28,,,1),                                                  *
CRPLBUF=(60,,,1),                                                *
LFBUF=(300,288,,20),                                             *
LPBUF=(12,,,6),                                                  *
SFBUF=(20,,,20),                                                 *
SPBUF=(210,,,32),                                                *
VFBUF=204800,                                                    *
VPBUF=528384,                                                    *
XDBUF=(6,,,1)
/+
/*
/&
* $$ EOJ
```

Figure 71. VTAM Startup Procedure ATCSTR04.B: CICS/VSE-SDLC-Client Using APPC NS/Windows

PU, ADDR, and LU

Figure 72 shows the VTAM PU, ADDR **1**, and LU **2** definitions we used in the sample configuration.

Sample Definitions

```
CCLICA    VBUILD TYPE=CA
CCLICAGR  GROUP  LNCTL=SDLC,
                 DIAL=NO,
                 ISTATUS=INACTIVE
CCLICALI  LINE   ADDRESS=B40,
                 CORNUM=(1,2),
                 MAXBFRU=(2,8),
                 PORT=A
CCLICAPU  PU     ADDR=C1,
                 XID=YES,
                 PUTYPE=2,MAXDATA=265
CCLICALU  LU     LOCADDR=0,
                 ISTATUS=ACTIVE,MODETAB=IESINCLM
          ...
```

Figure 72. PU, ADDR, and LU Definitions in VTAM CA Major Node: CICS/VSE-SDLC-Client Using APPC NS/Windows

Notes:

- You must specify XID=YES for PU Type 2.1 nodes to enable parallel sessions communication.
- The LU, CCLICALU **2**, is defined as an independent LU, specifying **0** in the LOCADDR parameter.

APPL

Figure 73 shows the VTAM APPL **3** definition required for the sample configuration.

```
          ...
BOEAPPL    VBUILD TYPE=APPL
CICSSA22   APPL   AUTH=(PASS,ACQ,VPACE),ACBNAME=CICSSA22,
                  EAS=4000,APPC=NO,PARSESS=YES,
                  SONSCIP=YES,VPACING=3
```

Figure 73. VTAM APPL Major Node Definition: CICS/VSE-SDLC-Client Using APPC NS/Windows

Generally, LU6.2 parallel rather than single sessions are used, in which case you must set PARSESS to YES to allow LU 6.2 parallel sessions.

Although the communication between the client and the server uses APPC, you must specify **APPC=NO** in the APPL definition.

APPC=YES indicates that the application uses the ACF/VTAM APPC-CMD programming interface. CICS does not use this VTAM function. Instead it has implemented its support of APPC through the traditional VTAM macro interface. Coding APPC=YES not only indicates that the application uses the new interface, but also causes VTAM not

Sample Definitions

to allow the application to use the traditional macros to manipulate an LU6.2 APPC session. So, not only is APPC=YES not needed for CICS coding, it also actually stops the existing CICS support from working.

CICS/VSE

In this section we present the CICS/VSE definitions for the server.

System Initialization Table Parameters

Figure 74 shows the SIT parameters to enable ISC.

```
   ...
   ISC=YES,
   APPLID=CICSSA22
   ...
```

Figure 74. System Initialization Table Definitions: CICS/VSE-SDLC-Client Using APPC NS/Windows

DFHISC Group

To enable ISC on CICS/VSE, you must install the DFHISC group (see Figure 75).

```
Either:     CEDA INSTALL GROUP(DFHISC)
And/or:     CEDA ADD LIST(grplist) GROUP(DFHISC)
            where 'grplist' is the list of groups
            CICS installs during start-up.
```

Figure 75. Install DFHISC: CICS/VSE-SDLC-Client Using APPC NS/Windows

LU6.2 Connection

Figure 76 on page 102 shows the LU6.2 connection definition we installed on CICS/VSE by using RDO.

Sample Definitions

```
OBJECT CHARACTERISTICS
 CEDA  View
   Connection    : CCLS
   Group         : CCLSDLC
 CONNECTION IDENTIFIERS
   Netname       : CCLICALU
   INDsys        :
 REMOTE ATTRIBUTES
   REMOTESystem  :
   REMOTEName    :
 CONNECTION PROPERTIES
   ACcessmethod  : Vtam         Vtam ] IRc ] INdirect
   Protocol      : Appc         Appc ] Lu61
   SInglesess    : No           No ] Yes
   Datastream    : User         User ] 3270 ] SCs ] STrfield ] Lms
   RECordformat  : U            U ] Vb
 OPERATIONAL PROPERTIES
   AUtoconnect   : Yes          No ] Yes ] All
 + INService     : Yes          Yes ] No
```

Figure 76. LU6.2 Connection Definition: CICS/VSE-SDLC-Client Using APPC NS/Windows

Note: The LU6.2 connection definition and the LU6.2 sessions definition must reside in the same group and be installed simultaneously.

LU6.2 Sessions

Figure 77 on page 103 shows the LU6.2 sessions definition we installed on CICS/VSE by using RDO.

```
OBJECT CHARACTERISTICS
 CEDA  View
   Sessions        : CCLS
   Group           : CCLSDLC
 SESSION IDENTIFIERS
   Connection      : CCLS
   SESSName        :
   NETnameq        :
   MOdename        :
 SESSION PROPERTIES
   Protocol        : Appc              Appc ] Lu61
   MAximum         : 00012 , 00004     0-32767
   RECEIVEPfx      :
   RECEIVECount    : No                No ] 1-999
   SENDPfx         :
   SENDCount       : No                No ] 1-999
   SENDSize        : 04096             1-30720
   RECEIVESize     : 04096             1-30720
+ OPERATOR DEFAULTS
```

Figure 77. LU6.2 Sessions Definition: CICS/VSE-SDLC-Client Using APPC NS/Windows

Note: The LU6.2 connection definition and the LU6.2 sessions definition must reside in the same group and be installed simultaneously.

APPC NS/Windows

In this section we explain in detail how to define your values to APPC NS/Windows.

For the sample configuration you must install the following APPC NS/Windows components:

BASE   required for networking modules

SDLC   enables connections to use SDLC

During installation of APPC NS/Windows you are asked the following question:

   Do you wish to run configuration at this time?

Select **Yes**.

Note: If you have already installed the product, you can run the configuration utility by clicking on the **Configure** icon from the IBM APPC Networking Services application group.

Sample Definitions

After the BASE and SDLC components have been installed, you are presented with the Networking Services Configuration window (see Figure 78 on page 104).

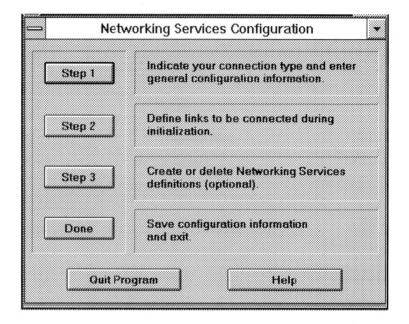

Figure 78. Networking Services Configuration Window: CICS/VSE-SDLC-Client Using APPC NS/Windows

Select **Step 1** to get to the General Configuration window.

General Configuration Window

On the General Configuration window (Figure 79 on page 105):

1. Specify your fully qualified local LU name, which is your Network ID 4 and Local LU name 2 separated by a period.
2. Select the connection type to be used by Networking Services. For the sample configuration you should select **Synchronous (SDLC)** for an SDLC network.
3. Select **OK** to return to the Networking Services Configuration window (Figure 78).

Sample Definitions

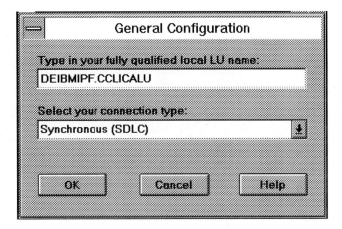

Figure 79. General Configuration Window

On the Networking Services Configuration window select **Step 2** to get to the Remote Configuration window.

Remote Configuration Window

Figure 80 on page 106 shows the Remote Configuration window.

Sample Definitions

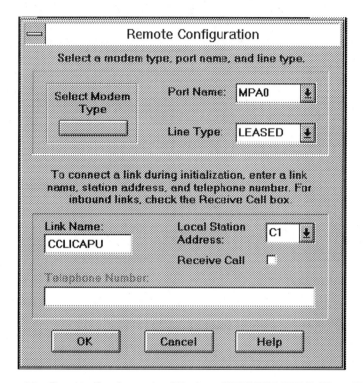

Figure 80. Remote Configuration Window: CICS/VSE-SDLC-Client Using APPC NS/Windows

On the Remote Configuration window:

1. Select **Select Modem Type** to get a list of available modems.

    - Select **YES** for the existing modem list.
    - Select the modem you are using. For the sample configuration we used a modem eliminator (**Null Modem**). See Figure 81 on page 107.

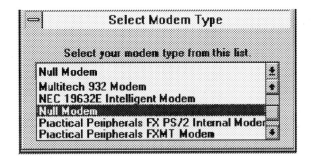

Figure 81. Select Modem Type Window

2. Select **MPA0** for port 0.
3. Select **LEASED** for dedicated lines.
4. Specify a name (that will be used only by your workstation) to refer to the link between your workstation and the server system. You can make this name meaningful to the end user, for example, CCLICAPU.
5. Specify the Local Station Address **1**. This parameter is required to activate the link connection.
6. Select **OK** to return to the Networking Services Configuration window (Figure 78 on page 104).

CRSR Transaction Program

The CRSR transaction program is required if the CICS server supports CICS 3270 terminal emulation. It is used to perform ATI against the CICS client terminals. CICS/VSE V2.2 does not support CICS 3270 terminal emulation, so for this sample configuration you do not need to define the CRSR transaction to APPC NS/Windows.

For those CICS servers that support CICS 3270 terminal emulation, see "CRSR Transaction Program" on page 43 for details on how to define the CRSR transaction to CM/2; or "Defining the Mode and CRSR Transaction Program" on page 59 for details on how to define the CRSR transaction to APPC NS/Windows V1.0.

On the Networking Services Configuration window select **Done** to complete your configuration.

Station Role Definition

For the sample configuration you must specify the station role of your workstation in the NSD.INI file. The station role must be set to secondary.

Sample Definitions

The NSD.INI file is found in your WINDOWS directory. Using an ASCII editor, edit the NSD.INI file and enter secondary on the SDLC statement within the [Remote] section. For example:

```
  :::         :::
[Remote]
SDLD=CCLICAPU, C1, , , , secondary,
SDDI=66
SDMT=NULMODEM
SDLT=NONSWTPP
  :::         :::
```

For this change to take effect:

1. On the Networking Services Configuration window double-click on the **Configure** icon.
2. Click on **Done**.

CICSCLI.INI

The CICSCLI.INI file is found in the CICS Client for Windows BIN subdirectory. Figure 82 shows the definitions required for the sample configuration.

```
    :::
  Server           = CICSVSE
  Netname          = DEIBMIPF.CICSSA22    4 3
  Protocol         = APPC
  LocalLUName      = CCLICALU             2
  ModeName         = *
    :::
  Driver           = APPC
  DriverName       = CCLIBMSN
```

Figure 82. CICSCLI.INI Definitions: CICS/VSE-SDLC-Client Using APPC NS/Windows

Notes:

1. A separate **Server** definition is required for each server to which the client needs to connect. You can make this value meaningful to the end user, for example, CICSVSE.

2. The **Netname** is the fully qualified applid of the server, that is, your Network ID and Local LU separated by a period.

3. The value of **Protocol** identifies the communication protocol to be used between the client and the server. This value must match the value you have assigned to **Driver**. You can make this value meaningful to the enduser, for example, SNA or APPC.
4. The **LocalLUName** is the local LU to be used when connecting to the server. The same LU can be used for all server connections.
5. The **ModeName** in the sample configuration has a value of * (asterisk). This indicates that a blank modename is to be used.
6. **Driver** must be the same as **Protocol**.
7. The device driver used by APPC NS/Windows in the sample configuration is **CCLIBMSN**.

Testing Your Configuration

After you have installed and configured all relevant products for this sample configuration, we recommend that you do the following:

Step 1. Start the CICS server.

Step 2. Start NS/Windows on the client workstation.
→ See "SNA" on page 341.

Step 3. Start the CICS Client for Windows.
Issue **CICSCLI /S=CICSVSE**.
→ See "Starting and Stopping Your CICS Client" on page 321.

Step 4. Check the status of the CICS Client for Windows.
Issue **CICSCLI /L**.
→ See "Checking the Status of Your CICS Client" on page 322.

Step 5. Prepare for data conversion.
→ See "Data Conversion: ASCII to EBCDIC" on page 326.

Step 6. Run a simple ECI application.
→ See "Sample Implementation" on page 277.

Step 7. Problems?
→ See Chapter 21, "Problem Determination," on page 293.
→ See Appendix C, "Common Problems: Symptoms and Solutions," on page 339.
→ See Appendix F, "CM/2 .NDF and APPC NS/Windows NSD.INI Files," on page 367.

Testing Your Configuration

Step 8. Need further information?
→ See Appendix B, "Frequently Asked Questions," on page 331.

8

CICS/VSE • Ethernet • Client Using APPC NS/Windows

> **This chapter covers the following topics:**
> - "Software Checklist" on page 112
> - "Definitions Checklist" on page 113
> - "Matching Definitions" on page 114
> - "Sample Definitions" on page 115
>   - VTAM
>   - IBM 3172 Configuration
>   - CICS/VSE
>   - LSP
>   - APPC Networking Services for Windows V1.0 (detailed step-by-step example)
>   - IBM CICS Client for Windows
> - "Testing Your Configuration" on page 128

This sample configuration (see Figure 83) consists of an IBM CICS Client for Windows[1] connecting to a CICS mainframe using SNA LU6.2 (APPC) communication provided by APPC Networking Services for Windows V1.0[2] on the client workstation and VTAM on the mainframe server.

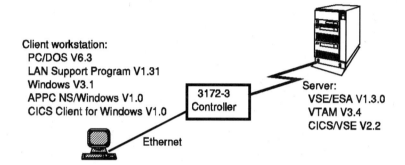

Figure 83. Ethernet Configuration: CICS/VSE-Ethernet-Client Using APPC NS/Windows

Although the sample configuration uses CICS/VSE V2.2 as the mainframe server, you could use CICS/MVS V2.1.2, CICS/ESA V3.3, or CICS/ESA V4.1 (or later).

We used an Ethernet LAN for this configuration, but you can use other physical links, for example, SDLC or token-ring connections.

Software Checklist

The levels of software used in the sample configuration are not necessarily the latest levels available. You should check the relevant products for levels of compatible software.

The software required on the server is:

- ❏ VSE/ESA operating system V1.3.0
- ❏ VTAM V3.4
- ❏ CICS/VSE V2.2

The software required on the client workstation is:

- ❏ PC DOS V6.3 operating system

---

[1] Hereafter referred to as CICS Client for Windows.
[2] Hereafter referred to as APPC NS/Windows.

- ❏ LAN Support Program V1.31
- ❏ Windows V3.1
- ❏ APPC NS/Windows V1.0
- ❏ IBM CICS Client for Windows V1.0

Note: When installing the LAN Support Program on the client workstation you must select the **802.2 interface support** option (see "LAN Support Program" on page 238). If you attempt to run APPC NS/Windows without the 802.2 interface support, you receive the following error message: Adapter not present.

Definitions Checklist

Before you configure the products, we recommend that you acquire definitions for the parameters listed in the tables that follow. Reference keys are assigned to definitions that must contain the same value in more than one product. For example, CUADDR has the reference key **1**. These reference keys are used in later sections of this chapter.

- ❏ VTAM
  - ➢ CUADDR **1**
  - ➢ XID (IDBLK+IDNUM) **2**
  - ➢ PU
  - ➢ LU **3**
  - ➢ APPL **4**
  - ➢ DIALNO **5**
  - ➢ NETID **7**
- ❏ Interconnect control program (ICP) definitions for the 3172 interconnect controller
  - ➢ Node address **6**
  - ➢ Subchannel **1**
- ❏ CICS/ESA V2.2
  - ➢ ISC SIT override
  - ➢ DFHISC group
  - ➢ Applid **4**
  - ➢ Netname in the LU6.2 connection definition **3**
- ❏ LAN Support Program
  - ➢ MAC address **5**
- ❏ APPC NS/Windows

Matching Definitions

- Network ID **7**
- Local LU name **3**
- Connection type
- Link name
- Remote address **6**
- Transaction program (CRSR)
- Node ID (in NSD.INI file) **2**

Note: APPC NS/Windows dynamically creates a partner LU definition when the first session with a partner LU is activated. The CICS Client for Windows automatically issues an allocate (CMALLC) request for a partner LU that is not defined to establish this connection. Alternatively, you can manually establish the connection by using the **Advanced Operations** program to request activation of sessions with a partner LU that is not yet defined. (See "Testing Your Configuration" on page 128 to see how this is done.)

❑ Workstation definitions. These entries are defined in the CICS-CLI.INI initialization file, generally found in the \CICSCLI\BIN subdirectory:

- Server
- Network.Netname **7**.**4**
- Protocol
- LocalLUName **3**
- Driver
- DriverName

Matching Definitions

In the sample configuration a number of definitions must match. Table 11 shows the definitions that must be the same. The last column (Example) shows the values we used in our configuration (see "Sample Definitions" on page 115).

Table 11. Matching Definitions: CICS/VSE-Ethernet-Client Using APPC NS/Windows

	VTAM	ICP 3172	CICS/VSE V2.2	LAN Support Program	APPC NS/ Windows	CICSCLI. INI	Example
1	CUADDR	Subchannel	-	-	-	-	961
2	XID	-	-	-	Node ID	-	05DE000B

Table 11. Matching Definitions: CICS/VSE-Ethernet-Client Using APPC NS/Windows

	VTAM	ICP 3172	CICS/VSE V2.2	LAN Support Program	APPC NS/ Windows	CICSCLI. INI	Example
3	LU	-	Netname	-	Local LU	LocalLU Name	CCLXL001
4	APPL	-	Applid	-	-	Netname	CICSSA22
5	DIALNO	-	-	MAC address	-	-	40001010100B
6	-	Node address	-	-	Remote address	-	020040400820 400002021004 See **Note:**
7	NETID	-	-	-	Network ID	Network	DEIBMIPF

Note: The Ethernet/802.3 Adapter address appears on the IBM 3172 in IEEE illustrative or canonical form, where the most significant bit is on the right (within each byte). For APPC NS/Windows, the address is shown in medium access control (MAC) bit order, where the most significant bit is on the left (within each byte). To convert from one form to the other, refer to Appendix B, "Address Conversion," in the *IBM 3172 Interconnect Controller Program Version 3.3 User's Guide*.

Sample Definitions

In this section we present examples of each of the definitions mentioned in "Definitions Checklist" on page 113. The values highlighted in the figures refer to the Example column of Table 11.

VTAM

In this section we present the VTAM definitions for the server.

XCA Major Node

An External Communication Adapter (XCA) major node is required to enable VTAM to use an IBM 3172. Figure 84 describes our IBM 3172 XCA major node.

Sample Definitions

```
CCLXCAET VBUILD TYPE=XCA
*
* DEFINITION FOR IBM 3172 ETHERNET
*
CET3172   PORT   CUADDR=961 ,
                 MEDIUM=CSMACD,
                 ADAPNO=0,
                 TIMER=60
G3172ET   GROUP  DIAL=YES
L3172ET   LINE   ISTATUS=ACTIVE,CALL=INOUT,ANSWER=ON
P3172ET   PU     ISTATUS=ACTIVE
```

Figure 84. VSE/VTAM XCA Major Node for the IBM 3172

The CUADDR **1** must match the virtual address ADDed in the VSE/ESA IPL procedure (see Appendix G, "IBM 3172 Customization," on page 377).

XID, PU, LU, and DIALNO

Figure 85 shows the VTAM XID **2**, PU, LU **3**, and DIALNO **5** definitions we used in the sample configuration.

```
CCLXCASW VBUILD TYPE=SWNET
*
CCLCPX01  PU    ADDR=01,
                LANSW=YES,
                IDBLK=05D ,IDNUM=E000B ,
                DISCNT=NO,
                ISTATUS=ACTIVE,PACING=1,VPACING=2,
                PUTYPE=2,
                MAXDATA=265,
                MAXOUT=1,
                MAXPATH=1,
                SAPADDR=4
*
          PATH  DIALNO=0104 40001010100B
*
CCLXL001  LU    LOCADDR=0,
                ISTATUS=ACTIVE,MODETAB=IESINCLM
          ...
```

Figure 85. VTAM XID, PU, LU and DIALNO Definitions

Note: The XID **2** is split into two parts: IDBLK and IDNUM.

The LU, CCLXL001 **3**, is defined as an independent LU, specifying **0** in the LOCADDR parameter.

APPL

Figure 86 shows the VTAM APPL ◧4 definition required for the sample configuration.

```
            ...
BOEAPPL     VBUILD TYPE=APPL
CICSSA22 APPL  AUTH=(PASS,ACQ,VPACE),ACBNAME=CICSSA22,
               EAS=4000,APPC=NO,PARSESS=YES,
               SONSCIP=YES,VPACING=3
```

Figure 86. VTAM APPL Definition: CICS/VSE-Ethernet-Client Using APPC NS/Windows

Generally, LU6.2 parallel rather than single sessions are used, in which case you must set PARSESS to YES to enable LU 6.2 parallel session support.

Although the communication between the client and the server uses APPC, you must specify **APPC=NO** in the APPL definition.

APPC=YES indicates that the application uses the ACF/VTAM APPC-CMD programming interface. CICS does not use this VTAM function. Instead it has implemented its own support of APPC through the traditional VTAM macro interface. Coding APPC=YES not only indicates that the application uses the new interface, but also causes VTAM to not allow the application to use the traditional macros to manipulate an LU6.2 APPC session. So, not only is APPC=YES not needed for CICS coding, it also actually stops the existing CICS support from working.

NETID

You specify the NETID ◧7 for VTAM in the VTAM startup procedure. Figure 87 on page 118 shows the VTAM startup procedure, ATCSTR04.B, that we used in the sample configuration.

Sample Definitions

```
* $$ JOB JNM=BOESTR04,DISP=D,PRI=3,                              C
* $$ NTFY=YES                                                    C
* $$ LDEST=*,                                                    C
* $$ CLASS=0
// JOB BOESTR04 CATALOG VTAM START OPTION LIST
// EXEC LIBR,PARM='MSHP'
ACCESS SUBLIB=PRD2.CONFIG
CATALOG    ATCSTR04.B    REPLACE=YES
SSCPID=22,                                                       *
HOSTSA=22,                                                       *
SSCPNAME=IPFV2B,                                                 *
HOSTPU=IPFVM22,                                                  *
NETID=DEIBMIPF,                                                  *
MAXSUBA=255,                                                     *
CONFIG=04,                                                       *
IOINT=0,                                                         *
SGALIMIT=1M,                                                     *
BSBUF=(28,,,1),                                                  *
CRPLBUF=(60,,,1),                                                *
LFBUF=(300,288,,20),                                             *
LPBUF=(12,,,6),                                                  *
SFBUF=(20,,,20),                                                 *
SPBUF=(210,,,32),                                                *
VFBUF=204800,                                                    *
VPBUF=528384,                                                    *
XDBUF=(6,,,1)
/+
/*
/&
* $$ EOJ
```

Figure 87. VTAM Startup Procedure ATCSTR04.B: CICS/VSE-Ethernet-Client Using APPC NS/Windows

IBM 3172 Configuration

Figure 88 on page 119 shows the parameters used in the customization of the ICP for the IBM 3172. There are two parameters that must match other definitions in our example:

> **Subchannel.** This value must match the control unit and unit portion of the real address defined to the host for the 3172. See "IOCDS and VM/ESA Definitions" on page 378.
>
> **Node Address.** This value is the **MAC address** used by APPC NS/Windows to find the IBM 3172 gateway to our CICS/VSE host.

For instructions on how to customize the IBM 3172 please refer to Appendix G, "IBM 3172 Customization," on page 377 .

```
3172-3 Configuration Summary
3172 Name ................. : ETHTOK
3172 Type ................. : 3172-3 Lan Gateway
Int Enhancement Feature (IEF) : Yes
User Data ................. : Ethernet + Token Ring Connection
Location .................. : ITSO Boeblingen
ICP Base Code Version...... : 3.02.00
ICP IEF Code Version....... : 3.02.00
APARs/Patches applied...... : None
Profile Name............... : ETHTOK
Slot    Name        Adapter Type
----    ----------  --------------------
  1     Unassigned
  2     Unassigned
  3     Unassigned
  4     CHAN1       Parallel Channel
  5     Reserved
  6     ETH1        Ethernet/802.3
  7     TOK1        Token-Ring 16/4
  8     Fixed Disk
LAN Function Name ......... : SNAGATE
Channel Adapter Name ...... : CHAN1
                To       To      LAN       Block   Maximum
Subchannels   Channel    LAN    Adapter    Delay   Response
-----------   -------   -------  -------   -----   --------
    60        TOCHN060  TOLAN060  TOK1      10      100
    61        TOCHN061  TOLAN061  ETH1      10      100
Slot ...................... : 4
Adapter Name .............. : CHAN1
Adapter Type .............. : Parallel Channel
Transfer Mode and Speed ... : 4.5 MB Data Streaming
SNA Management Services ... : No
Slot ...................... : 6
Adapter Name .............. : ETH1
Adapter Type .............. : Ethernet/802.3
Node Address .............. : **400020201004**
Transceiver Type .......... : BNC
Receive Mode .............. : S
To Operator FAcility ...... : No
Slot ...................... : 7
Adapter Name .............. : TOK1
Adapter Type .............. : Token-Ring 16/4
Node Address .............. : 400020201003
Data Rate (Mbps) .......... : 4
To Operator FAcility ...... : No
Combined Functional Addresses : 000000000000
```

Figure 88. IBM 3172 ICP Configuration

CICS/VSE

In this section we present the CICS/VSE definitions for the server.

System Initialization Table Parameters

Figure 89 shows the SIT parameters to enable ISC.

```
   ...
   ISC=YES,
   APPLID=CICSSA22
   ...
```

Figure 89. System Initialization Table Definitions: CICS/VSE-Ethernet-Client Using APPC NS/Windows

DFHISC Group

To enable ISC on CICS/VSE, you must install the DFHISC group (see Figure 90).

```
   Either:    CEDA INSTALL GROUP(DFHISC)
   And/or:    CEDA ADD LIST(grplist) GROUP(DFHISC)
              where 'grplist' is the list of groups
              CICS installs during start-up.
```

Figure 90. Install DFHISC: CICS/VSE-Ethernet-Client Using APPC NS/Windows

LU6.2 Connection

Figure 91 on page 121 shows the LU6.2 connection definition that we installed on CICS/VSE by using RDO.

Sample Definitions

```
OBJECT CHARACTERISTICS
 CEDA  View
   Connection    : CCLW
   Group         : CCLWIN
 CONNECTION IDENTIFIERS
   Netname       : CCLXL001
   INDsys        :
 REMOTE ATTRIBUTES
   REMOTESystem  :
   REMOTEName    :
 CONNECTION PROPERTIES
   ACcessmethod  : Vtam       Vtam ] IRc ] INdirect
   Protocol      : Appc       Appc ] Lu61
   SInglesess    : No         No ] Yes
   Datastream    : User       User ] 3270 ] SCs ] STrfield ] Lms
   RECordformat  : U          U ] Vb
 OPERATIONAL PROPERTIES
   AUtoconnect   : Yes        No ] Yes ] All
 + INService     : Yes        Yes ] No
```

Figure 91. LU6.2 Connection Definition: CICS/VSE-Ethernet-Client Using APPC NS/Windows

Note: The LU6.2 connection definition and the LU6.2 sessions definition must reside in the same group and be installed simultaneously.

LU6.2 Sessions

Figure 92 on page 122 shows the LU6.2 sessions definition that we installed on CICS/VSE by using RDO.

Sample Definitions

```
OBJECT CHARACTERISTICS
 CEDA  View
   Sessions        : CCLW
   Group           : CCLWIN
 SESSION IDENTIFIERS
   Connection      : CCLW
   SESSName        :
   NETnameq        :
   MOdename        :
 SESSION PROPERTIES
   Protocol        : Appc              Appc ] Lu61
   MAximum         : 00012 , 00004     0-32767
   RECEIVEPfx      :
   RECEIVECount    : No                No ] 1-999
   SENDPfx         :
   SENDCount       : No                No ] 1-999
   SENDSize        : 04096             1-30720
   RECEIVESize     : 04096             1-30720
 + OPERATOR DEFAULTS
```

Figure 92. LU6.2 Sessions Definition: CICS/VSE-Ethernet-Client Using APPC NS/Windows

Note: The LU6.2 connection definition and the LU6.2 sessions definition must reside in the same group and be installed simultaneously.

LAN Support Program

For a step-by-step guide to installing the LAN Support Program, see "LAN Support Program" on page 238 .

For the sample configuration you must specify the correct MAC address 5 of the workstation in the CONFIG.SYS file. The MAC address must match the address configured on VTAM (see Figure 85 on page 116).

Using an ASCII editor, edit the CONFIG.SYS file and enter the MAC address on the DXME0MOD.SYS statement (see Figure 93 on page 123).

```
.
.
.
DEVICE=\LSP\PROTMAN.DOS /I:\LSP
DEVICE=\LSP\MACETH.DOS
DEVICE=\LSP\DXMAOMOD.SYS 001
DEVICE=\LSP\DXMEOMOD.SYS 40001010100B
DEVICE=\LSP\DXMTOMOD.SYS O=N
.
.
.
```

Figure 93. CONFIG.SYS Definitions: LAN Support Program

APPC NS/Windows

In this section we explain in detail how to define your values to APPC NS/Windows.

For the sample configuration you must install the following APPC NS/Windows components:

BASE   required for networking modules

LAN   enables connections to token-ring, Ethernet, PC Network, and mobile LANs

During installation of APPC NS/Windows you are asked the following question:

   Do you wish to run configuration at this time?

Select **Yes**.

Note: If you have already installed the product, you can run the configuration utility by clicking on the **Configure** icon from the IBM APPC Networking Services application group.

After the BASE and LAN components have been installed, you are presented with the Networking Services Configuration window (see Figure 94 on page 124).

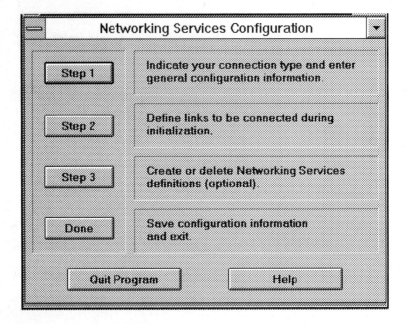

Figure 94. Networking Services Configuration Window: CICS/VSE-Ethernet-Client Using APPC NS/Windows

Select **Step 1** to get to the General Configuration window.

General Configuration Window

On the General Configuration window (Figure 95 on page 125):

1. Specify your fully qualified local LU name, which is your Network ID 7 and Local LU 8 separated by a period.
2. Select the connection type to be used by Networking Services. For the sample configuration you should select **Local Area Network (LAN)** for an Ethernet network.
3. Select **OK** to return to the Networking Services Configuration window (Figure 94).

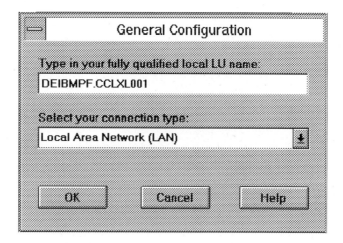

Figure 95. General Configuration Window: CICS/VSE-Ethernet-Client Using APPC NS/Windows

4. Select **Step 2** to get to the LAN Configuration window.

LAN Configuration Window

On the LAN Configuration window (Figure 96 on page 126):

1. Specify a name (that will only be used by your workstation) to refer to the link between your workstation and the server system. You can make this name meaningful to the end user, for example, CICSVSE.
2. Specify the LAN address of the remote system 6 as a MAC address (see note to Table 11 on page 114).
3. Select **OK** to return to the Networking Services Configuration window (Figure 94 on page 124).

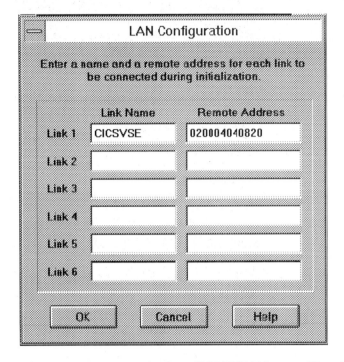

Figure 96. LAN Configuration Window: CICS/VSE-Ethernet-Client Using APPC NS/Windows

CRSR Transaction Program

The CRSR transaction program is required if the CICS server supports CICS 3270 terminal emulation. It is used to perform ATI against the CICS client terminals. CICS/VSE V2.2 does not support CICS 3270 terminal emulation, so for this sample configuration you do not need to define the CRSR transaction to APPC NS/Windows.

For those CICS servers that support CICS 3270 terminal emulation, see "CRSR Transaction Program" on page 43 for details on how to define the CRSR transaction to CM/2; or "Defining the Mode and CRSR Transaction Program" on page 59 for details on how to define the CRSR transaction to APPC NS/Windows V1.0.

On the Networking Services Configuration window select **Done** to complete your configuration.

Node ID Definition

For the sample configuration you must specify the correct node ID **2** of your workstation in the NSD.INI file. The node ID must match the Node ID configured in VTAM; otherwise your workstation may be unresponsive after it attempts to connect to the server system.

The NSD.INI file is found in your WINDOWS directory. Using an ASCII editor, edit the NSD.INI file and enter your Node ID on the NODEID= statement within the [Configuration] section. For example:

```
[Configuration]
DLCTYPE=LAN
  :::         :::
LOCALLUNAME=DEIBMIPF.CCLXL001
NODEID=05DE000B  2
  :::         :::
```

The LOCALLUNAME definition was added automatically during general configuration (see Figure 95 on page 125).

CICSCLI.INI

The CICSCLI.INI file is found in the CICS Client for Windows BIN subdirectory. Figure 97 shows the definitions required for the sample configuration.

```
   :::
  Server        = CICSVSE
  Netname       = DEIBMIPF.CICSSA22    7 4
  Protocol      = APPC
  LocalLUName   = CCLXL001             3
  ModeName      = *

   :::

  Driver        = APPC
  DriverName    = CCLIBMSN
```

Figure 97. CICSCLI.INI Definitions: CICS/VSE-Ethernet-Client Using APPC NS/Windows

Notes:

1. A separate **Server** definition is required for each server to which the client needs to connect. You can make this value meaningful to the end user, for example, CICSVSE.

2. The **Netname** is the fully qualified applid of the server, that is, your Network ID and Local LU separated by a period.

3. The value of **Protocol** identifies the communication protocol to be used between the client and the server. This value must match the value you have assigned to **Driver**. You can make this value meaningful to the enduser, for example, SNA or APPC.

4. The **LocalLUName** is the local LU to be used when connecting to the server. The same LU can be used for all server connections.

5. The **ModeName** in the sample configuration has a value of * (asterisk). This value indicates that a blank modename is to be used.

6. **Driver** must be the same as **Protocol**.

7. The device driver used by APPC NS/Windows in the sample configuration is **CCLIBMSN**.

Testing Your Configuration

After you have installed and configured all relevant products for this sample configuration, we recommend that you do the following:

Step 1. Start the CICS server.

Step 2. Start NS/Windows on the client workstation.
→ See "SNA" on page 341.

Step 3. Start the CICS Client for Windows.
Issue **CICSCLI /S=CICSVSE**
→ See "Starting and Stopping Your CICS Client" on page 321.

Step 4. Check the status of the CICS Client for Windows.
Issue **CICSCLI /L**
→ See "Checking the Status of Your CICS Client" on page 322.

Step 5. Prepare for data conversion.
→ See "Data Conversion: ASCII to EBCDIC" on page 326.

Step 6. Run a simple ECI application.
→ See "Sample Implementation" on page 277.

Step 7. Problems?
→ See Chapter 21, "Problem Determination," on page 293.
→ See Appendix C, "Common Problems: Symptoms and

Solutions," on page 339.
→ See Appendix F, "CM/2 .NDF and APPC NS/Windows NSD.INI Files," on page 367.

Step 8. Need further information?
→ See Appendix B, "Frequently Asked Questions," on page 331.

Testing Your Configuration

9

CICS/VSE • CM/2 APPN Gateway • APPC NS/Windows

This chapter covers the following topics:
- "Software Checklist" on page 132
- "Definitions Checklist" on page 133
- "Matching Definitions" on page 135
- "Sample Definitions" on page 135
    - VTAM
    - CICS/VSE
    - Communications Manager/2 on the APPN OS/2 Gateway (detailed step-by-step example)
    - APPC Networking Services for Windows V1.0 (detailed step-by-step example)
    - IBM CICS Client for Windows
- "Testing Your Configuration" on page 150

Software Checklist

This sample configuration (see Figure 98) consists of an IBM CICS Client for Windows [1] connecting to a CICS mainframe through SNA LU6.2 (APPC) communication provided by APPC NS/Windows on the client workstation, CM/2 on the APPN OS/2 gateway, and VTAM on the mainframe server.

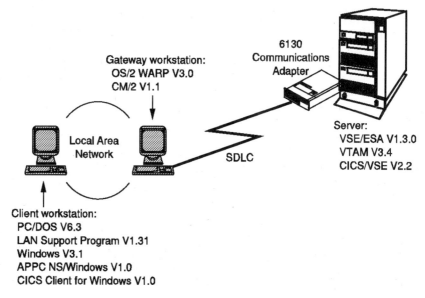

Figure 98. CM/2 APPN Gateway Configuration: CICS/VSE-CM/2 APPN Gateway-APPC NS/Windows

Although the sample configuration uses CICS/VSE V2.2 as the mainframe server, you could use CICS/MVS V2.1.2, CICS/ESA V3.3, or CICS/ESA V4.1 (or later).

We used a token-ring connection between the client workstation and the APPN OS/2 network node and an SDLC connection between the APPN OS/2 network node and the mainframe server for this configuration, but you can use other physical links, for example, Ethernet or coaxial.

Software Checklist

The levels of software used in the sample configuration are not necessarily the latest levels available. You should check the relevant products for levels of compatible software.

---

[1] Hereafter referred to as CICS Client for Windows.

The software required on the server is:
- ❏ VSE/ESA operating system V1.3.0
- ❏ VTAM V3.4
- ❏ CICS/VSE V2.2 + PTF UN63772

The software required on the gateway workstation is:
- ❏ OS 2 WARP V3.0 operating system
- ❏ CM/2 V1.1

The software required on the client workstation is:
- ❏ PC DOS V6.3 operating system
- ❏ LAN Support Program V1.31
- ❏ Windows V3.1
- ❏ APPC NS/Windows V1.0
- ❏ IBM CICS Client for Windows V1.0

Note: When installing the LAN Support Program on the client workstation you must select the **802.2 interface support** option (see "LAN Support Program" on page 238). If you attempt to run APPC NS/Windows without the 802.2 interface support, you receive the error message: Adapter not present.

Definitions Checklist

Before you configure the products, we recommend that you acquire definitions for the parameters listed below. Reference keys are assigned to definitions that must contain the same value in more than one product. For example, NETID has the reference key **1**. These reference keys are used in later sections of this chapter.

- ❏ VTAM
   - ➣ NETID **1**
   - ➣ ADDR **2**
   - ➣ PU
   - ➣ LU **3**
   - ➣ APPL **4**
- ❏ CICS/VSE V2.2
   - ➣ ISC SIT override
   - ➣ DFHISC group
   - ➣ Applid **4**

Definitions Checklist

- Netname in the LU6.2 connection definition **3**
- ❏ CM/2
  - Local station address **2**
  - Local node name
  - Partner network ID **1**
  - Partner LU **4**
- ❏ APPC NS/Windows
  - Network ID **1**
  - Local node name
  - Local LU name **3**
  - Connection type
  - Link name
  - Remote address

Note: APPC NS/Windows dynamically creates a partner LU definition when the first session with a partner LU is activated. The CICS Client for Windows automatically issues an allocate (CMALLC) request for a partner LU that is not defined to establish this connection. Alternatively, you can manually establish the connection by using the **Advanced Operations** program to request activation of sessions with a partner LU that is not yet defined. (See "Testing Your Configuration" on page 150 to see how this is done.).

- ❏ Workstation definitions. These entries are defined in the CICSCLI.INI initialization file, generally found in the \CICSCLI\BIN subdirectory:
  - Server
  - Network.Netname **1**,**4**
  - Protocol
  - LocalLUName **3**
  - Driver
  - DriverName

Matching Definitions

In the sample configuration a number of definitions must match. Table 12 shows the definitions that must be the same. The last column (Example) shows the values we used in our configuration (see "Sample Definitions" on page 135).

Table 12. Matching Definitions: CICS/VSE-CM/2 APPN Gateway-APPC NS/Windows

	VTAM	CICS/VSE V2.2	CM/2	APPC NS/Windows	CICSCLI.INI	Example
1	NETID	-	Partner network ID	Network ID	Network ID	DEIBMIPF
2	ADDR	-	Local station address	-	-	C1
3	LU	Netname	-	Local LU name	LocalLUName	CCLICAL1
4	APPL	Applid	Partner LU	-	Netname	CICSSA22

Sample Definitions

In this section we present the values of each of the definitions mentioned in "Definitions Checklist" on page 133. The values highlighted in the figures refer to the Example column of Table 12 .

VTAM

In this section we present the VTAM definitions for the server.

NETID

You specify the NETID for VTAM in the VTAM startup procedure. Figure 99 shows the VTAM startup procedure, ATCSTR04.B, that we used in the sample configuration.

Sample Definitions

```
* $$ JOB JNM=BOESTR04,DISP=D,PRI=3,                    C
* $$ NTFY=YES                                          C
* $$ LDEST=*,                                          C
* $$ CLASS=0
// JOB BOESTR04 CATALOG VTAM START OPTION LIST
// EXEC LIBR,PARM='MSHP'
ACCESS SUBLIB=PRD2.CONFIG
CATALOG    ATCSTR04.B    REPLACE=YES
SSCPID=22,                                             *
HOSTSA=22,                                             *
SSCPNAME=IPFV2B,                                       *
HOSTPU=IPFVM22,                                        *
NETID=DEIBMIPF,                                        *
MAXSUBA=255,                                           *
CONFIG=04,                                             *
IOINT=0,                                               *
SGALIMIT=1M,                                           *
BSBUF=(28,,,1),                                        *
CRPLBUF=(60,,,1),                                      *
LFBUF=(300,288,,20),                                   *
LPBUF=(12,,,6),                                        *
SFBUF=(20,,,20),                                       *
SPBUF=(210,,,32),                                      *
VFBUF=204800,                                          *
VPBUF=528384,                                          *
XDBUF=(6,,,1)
/+
/*
/&
* $$ EOJ
```

Figure 99. VTAM Startup Procedure ATCSTR04.B: CICS/VSE-CM/2 APPN Gateway-APPC NS/Windows

PU, ADDR, and LU

Figure 100 on page 137 shows the VTAM PU, ADDR **2**, and LU **3** definitions we used in the sample configuration.

```
CCLICA   VBUILD TYPE=CA
CCLICAGR GROUP  LNCTL=SDLC,
                DIAL=NO,
                ISTATUS=INACTIVE
CCLICALI LINE   ADDRESS=B40,
                CORNUM=(1,2),
                MAXBFRU=(2,8),
                PORT=A
CCLICAPU PU     ADDR=C1,
                XID=YES,
                PUTYPE=2,MAXDATA=265
CCLICALU LU     LOCADDR=0,
                ISTATUS=ACTIVE,MODETAB=IESINCLM
CCLICAL1 LU     LOCADDR=0,
                ISTATUS=ACTIVE,MODETAB=IESINCLM
                ...
```

Figure 100. PU, ADDR, and LU Definitions in VTAM CA Major Node: CICS/VSE-CM/2 APPN Gateway-APPC NS/Windows

Note: You must specify XID=YES in the PU definition for PU Type 2.1 nodes to enable parallel sessions communication.

The LU, CCLICAL1 **3**, is defined as an independent LU, specifying **0** in the LOCADDR parameter.

APPL

Figure 101 shows the VTAM APPL **4** definition required for the sample configuration.

```
         ...
BOEAPPL   VBUILD TYPE=APPL
CICSSA22  APPL   AUTH=(PASS,ACQ,VPACE),ACBNAME=CICSSA22,
                 EAS=4000,APPC=NO,PARSESS=YES,
                 SONSCIP=YES,VPACING=3
```

Figure 101. VTAM APPL Major Node Definition: CICS/VSE-CM/2 APPN Gateway-APPC NS/Windows

Generally, LU6.2 parallel rather than single sessions are used, in which case you must set PARSESS to YES to allow LU 6.2 parallel sessions.

Although the communication between the client and the server is through APPC, you must specify **APPC=NO** in the APPL definition.

APPC=YES indicates that the application uses the ACF/VTAM APPC-CMD programming interface. CICS does not use this VTAM function. Instead it has implemented its own support of APPC through the traditional VTAM macro interface. Coding APPC=YES not only indicates that the application uses the new interface, but also causes VTAM not to allow the application to use the traditional macros to manipulate an LU6.2 APPC session. So, not only is APPC=YES not needed for CICS coding, it also actually stops the existing CICS support from working.

CICS/VSE

In this section we present the CICS/VSE definitions for the server.

System Initialization Table Parameters

Figure 102 shows the SIT parameters to enable ISC.

```
    ...
    ISC=YES,
    APPLID=CICSSA22
    ...
```

Figure 102. System Initialization Table Definitions: CICS/VSE-CM/2 APPN Gateway-APPC NS/Windows

DFHISC Group

To enable ISC on CICS/VSE, you must install the DFHISC group (see Figure 103).

```
Either:     CEDA INSTALL GROUP(DFHISC)
And/or:     CEDA ADD LIST(grplist) GROUP(DFHISC)
            where 'grplist' is the list of groups
            CICS installs during start-up.
```

Figure 103. Install DFHISC: CICS/VSE-CM/2 APPN Gateway-APPC NS/Windows

LU6.2 Connection

Figure 104 on page 139 shows the LU6.2 connection definition that we installed on CICS/VSE by using RDO.

```
OBJECT CHARACTERISTICS
 CEDA   View
   Connection     : CCLN
   Group          : CCLNETN
 CONNECTION IDENTIFIERS
   Netname        : CCLICAL1
   INDsys         :
 REMOTE ATTRIBUTES
   REMOTESystem   :
   REMOTEName     :
 CONNECTION PROPERTIES
   ACcessmethod   : Vtam        Vtam ] IRc ] INdirect
   Protocol       : Appc        Appc ] Lu61
   SInglesess     : No          No ] Yes
   Datastream     : User        User ] 3270 ] SCs ] STrfield ] Lms
   RECordformat   : U           U ] Vb
 OPERATIONAL PROPERTIES
   AUtoconnect    : Yes         No ] Yes ] All
+  INService      : Yes         Yes ] No
```

Figure 104. LU6.2 Connection Definition: CICS/VSE-CM/2 APPN Gateway-APPC NS/Windows

Note: The LU6.2 connection definition and the LU6.2 sessions definition must reside in the same group and be installed simultaneously.

LU6.2 Sessions

Figure 105 on page 140 shows the LU6.2 sessions definition that we installed on CICS/VSE by using RDO.

Sample Definitions

```
 OBJECT CHARACTERISTICS
  CEDA  View
    Sessions        : CCLN
    Group           : CCLNETN
  SESSION IDENTIFIERS
    Connection      : CCLN
    SESSName        :
    NETnameq        :
    MOdename        :
  SESSION PROPERTIES
    Protocol        : Appc              Appc ] Lu61
    MAximum         : 00012 , 00004     0-32767
    RECEIVEPfx      :
    RECEIVECount    : No                No ] 1-999
    SENDPfx         :
    SENDCount       : No                No ] 1-999
    SENDSize        : 04096             1-30720
    RECEIVESize     : 04096             1-30720
+ OPERATOR DEFAULTS
```

Figure 105. LU6.2 Sessions Definition: CICS/VSE-CM/2 APPN Gateway-APPC NS/Windows

Note: The LU6.2 connection definition and the LU6.2 sessions definition must reside in the same group and be installed simultaneously.

Communications Manager/2

In this section we explain in detail how to define your values to CM/2.

We recommend that you use a new configuration file because adding values to an existing configuration file may cause conflicts with existing values.

To configure CM/2 as in our example, follow these steps:

1. Run Communications Manager Setup from the Communications Manager/2 folder on the OS/2 desktop.
2. Follow through the windows to display the Communications Manager Configuration Definition window (see Figure 106 on page 141).
3. Click on the **SDLC** option in the Workstation Connection Type list box.
4. Click on the **APPC APIs** in the Feature or Application list box.
5. Click on **Configure...** to get to the Communications Manager Profile List (see Figure 107 on page 141).

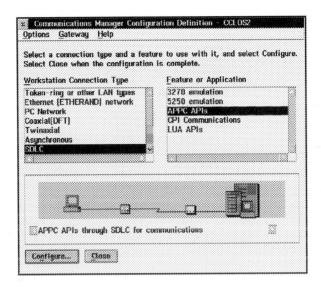

Figure 106. Communications Manager Configuration Definition Window: CICS/VSE-CM/2 APPN Gateway-APPC NS/Windows

Figure 107 shows the Communications Manager Profile List. For our sample configuration the first three profiles must be configured. To configure the DLC-SDLC profile, follow these steps:

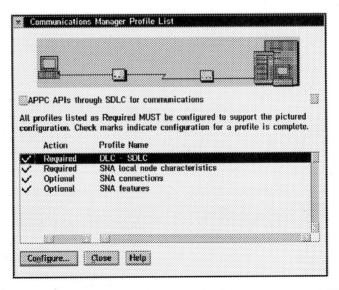

Figure 107. Communications Manager Profile List Window: CICS/VSE-CM/2 APPN Gateway-APPC NS/Windows

Sample Definitions

1. Click on **DLC - SDLC**, then on **Configure...**
2. On the SDLC DLC Adapter Parameters window (Figure 108) select:
   - Adapter **0**
   - Line type as **Non-switched**
   - Link station role as **Secondary**

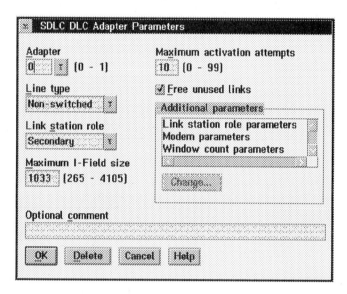

Figure 108. SDLC DLC Adapter Parameters Window: CICS/VSE-CM/2 APPN Gateway-APPC NS/Windows

3. Click on **Link station role parameters** in the Additional parameters list.
4. Click on **Change** to get the Link Station Role Parameters window (not shown). The only field that requires an entry for our sample configuration is Local station address 2.
5. Return to the Communications Manager Profile List (Figure 107 on page 141).
6. Double-click on **SNA local node characteristics**.

Local Node Characteristics

Figure 109 on page 143 shows the Local Node Characteristics configuration on CM/2. This window contains definitions for the:

- Network ID 1
- Local node name

❏ Local node ID.

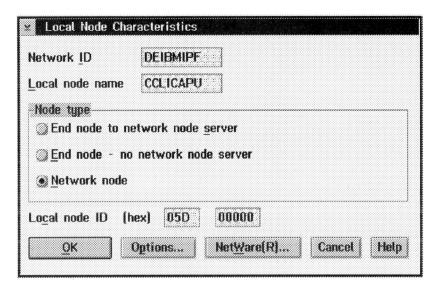

Figure 109. Local Node Characteristics Window: CICS/VSE-CM/2 APPN Gateway-APPC NS/Windows

The Local node name must be a unique name. It is the name other nodes in your network use to address your APPN node. For the sample configuration the name is unimportant, but you can enter a value meaningful to the end user, for example, the name of the VTAM PU.

In a leased SDLC connection, a value for Local node ID is not required. You can accept the default value supplied by the configuration program.

You must select the **Network node** radio button to get all APPN capabilities for this station.

After entering your local node characteristics, return to the Communications Manager Profile List window (Figure 107 on page 141):

1. Double-click on **SNA connections**
2. On the Connections List window (not shown), click on the **To Host** radio button.
3. Click on **Create**.
4. On the Adapter List window (not shown), **SDLC Adapter 0, 1 Regular...** is highlighted. Click on **Continue...** to display the Connection to a Host window (Figure 110 on page 144).

Sample Definitions

On the Connection to a Host window:

- Link name must be unique within CM/2. You can make this value meaningful to the end user.
- Local PU name allows you to specify a PU name for each connection you want to define. It must be unique within CM/2, and you can make this value meaningful to the end user.
- Partner network ID in the sample configuration is our Network ID **1**.
- Partner node name is required in an APPN. For our sample configuration we used the SSCPNAME (IPFV2B) as specified in our VTAM definitions (see Figure 99 on page 136).

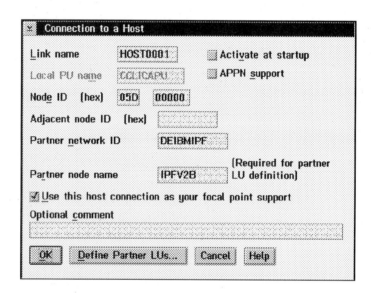

Figure 110. Connection to a Host Window: CICS/VSE-CM/2 APPN Gateway-APPC NS/Windows

Click on **Define Partner LUs...** to get to Partner LUs window (Figure 111 on page 145).

Enter the Network ID **1** and LU name **4** of your partner.

Note: Be careful when using aliases for LU names, as they can often cause confusion when configuring your setup for the first time. If you are unsure whether or not to use an alias, use the same value for the LU name and its alias.

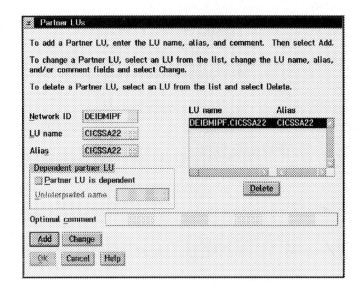

Figure 111. Partner LUs Window: CICS/VSE-CM/2 APPN Gateway-APPC NS/Windows

Communications Manager Configuration Definition window (Figure 106 on page 141).

Until now we have only defined the link between CM/2 and VTAM. As a second step, we must define the link to the client workstation.

1. Click on the **Token-ring or other LAN types** option in the Workstation Connection Type list box in the Communications Manager Configuration Definition Window (see Figure 106 on page 141).
2. Click on the **APPC APIs** in the Feature or Application list box.
3. Click on **Configure...** to get to the Communications Manager Profile List (see Figure 112 on page 146).

Sample Definitions

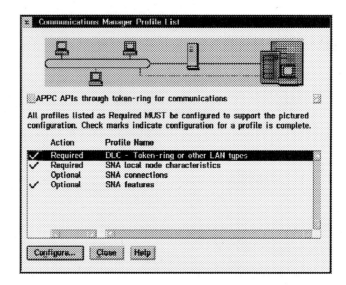

Figure 112. Communications Manager Profile List: CICS/VSE-CM/2 APPN Gateway-APPC NS/Windows

Figure 112 shows the Communications Manager Profile List. For our sample configuration the DLC - Token-ring or other Lan types profile must be configured. Follow these steps:

1. Click on **DLC - Token-ring or other LAN types**, then on **Configure...**
2. On the DLC - Token-ring or other LAN types window (not shown), the only field that requires an entry for our sample configuration is C&SM LAN ID. You can enter the value *CSMLANID* in this field.

There is no need to define a link to the CICS Client workstation. APPN manages this link for you.

APPC NS/Windows

In this section we explain in detail how to define your values to APPC NS/Windows.

For the sample configuration you must install the following APPC NS/Windows components:

BASE required for networking modules

LAN enables connections to token-ring, Ethernet, PC Network, and mobile LANs

During installation of APPC NS/Windows you are asked the following question:

```
Do you wish to run configuration at this time?
```

Select **Yes**.

Note: If you have already installed the product you can run the configuration utility by clicking on the **Configure** icon from the IBM APPC Networking Services application group.

After the BASE and LAN components have been installed, you are presented with the Networking Services Configuration window (see Figure 113 on page 147).

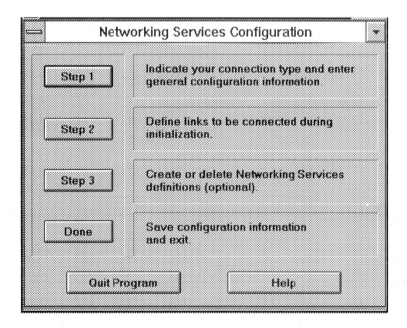

Figure 113. Networking Services Configuration Window: CICS/VSE-CM/2 APPN Gateway-APPC NS/Windows

Select **Step 1** to get to the General Configuration window.

General Configuration Window

On the General Configuration window (Figure 114):

1. Specify your fully qualified local LU name, which is your Network ID ▌1 and Local LU ▌3 separated by a period.
2. Select the connection type to be used by Networking Services. For the sample configuration you should select **Local Area Network (LAN)** for a token-ring network.
3. Select **OK** to return to the Networking Services Configuration window (Figure 113).

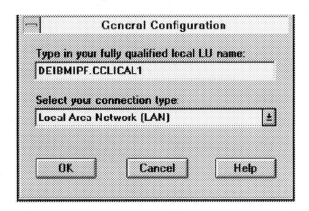

Figure 114. General Configuration Window: CICS/VSE-CM/2 APPN Gateway-APPC NS/Windows

4. Select **Step 2** to get to the LAN Configuration window.

LAN Configuration Window

On the LAN Configuration window (Figure 115 on page 149):

1. Specify a name (that will only be used by your workstation) to refer to the link between your workstation and the server system. You can make this name meaningful to the end user, for example, CICSVSE.
2. Specify the LAN address of the OS/2 APPN network node.

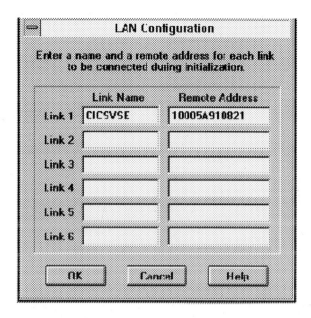

Figure 115. LAN Configuration Window: CICS/VSE-CM/2 APPN Gateway-APPC NS/Windows

   3. Select **OK** to return to the Networking Services Configuration window (Figure 113 on page 147).

On the Networking Services Configuration window select **Done** to complete your configuration.

CICSCLI.INI

The CICSCLI.INI file is found in the CICS Client for Windows BIN subdirectory. Figure 116 on page 150 shows the definitions required for the sample configuration.

```
   :::
   Server              = CICSVSE
   Netname             = DEIBMIPF.CICSSA22    1,4
   Protocol            = APPC
   LocalLUName         = CCLICAL1             3
   ModeName            = *
   :::
   Driver              = APPC
   DriverName          = CCLIBMSN
```

Figure 116. CICSCLI.INI Definitions: CICS/VSE-CM/2 APPN Gateway-APPC NS/Windows

Notes:

1. A separate **Server** definition is required for each server to which the client needs to connect. You can make this value meaningful to the end user, for example, CICSVSE.

2. The **Netname** is the fully qualified applid of the server.

3. The value for **Protocol** identifies the communication protocol to be used to communicate between the client and the server. This value must match the value you have assigned to **Driver**. You can make this value meaningful to the end user, for example, SNA or APPC.

4. The **LocalLUName** is the name of the local LU to be used when connecting to the server. The same LU can be used for all server connections.

5. The **ModeName** specifies the user mode name to be used when connecting to the server. If you choose to use a blank mode name, you can specify a value of * (asterisk).

6. **Driver** must be the same as **Protocol**.

7. The device driver used by APPC NS/Windows in the sample configuration is **CCLIBMSN**.

Testing Your Configuration

After you have installed and configured all relevant products for this sample configuration, we recommend that you do the following:

Step 1. Start the CICS server.

Step 2. Start CM/2 on the OS/2 network node workstation.

Step 3. Start NS/Windows on the client workstation.
→ See "SNA" on page 341.

Step 4. Start the CICS Client for Windows.
Issue **CICSCLI /S=CICSVSE**.
→ See "Starting and Stopping Your CICS Client" on page 321.

Step 5. Check the status of the CICS Client for Windows.
Issue **CICSCLI /L**.
→ See "Checking the Status of Your CICS Client" on page 322.

Step 6. Prepare for data conversion.
→ See "Data Conversion: ASCII to EBCDIC" on page 326.

Step 7. Run a simple ECI application.
→ See "Sample Implementation" on page 277.

Step 8. Problems?
→ See Chapter 21, "Problem Determination," on page 293.
→ See Appendix C, "Common Problems: Symptoms and Solutions," on page 339.
→ See Appendix F, "CM/2 .NDF and APPC NS/Windows NSD.INI Files," on page 367.

Step 9. Need further information?
→ See Appendix B, "Frequently Asked Questions," on page 331.

Testing Your Configuration

10

CICS for OS/2 • CICS Client Using TCP/IP for OS/2

This chapter covers the following topics:
- "Software Checklist" on page 154
- "Definitions Checklist" on page 155
- "Matching Definitions" on page 156
- "Sample Definitions" on page 156
  - TCP/IP for OS/2
  - CICS for OS/2
  - CICS Client for OS/2
- "Testing Your Configuration" on page 162

This sample configuration (see Figure 117) consists of an IBM CICS Client for OS/2 [1] connecting to an IBM CICS for OS/2 [2] server using TCP/IP for OS/2.

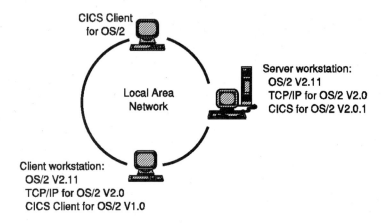

Figure 117. TCP/IP Configuration: CICS for OS/2-CICS Client Using TCP/IP for OS/2

We used a token-ring network in this configuration, but you can use other physical links, for example, Ethernet, FDDI, X.25, or asynchronous connections.

Software Checklist

The levels of software used in the sample configuration are not necessarily the latest levels available. You should check the relevant products for levels of compatible software.

The software required on the server workstation is:

- ❑ OS/2 V2.11
- ❑ TCP/IP for OS/2 V2.0
- ❑ CICS for OS/2 V2.0.1 Multi-user

The software required on the client workstation is:

- ❑ OS/2 V2.11
- ❑ TCP/IP for OS/2 V2.0
- ❑ CICS Client for OS/2 V1.0

---

[1] Hereafter referred to as CICS Client for OS/2.
[2] Hereafter referred to as CICS for OS/2.

Definitions Checklist

Before you configure the products, we recommend that you acquire the definitions for the parameters listed below. Reference keys are assigned to definitions that must contain the same value in more than one product. For example, hostname has the reference key **2**. These reference keys are used in subsequent sections of this chapter.

- ❏ TCP/IP for OS/2 V2.0
    - ➢ IP address of workstation **1**
    - ➢ IP address of domain nameserver **4**
    - ➢ IP address of router
    - ➢ Subnet mask
    - ➢ Hostname **2**
    - ➢ Port number **3**
- ❏ CICS for OS/2 Multi-user
    - ➢ TCP/IP local hostname **1** or **2**
    - ➢ TCP/IP local host port **3**
    - ➢ Maximum TCP/IP systems
- ❏ TCP/IP for OS/2 V2.0
    - ➢ IP address of workstation
    - ➢ IP address of domain nameserver **4**
    - ➢ Subnet mask
    - ➢ IP address of router
- ❏ CICSCLI.INI for the CICS Client for OS/2
    - ➢ Server
    - ➢ Protocol
    - ➢ Netname **1** or **2**
    - ➢ Port **3**
    - ➢ Driver
    - ➢ DriverName

Matching Definitions

In the sample configuration some definitions must match. Table 13 shows the definitions that must be the same. The last column (Example) shows the values we used in our configuration (see "Sample Definitions" on page 156).

Table 13. Matching Definitions: CICS for OS/2-CICS Client Using TCP/IP for OS/2

	TCP/IP on Server	CICS for OS/2 on Server	TCP/IP on Client	CICSCLI.INI on Client	Example
1	IP address	TCP/IP Local Host Name	-	Netname	9.113.36.31
2	Hostname	TCP/IP Local Host Name	-	Netname	giant
3	Port number	TCP/IP Local Host Port	-	Port	1435 (default)
4	IP address of domain nameserver	-	IP address of domain name server	-	9.113.42.250

Notes:

1. If you do not have a domain nameserver, ignore **2** and use **1**.
2. If you have a domain nameserver, you can to specify either **1** or **2**.
3. The IP address of the domain nameserver on the server and client workstations are the same if both workstations are on the same token-ring network.

Sample Definitions

In this section we present examples of the definitions mentioned in section "Definitions Checklist" on page 155. The values highlighted in the figures refer to the Example column of Table 13.

TCP/IP for OS/2 V2.0 on Server

In this section we explain in detail how to configure TCP/IP for OS/2 V2.0 for the sample configuration. We assume that you have successfully installed TCP/IP for OS/2 V2.0 on the server workstation.

Configure Network Interface Parameters

To configure the network interface parameters, follow these steps:

1. Double-click on the **TCP/IP** folder on the OS/2 desktop.
   The **TCP/IP - Icon View** window is presented.
2. Double-click on **TCP/IP Configuration**.
   Configure Network Interface Parameters is presented as shown in Figure 118.
3. Set the **IP Address** of the server workstation **1**.
4. Set the **Subnet Mask**.

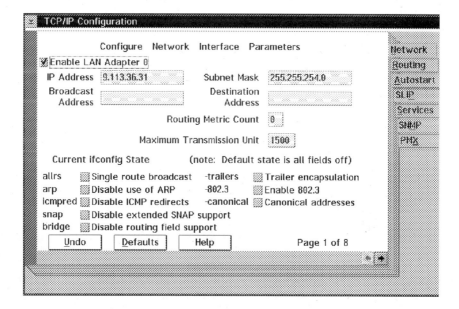

Figure 118. TCP/IP for OS/2 Configure Network Interface Parameters

Configure Routing Information

Routing is the process of deciding where to send a packet on the basis of its destination address. To define the IP address of your router, follow these steps:

1. Click on **Routing** in the TCP/IP Configuration Window.
   Configure Routing Information is presented as shown in Figure 119 on page 158.
2. Enter the **Route Type**.
3. Enter the **Destination**.
4. Enter the **Router**.

Sample Definitions

5. Enter the **Metric**.

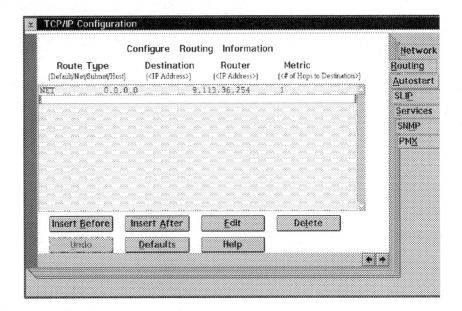

Figure 119. TCP/IP for OS/2 Routing Information

Configure Services for Hostname

To define your hostname, domain name, and domain nameserver address, follow these steps:

1. Click on **Services** in the TCP/IP Configuration Window.
   Configure Services (FTP, DOMAIN NAME SERVICES) is presented as shown in Figure 120 on page 159.
2. Enter **This Machine's Hostname**.
3. Enter the **Domain Name**.
4. Enter the **Domain Nameserver(s) (address)**.

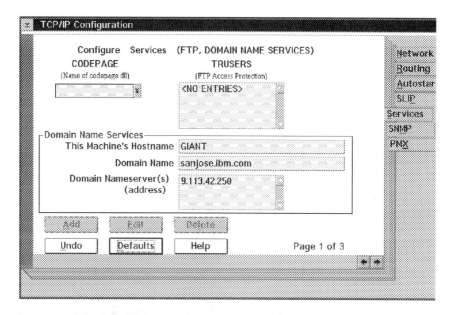

Figure 120. TCP/IP for OS/2 Services Definitions

Define Port Number to TCP/IP

The default port number for all CICS products supporting TCP/IP is 1435. If a non-CICS product is already using this port number, you must define a different port number for both the CICS for OS/2 server and CICS Client for OS/2 to use. Perform the following steps to define a port number to TCP/IP:

1. Decide on a port number to be used for both the CICS for OS/2 server and CICS Client for OS/2, for example, 2001.
2. Select the \TCPIP\ETC directory from the OS/2 command line.
3. Edit the **Services** file using an editor of your choice.
4. Ensure that the port number you want to add is not already in use.
5. Add a line containing the parameters shown in Figure 121 on page 160.
6. Save the file and exit.

Figure 121 on page 160 shows the **Services** file with the port number 2001 defined for CICS. You must define the port number on both the server and the client workstations. The port number that you specify must be the same on both the server and the client workstations.

```
#
# Start of IBM added services
#
  :::
  :::
  cicstcp    2001/tcp
  :::
```

Figure 121. Port Number Definition in Services File

CICS for OS/2 on Server

You must provide three values in the SIT to enable TCP/IP support for CICS for OS/2:

- ❑ TCP/IP Local Host Name
- ❑ TCP/IP Local Host Port
- ❑ Maximum TCP/IP Systems

TCP/IP Local Host Name allows the local TCP/IP address to be specified. The host name can be of the form 9.113.36.31, giant, giant.sanjose.ibm.com, or *. If you specify an asterisk, the host name defined in TCP/IP will be used (see Figure 120 on page 159).

TCP/IP Local Host Port specifies the TCP/IP port on the local system that receives incoming connections to the CICS system. The valid range is 1 - 65535, or *.
Choose * for the CICS default port 1435 unless you have decided not to use the default port number (see "Define Port Number to TCP/IP" on page 159).

Maximum TCP/IP Systems determines the maximum number of remote systems with which the local system can concurrently communicate over TCP/IP. A TCP/IP system in this context can be a CICS client or server connected to the local system using TCP/IP.

Figure 122 on page 161 shows the second page of the SIT containing the parameters required to enable TCP/IP support for CICS for OS/2.

```
  Update    Add     View    Delete                      Exit
FAASIT3             System Initialization Table-2
                                                        More :
      Group Name . . . . . . . . : FAASYS
  System Communications
      Local System ID. . . . . . : CICS
      Local System Appl ID . . . : CICSSRV1
      Default Remote System ID . :
  NETBIOS Support
      NETBIOS Listener Adapter . :           (0, 1 or B)
      Maximum NETBIOS Systems. . :           (0-254)
  TCP/IP Support
      TCP/IP Local Host Name . . : *
      TCP/IP Local Host Port . . : *         (* or 1-65535)
      Maximum TCP/IP Systems . . : 5         (0-255)
  PNA Support
      Load PNA Support . . . . . : N         (Y or N)
      PNA Model Terminal . . . . : MPNA

  Enter F1=Help F3=Exit F7=Bkwd F8=Fwd F10=Actions F12=Cancel
```

Figure 122. SIT Parameters to Enable TCP/IP Support for CICS for OS/2

For CICS for OS/2 V2.0.1 you will need to shut down CICS and restart the system for the changes to take effect.

If you have configured TCP/IP correctly, you will see the messages shown in Figure 123 when CICS for OS/2 is started.

```
.....
.....
FAA5780I  TCP/IP Listener started
FAA5781I  Hostname:(GIANT) (9.113.36.31) Listen:ANY Port:1435
.....
```

Figure 123. TCP/IP Messages in CICS for OS/2 Message Log

TCP/IP for OS/2 V2.0 on Client

You must define the following values to TCP/IP for OS/2 V2.0 on the client workstation:

- IP address of workstation
- IP address of domain nameserver
- Subnet Mask
- IP address of router

CICSCLI.INI for CICS Client for OS/2

The CICSCLI.INI file is found in the BIN subdirectory. Figure 124 shows the definitions required for this sample configuration.

```
   :::
   Server         = CICSOS2
   Netname        = 9.113.36.31        ▌1▐ or ▌2▐
   Protocol       = TCPIP
   Port           = 0                  ▌3▐
   :::
   Driver         = TCPIP
   DriverName     = CCLIBMIP
```

Figure 124. CICSCLI.INI Definitions: CICS for OS/2-CICS Client Using TCP/IP for OS/2

Notes:

1. A separate **Server** definition is required for each server to which the client needs to connect. You can make this value meaningful to the end user, for example, CICSOS2.

2. The **Netname** should be either the IP address or the symbolic hostname of the server. If you are using a domain nameserver, you can specify the symbolic hostname (giant) rather than the IP address of the server (9.113.36.31). Hostnames allow greater flexibility, can be made meaningful, and are easier for an administrator to remember.

3. The value of **Protocol** identifies the communication protocol to be used between the client and the server. This value must match the value you have assigned to **Driver**. You can make this value meaningful to the end user, for example, TCPIP.

4. The **Port** specifies the port number you are using on the server.

5. **Driver** must be the same as **Protocol**.

6. The TCP/IP device driver for the CICS Client for OS/2 is **CCLIBMIP**.

Testing Your Configuration

After you have installed and configured all relevant products for this sample configuration, we recommend that you do the following:

Testing Your Configuration

Step 1. Start the CICS server.

Step 2. Start TCP/IP on the client workstation.

Step 3. Start the CICS Client for OS/2.
Issue **CICSCLI /S=CICSTCP**.
→ See "Starting and Stopping Your CICS Client" on page 321.

Step 4. Check the status of the CICS Client for OS/2.
Issue **CICSCLI /L**.
→ See "Checking the Status of Your CICS Client" on page 322.

Step 5. Run the ping utility successfully.
Issue **ping 9.113.36.31**.

Step 6. Start a 3270 emulator session.
Issue **CICSTERM /s=CICSTCP**.

Step 7. Problems?
→ See Chapter 21, "Problem Determination," on page 293.
→ See Appendix C, "Common Problems: Symptoms and Solutions," on page 339.

Step 8. Need further information?
→ See Appendix B, "Frequently Asked Questions," on page 331.

Testing Your Configuration

11

CICS for OS/2 • CICS Client for Macintosh • TCP/IP

This chapter covers the following topics:
- "Software Checklist" on page 166
- "Definitions Checklist" on page 167
- "Matching Definitions" on page 168
- "Sample Definitions" on page 168
    - TCP/IP for OS/2
    - CICS for OS/2
    - MacTCP
    - CICS Client for Macintosh
- "Testing Your Configuration" on page 177

This sample configuration (see Figure 125) consists of an IBM CICS Client for Macintosh [1] connecting to an IBM CICS for OS/2 [2] server using the IBM TCP/IP for OS/2 on the server and MacTCP on the Macintosh.

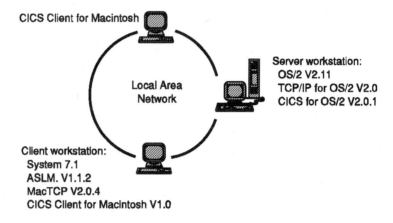

Figure 125. TCP/IP Configuration Using MacTCP

Software Checklist

The levels of software used in the sample configuration are not necessarily the latest levels available. You should check the relevant products for levels of compatible software.

The software required on the server workstation is:

- ❑ OS/2 V2.11
- ❑ TCP/IP for OS/2 V2.0
- ❑ CICS for OS/2 V2.0.1 Multi-user

The software required on the client workstation is:

- ❑ System 7.1 operating system
- ❑ Apple Shared Library Manager V1.1.2
- ❑ MacTCP V2.0.4
- ❑ CICS Client for Macintosh V1.0

---

[1] Hereafter referred to as CICS Client for Macintosh.
[2] Hereafter referred to as CICS for OS/2.

Definitions Checklist

Before you configure the products, we recommend that you acquire the definitions for the parameters listed below. Reference keys are assigned to definitions that must contain the same value in more than one product. For example, hostname has the reference key **2**. These reference keys are used in subsequent sections of this chapter.

- ❑ TCP/IP for OS/2 V2.0
    - ➢ IP address of workstation **1**
    - ➢ IP address of domain nameserver **4**
    - ➢ IP address of router
    - ➢ Subnet Mask
    - ➢ Hostname **2**
    - ➢ Port number **3**
- ❑ CICS for OS/2 Multi-user
    - ➢ TCP/IP Local Host Name **1** or **2**
    - ➢ TCP/IP Local Host Port **3**
    - ➢ Maximum TCP/IP systems
- ❑ MacTCP
    - ➢ IP address of workstation
    - ➢ IP address of domain nameserver **4**
    - ➢ Subnet mask
    - ➢ IP address of router
- ❑ CICSCLI.INI for the CICS Client for Macintosh
    - ➢ Server
    - ➢ Protocol
    - ➢ Netname **1** or **2**
    - ➢ Port **3**
    - ➢ Driver
    - ➢ DriverName

Matching Definitions

In the sample configuration some definitions must match. Table 14, "Matching Definitions: CICS for OS/2-CICS Client for Macintosh-TCP/IP," on page 168 shows the definitions that must be the same. The last column (Example) shows the values we used in our configuration (see "Sample Definitions" on page 168).

Table 14. Matching Definitions: CICS for OS/2-CICS Client for Macintosh-TCP/IP

	TCP/IP on Server	CICS for OS/2 on Server	MacTCP on Client	CICSCLI.INI on Client	Example
1	IP address	TCP/IP Local Host Name	-	Netname	9.113.36.48
2	Hostname	TCP/IP Local Host Name	-	Netname	giant
3	Port number	TCP/IP Local Host Port	-	Port	1435 (default)
4	IP address of domain nameserver	-	IP address of domain nameserver	-	9.113.42.250

Notes:

1. If you do not have a domain nameserver, ignore **2** and use **1**.
2. If you have a domain nameserver you can specify either **1** or **2**.
3. The IP address of the domain nameserver on the server and client workstations is the same if both workstations are on the same token-ring network.

Sample Definitions

In this section we present examples of the definitions mentioned in section "Definitions Checklist" on page 167. The values highlighted in the figures refer to the Example column of Table 14.

TCP/IP for OS/2 V2.0 on Server

In this section we explain in detail how to configure TCP/IP for OS/2 V2.0 for the sample configuration. We assume that you have successfully installed TCP/IP for OS/2 V2.0 on the server workstation.

Configure Network Interface Parameters

To configure the network interface parameters, follow these steps:

1. Double-click on the **TCP/IP** folder on the OS/2 desktop.
   The **TCP/IP - Icon View** window is presented.
2. Double-click on **TCP/IP Configuration**.
   Configure Network Interface Parameters is presented as shown in Figure 126.
3. Set the **IP Address** of the server workstation **1**.
4. Set the **Subnet Mask**.

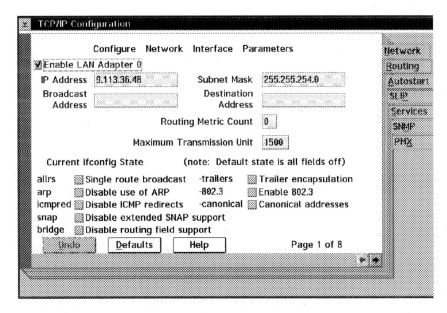

Figure 126. TCP/IP for OS/2 Configure Network Interface Parameters: CICS for OS/2-CICS Client for Macintosh-TCP/IP

Configure Routing Information

Routing is the process of deciding where to send a packet on the basis of its destination address. To define the IP address of your router, follow these steps:

1. Click on **Routing** in the TCP/IP Configuration window.
   Configure Routing Information is presented as shown in Figure 127.
2. Enter the **Route Type**.
3. Enter the **Destination**.
4. Enter the **Router**.

5. Enter the **Metric**.

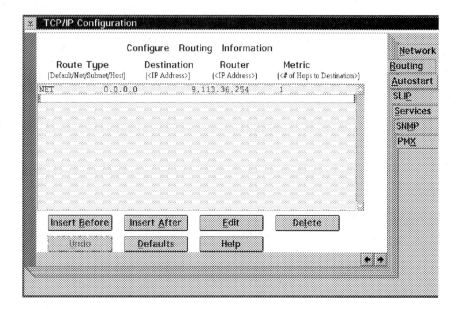

Figure 127. TCP/IP for OS/2 Routing Information: CICS for OS/2-CICS Client for Macintosh-TCP/IP

Configure Services for Hostname

To define your Hostname, Domain Name, and Domain Nameserver address, follow these steps:

1. Click on **Services** in the TCP/IP Configuration window.
   Configure Services (FTP, DOMAIN NAME SERVICES) is presented as shown in Figure 128 on page 171.
2. Enter **This Machine's Hostname**.
3. Enter the **Domain Name**.
4. Enter the **Domain Nameserver(s) (address)**.

Sample Definitions

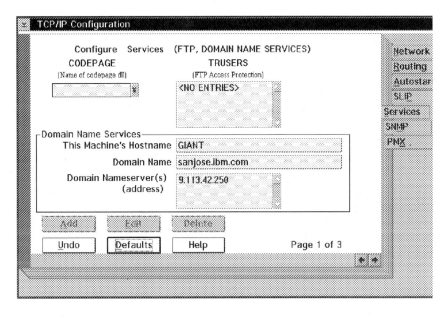

Figure 128. TCP/IP for OS/2 Services Definitions: CICS for OS/2-CICS Client for Macintosh-TCP/IP

Define Port Number to TCP/IP

The default port number for all CICS products supporting TCP/IP is 1435. If a non-CICS product is already using this port number, you must define a different port number for both the CICS for OS/2 server and CICS Client for Macintosh to use. Perform the following steps to define a port number to TCP/IP:

1. Decide on a port number to be used for both the CICS for OS/2 server and CICS Client for Macintosh, for example, 2001.
2. On the CICS for OS/2 server select the \TCPIP\ETC\ directory from the OS/2 command line.
3. Edit the **Services** file using an editor of your choice.
4. Ensure that the port number you want to add is not already in use.
5. Add a line containing the parameters shown in Figure 129 on page 172.
6. Save the file and exit.

Figure 129 shows the **Services** file with the port number 2001 defined for the CICS for OS/2 server. The CICS Client for Macintosh does not have an equivalent services file. The port number is specified in the CICSCLI.INI file only (see "CICSCLI.INI for CICS Client for Macintosh" on page 176).

```
#
# Start of IBM added services
#
  :::
  :::
  cicstcp   2001/tcp
  :::
```

Figure 129. Port Number Definition in Services File: CICS for OS/2-CICS Client for Macintosh-TCP/IP

CICS for OS/2 on Server

You must provide three values in the SIT to enable TCP/IP support for CICS for OS/2:

- ❑ TCP/IP Local Host Name
- ❑ TCP/IP Local Host Port
- ❑ Maximum TCP/IP Systems

TCP/IP Local Host Name allows the local TCP/IP address to be specified. The host name can be of the form 9.113.36.48, giant, giant.sanjose.ibm.com, or *. If you specify an asterisk, the host name defined in TCP/IP will be used (see Figure 120 on page 159).

TCP/IP Local Host Port specifies the TCP/IP port on the local system that receives incoming connections to the CICS system. The valid range is 1 - 65535, or *. Choose * for the CICS default port 1435 unless you have decided not to use the default port number (see "Define Port Number to TCP/IP" on page 171).

Maximum TCP/IP Systems determines the maximum number of remote systems with which the local system can concurrently communicate over TCP/IP. A TCP/IP system in this context can be a CICS client or server connected to the local system using TCP/IP.

Figure 130 on page 173 shows the second page of the SIT containing the parameters required to enable TCP/IP support for CICS for OS/2.

```
    Update    Add     View    Delete                      Exit
    FAASIT3                   System Initialization Table-2
                                                                  More :
         Group Name . . . . . . . . : FAASYS
    System Communications
         Local System ID. . . . . . : CICS
         Local System Appl ID . . . : CICSSRV1
         Default Remote System ID . :
    NETBIOS Support
         NETBIOS Listener Adapter . :            (0, 1 or B)
         Maximum NETBIOS Systems. . :            (0-254)
    TCP/IP Support
         TCP/IP Local Host Name . . : *
         TCP/IP Local Host Port . . : *          (* or 1-65535)
         Maximum TCP/IP Systems . . :   5        (0-255)
    PNA Support
         Load PNA Support . . . . . : N          (Y or N)
         PNA Model Terminal . . . . : MPNA

    Enter F1=Help F3=Exit F7=Bkwd F8=Fwd F10=Actions F12=Cancel
```

Figure 130. SIT Parameters to Enable TCP/IP Support for CICS for OS/2: CICS for OS/2-CICS Client for Macintosh-TCP/IP

For CICS for OS/2 V2.0.1 you will need to shut down CICS and restart the system for the changes to take effect.

If you have configured TCP/IP correctly, you will see the messages shown in Figure 131 when CICS for OS/2 is started.

```
    .....
    .....
    FAA5780I  TCP/IP Listener started
    FAA5781I  Hostname:(GIANT) (9.113.36.48) Listen:ANY Port:1435
    .....
```

Figure 131. TCP/IP Messages in CICS for OS/2 Message Log: CICS for OS/2-CICS Client for Macintosh-TCP/IP

MacTCP on Client

To configure MacTCP for your workstation, follow these steps:

1. Select the **MacTCP** icon. This is generally found within **Control Panels**.
2. Select **Token Ring** (see Figure 132 on page 174).

Sample Definitions

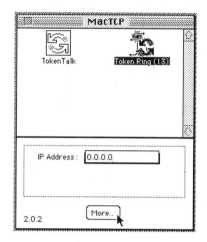

Figure 132. MacTCP Token-Ring Panel

3. At this point you cannot enter your IP Address.
   Select **More...** to get to the MacTCP Configuration Panel (see Figure 133).

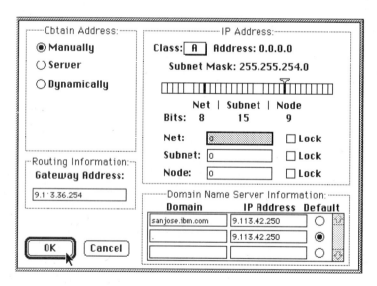

Figure 133. MacTCP Configuration Panel

4. Within **Obtain Address** select **Manually**.
5. Within **Routing Information** enter your **Gateway Address**.

6. Within **IP Address** enter your **Subnet Mask** by sliding the pointer from left to right.

7. If you are using a Domain Nameserver, within **Domain Name Server Information**, on the first line enter your **Domain** and corresponding **IP Address**. On the second line enter a fullstop for the Domain and the IP Address as in the first line. Make the second line the default by highlighting the second radio button. This will enable you to specify your server by name rather than by IP address.

8. Select **OK** to return to the MacTCP Token-Ring panel (Figure 132 on page 174).

9. Enter your workstation **IP Address** as shown in Figure 134.

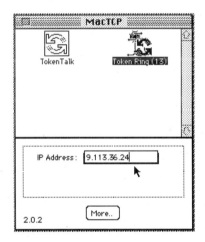

Figure 134. Workstation IP Address: MacTCP

10. Select **More...**.
    Your IP address now appears under IP Address in the MacTCP Configuration panel (see Figure 135 on page 176). The sample configuration uses a **Class A** IP address. If required you can change the class by selecting the boxed 'A'.

Sample Definitions

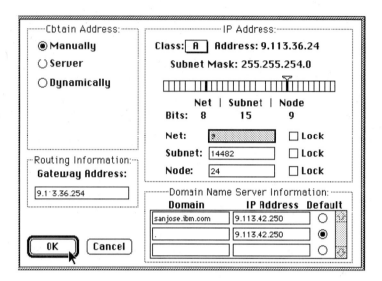

Figure 135. MacTCP Configuration Panel with IP Address

11. Select **OK** to complete your configuration.
12. After closing the MacTCP window you have to restart your workstation.

CICSCLI.INI for CICS Client for Macintosh

The default location of the CICSCLI.INI file is in the CICSCLI BIN folder. Figure 136 shows the definitions required for this sample configuration.

```
   :::
   Server        = CICSOS2
   Netname       = 9.113.36.48      1 or 2
   Protocol      = TCPIP
   Port          = 0                3
   :::
   Driver        = TCPIP
   DriverName    = CCLMACIP
```

Figure 136. CICSCLI.INI Definitions: CICS for OS/2-CICS Client for Macintosh-TCP/IP

Notes:

1. A separate **Server** definition is required for each server to which the client needs to connect. You can make this value meaningful to the end user, for example, CICSOS2.
2. The **Netname** should be either the IP address or the symbolic hostname of the server. If you are using a Domain Nameserver, you can specify the symbolic hostname (giant) rather than the IP address of the server (9.113.36.48). Hostnames allow greater flexibility, can be made meaningful, and are easier for an administrator to remember.
3. The value of **Protocol** identifies the communication protocol to be used between the client and the server. This value must match the value you have assigned to **Driver**. You can make this value meaningful to the end-user, for example, TCPIP.
4. The **Port** specifies the port number you are using on the server. Specifying zero on the CICS Client for Macintosh indicates that you are using the default CICS value of 1435.
5. **Driver** must be the same as **Protocol**.
6. The device driver for clients using TCPIP to connect to a server is **CCLMACIP**.

Testing Your Configuration

After you have installed and configured all relevant products for this sample configuration, we recommend that you do the following:

Step 1. Start the CICS server.

Step 2. Start the CICS Client for Macintosh.
Select the **CICS Client Admin** icon.
→ See "CICS Client for Macintosh Operation" on page 323.

Step 3. Check the status of the CICS Client for Macintosh.
Select the **Client Status** icon.
→ See "Checking the Status of Your CICS Client" on page 322.

Step 4. Run the MacPing utility successfully.
Select IP Address **9.113.36.48**.

Step 5. Start a 3270 emulator session.
Select the **CICS Terminal** icon.

Step 6. Problems?
→ See Chapter 21, "Problem Determination," on page 293.
→ See Appendix C, "Common Problems: Symptoms and Solutions," on page 339.

Step 7. Need further information?
→ See Appendix B, "Frequently Asked Questions," on page 331.

12

CICS/6000 • CICS Client for OS/2 Using TCP/IP for OS/2

This chapter covers the following topics:

- "Software Checklist" on page 181
- "Definitions Checklist" on page 181
- "Matching Definitions" on page 182
- "Sample Definitions" on page 183
    - ➢ TCP/IP for AIX/6000
    - ➢ CICS/6000
    - ➢ TCP/IP for OS/2
    - ➢ CICS Client for OS/2
- "Testing Your Configuration" on page 189

This sample configuration (see Figure 137 on page 180) consists of an IBM CICS Client for OS/2 V1.0 [1] connecting to a CICS/6000 server through the TCP/IP transport protocol provided by IBM TCP/IP for OS/2 V2.0 [2] on the client workstation and TCP/IP for AIX/6000 on the server.

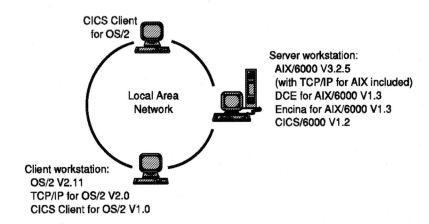

Figure 137. TCP/IP Configuration: CICS/6000-CICS Client for OS/2 Using TCP/IP for OS/2

Although we use CICS/6000 V1.2 as the CICS on Open Systems server in this sample configuration, you could use CICS for HP 9000 or CICS for DEC OSF/1 AXP.

We used a token-ring network for this configuration, but you can use other physical links, for example, Ethernet, FDDI, X.25, or asynchronous connections.

We did not use a domain nameserver for this configuration. However, if your network size is considerably large or a domain nameserver is already available, we recommend that you use a domain name server. We used a domain nameserver in Chapter 13, "CICS/6000 • Clients for DOS and Windows • TCP/IP for DOS," on page 191.

We installed the server and the client workstation on the same LAN. However your server and client workstation can be on separate LANs or even on a WAN.

---

[1] Hereafter referred to as CICS Client for OS/2.
[2] Hereafter referred to as TCP/IP for OS/2.

Software Checklist

The levels of software used in the sample configuration are not necessarily the latest levels available. You should check the relevant products for levels of compatible software.

The software required on the server is:

- AIX/6000 V3.2.5 (TCP/IP for AIX/6000 included)
- DCE for AIX/6000 V1.3
- Encina for AIX/6000 V1.3
- CICS/6000 V1.2

The software required on the client workstation is:

- OS/2 V2.11 operating system
- IBM TCP/IP for OS/2 V2.0
- IBM CICS Client for OS/2 V1.0

Definitions Checklist

Before you configure the products, we recommend that you acquire definitions for the parameters listed below. Reference keys are assigned to definitions that must contain the same value in more than one product. For example, HOSTNAME has the reference key **1**. These reference keys are used in later sections of this chapter.

- TCP/IP for AIX/6000
    - HOSTNAME **1**
    - Internet ADDRESS **2**
    - Network MASK **3**
    - Client Hostname **4**
    - Client Address **5**
    - TCP/IP service name **6**
    - Port number **7**
    - Protocol type (TCP only)
- CICS/6000 V1.2
    - Listener Identifier
    - Protocol type (TCP only)
    - TCP adapter address **2**
    - TCP service name **6**

Matching Definitions

- TCP/IP for OS/2
    - Host name **4**
    - IP address **5**
    - Subnet Mask **3**
    - Route type
    - Metric
    - Server IP address **2**
    - Server hostname **1**
- CICSCLI.INI for CICS Client for OS/2. These entries are defined in the CICSCLI.INI initialization file, generally found in the \CICSCLI\BIN subdirectory:
    - Server
    - Protocol
    - Netname (host name) **1**
    - Netname (IP address) **2**
    - Port **7**
    - Driver
    - DriverName

Matching Definitions

In this sample configuration a number of definitions must match. Table 15 shows definitions that must be the same. The last column (Example) shows the values we used in our configuration (see section "Sample Definitions" on page 183).

Table 15. Matching Definitions: CICS/6000-CICS Client for OS/2 Using TCP/IP for OS/2

	TCP/IP for AIX/6000	CICS/6000	TCP/IP for OS/2	CICSCLI.INI	Example
1	HOSTNAME	-	Server Hostname	Netname (host name)	giant
2	Internet ADDRESS	TCP adapter address	Server IP Address	Netname (IP address)	192.113.36.200
3	Network MASK	-	Subnet Mask	-	255.255.255.0
4	Client Hostname	-	hostname	-	dwarf

Table 15. Matching Definitions: CICS/6000-CICS Client for OS/2 Using TCP/IP for OS/2

	TCP/IP for AIX/6000	CICS/6000	TCP/IP for OS/2	CICSCLI.INI	Example
5	Client Address	-	IP Address	-	192.113.36.78
6	TCP/IP service name	TCP service name	-	-	cicstcp
7	Port number	-	-	Port	2345

Sample Definitions

In this section we present examples of the definitions mentioned in "Definitions Checklist" on page 181. The values highlighted in the figures refer to the Example column of Table 15.

TCP/IP for AIX/6000

In this section we present the TCP/IP for AIX/6000 definitions for the server.

We assume that the server is already running CICS/6000 V 1.2, and as a prerequisite for CICS/6000, TCP/IP for AIX/6000 is already configured and started.

We highly recommend that you not change the TCP/IP for AIX/6000 definitions, except for those covered in this section. For example, if you change the internet address of your server, you must reconfigure DCE, as the DCE Security Service maintains a degree of its integrity through the use of internet addresses.

---- **Authorization** ----
During the configuration on the server you must be logged in in AIX as privileged user **root**.

TCP/IP for AIX/6000 Definitions

To obtain the TCP/IP for AIX/6000 definitions, enter the command:

 # smit mktcpip

Figure 138 shows the definitions.

Press F3 or F10 to quit this screen without making any changes.

Sample Definitions

```
                    Minimum Configuration & Startup

  To Delete existing configuration data, please use Further Configuration menus


   Type or select values in entry fields.
   Press Enter AFTER making all desired changes.
                                                        [Entry Fields]
 * HOSTNAME                                             [giant]
 * Internet ADDRESS (dotted decimal)                    [192.113.36.200]
   Network MASK (dotted decimal)                        [255.255.255.0]
 * Network INTERFACE                                    tr0
   NAMESERVER
           Internet ADDRESS (dotted decimal)            []
           DOMAIN Name                                  []
   Default GATEWAY Address                              []
     (dotted decimal or symbolic name)
     RING Speed                                         4
     START Now                                          no


    F1=Help          F2=Refresh        F3=Cancel          F4=List
    F5=Reset         F6=Command        F7=Edit            F8=Image
    F9=Shell         F10=Exit          Enter=Do
```

Figure 138. TCP/IP for AIX/6000 Definitions

TCP/IP for AIX/6000 Name Resolution

To define the name resolution entry for your client workstation, enter the command:

 # smit mkhostent

Figure 139 shows you how to assign the host name dwarf 4 to the internet address, 192.113.36.78 5.

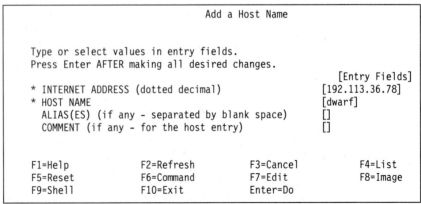

```
                          Add a Host Name


   Type or select values in entry fields.
   Press Enter AFTER making all desired changes.
                                                        [Entry Fields]
 * INTERNET ADDRESS (dotted decimal)                    [192.113.36.78]
 * HOST NAME                                            [dwarf]
   ALIAS(ES) (if any - separated by blank space)        []
   COMMENT (if any - for the host entry)                []


    F1=Help          F2=Refresh        F3=Cancel          F4=List
    F5=Reset         F6=Command        F7=Edit            F8=Image
    F9=Shell         F10=Exit          Enter=Do
```

Figure 139. TCP/IP for AIX/6000 Name Resolution Definitions

You can then find the entry **192.113.36.78 dwarf** in the **/etc/hosts** file. Alternatively, you can edit the **/etc/hosts** file and add this entry to achieve the same result.

TCP Service Definition for CICS/6000

> **Note**
>
> The default port number for CICS is **1435**. If you use this port number, you do not require this TCP service definition. However, you must ensure that no other TCP/IP service occupies this port.

You can add a TCP service entry by editing the **/etc/services** file:

 # vi /etc/services

Figure 140 shows the TCP service entry used for this sample. The port number 2345 **7** must be unique in this file.

```
:::

cicstcp     2345/tcp

:::
```

Figure 140. TCP Service Entry

CICS/6000

In this section we present the CICS/6000 definitions for the server.

To enable your CICS/6000 server for your CICS Clients, you must have a listener definition on your CICS/6000 server.

> **Note**
>
> If the default CICS port number **1435** is used, the default listener definition will be used, and you do not require this listener definition. However, you must ensure that the Protocol type in the default listener definition is TCP. The default listener identifier is ".".

You can add a listener definition using this command:

 # smit cicsaddld

When prompted to select a Model Listener Identifier, press Enter. The default listener definition will be used.

Figure 141 shows the CICS/6000 listener definition required for this sample configuration.

Sample Definitions

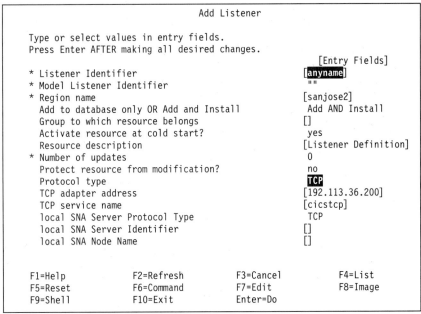

Figure 141. CICS/6000 Listener Definition

Notes:

1. We recommend that you use Add AND Install to make the listener definition available for the client workstation immediately.

2. If you do not specify a TCP adapter address, connection requests will be accepted on any installed and enabled adapter.

3. If you do not specify a TCP service name, the default ("") will be used, and that means the default CICS port number (1435) will be used.

TCP/IP for OS/2

In this section we present the TCP/IP definitions for the client workstation. We assume that your client workstation is running OS/2 and is physically connected to the same LAN as the server.

TCP/IP for OS/2 Installation and Network Configuration

To install TCP/IP for OS/2, insert the diskette labeled BASE-1. From an OS/2 Window, enter the command:

[C:\] A:\TCPINST

Sample Definitions

While installing TCP/IP for OS/2, you will be required to enter the following values for a basic network configuration:

1. Host name (required)
2. IP Address (required)
3. Subnet Mask (optional, you can define it later)

You can change these definitions after TCP/IP for OS/2 is installed successfully.

Figure 142 on page 187 shows the TCP/IP for OS/2 installation and network configuration required on the client workstation. The Host name is set to **dwarf** 4, the IP Address is set to **192.113.36.78** 5, and the Subnet Mask is set
to **255.255.255.0** 3.

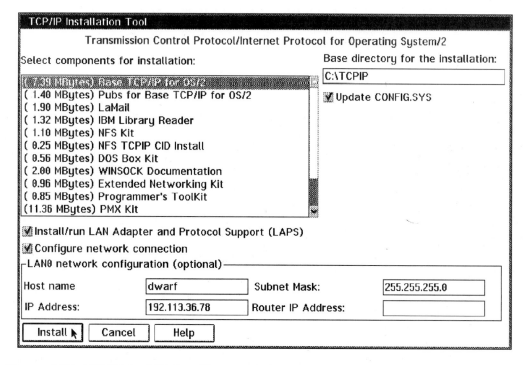

Figure 142. TCP/IP for OS/2 Installation and Network Configuration

TCP/IP for OS/2 Name Resolution

To define the name resolution between the server HOSTNAME 1 and the server Internet ADDRESS 2, follow these steps:

1. Click on the **TCP/IP** icon from the OS/2 Desktop.

Sample Definitions

2. Click on the **TCP/IP Configuration** icon.
3. From the **TCP/IP Configuration** window. click on N▶ twice to turn to **Page 3 of 3**.
4. Click on **HOSTS**.
5. In the **HOSTS Entry - Add** window (Figure 143 on page 188):
   - Set **IP Address** to **192.113.36.200** ▨.
   - Set **Hostname** to **giant** ▨.
6. Click on **Add**.

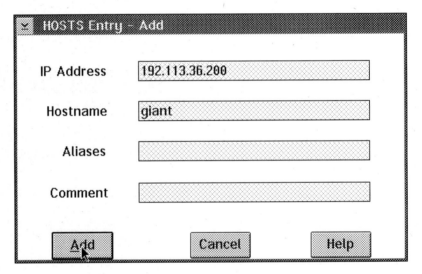

Figure 143. TCP/IP for OS/2 Name Resolution Definitions: CICS/6000-CICS Client for OS/2 Using TCP/IP for OS/2

The entry **192.113.36.200 giant** can then be found in the \TCPIP\ETC\HOSTS file. Alternatively, you can edit the \TCPIP\ETC\HOSTS file and add this entry to achieve the same result.

Save TCP/IP for OS/2 Definitions

To save your TCP/IP configuration: click on **V**. In the pop-up menu click on **Save**

You are asked whether you would like to update your CONFIG.SYS file; we recommend that you answer *Yes*.

TCP/IP for OS/2 Startup

There are two ways to start TCP/IP for OS/2. One is to return to the **TCP/IP - Icon View** window and click on the **TCP/IP Startup** icon; the other is to enter TCPSTART from an OS/2 window.

CICSCLI.INI

The CICSCLI.INI file is found in the BIN subdirectory. Figure 144 on page 189 shows the definitions required for the sample configuration.

```
    Server          = CICSTCP
(either)
    Netname         = giant              1
(or)
    Netname         = 192.113.36.200     2
    Protocol        = TCPIP
    Port            = 2345               7
    Driver          = TCPIP
    DriverName      = CCLIBMIP
```

Figure 144. CICSCLI.INI Definitions: CICS/6000-CICS Client for OS/2 Using TCP/IP for OS/2

1. The value of **Protocol** identifies the communication protocol to be used between the client and the server. This value must match the value you have assigned to **Driver**. This value can be up to eight characters long, and it can be made meaningful to the end user.
2. Select either a Netname (host name) 1 or a Netname (IP address) 2. Do not specify both for a given server.
3. If the default CICS port number **1435** is used, the Port in the CICSCLI.INI file does not need to be defined.

Testing Your Configuration

After you have installed and configured all relevant products for this sample configuration, we recommend that you do the following:

Step 1. Start TCP/IP for AIX on the server.

Step 2. Start the CICS/6000 region on the server.
→ See *AIX CICS / 6000 Installation and Configuration: A Guide to Implementation* for details.

Step 3. Start TCP/IP for OS/2 on the client workstation.

Testing Your Configuration

Step 4. Start CICS Client for OS/2 on the client workstation.
→ See "Starting and Stopping Your CICS Client" on page 321.

Step 5. Check the status of CICS Client for OS/2.
Issue **CICSCLI /L**.
→ See "Checking the Status of Your CICS Client" on page 322.

Step 6. Start a 3270 emulator session.
Issue **CICSTERM /S=CICSTCP**.
→ See "Using CICSTERM Commands" on page 322.

Step 7. Run a simple ECI application.
→ See "Sample Implementation" on page 277.

Step 8. Problems?
→ See Chapter 21, "Problem Determination," on page 293.
→ See Appendix C, "Common Problems: Symptoms and Solutions," on page 339.

Step 9. Need further information?
→ See Appendix B, "Frequently Asked Questions," on page 331.

13

CICS/6000 • Clients for DOS and Windows • TCP/IP for DOS

This chapter covers the following topics:
- "Software Checklist" on page 193
- "Definitions Checklist" on page 193
- "Matching Definitions" on page 195
- "Sample Definitions" on page 195
  - TCP/IP for AIX/6000
  - CICS/6000
  - TCP/IP for DOS
  - CICS Client for DOS/Windows
- "Testing Your Configuration" on page 202

This sample configuration is suitable for CICS Client for DOS and CICS Client for Windows. To facilitate your reading of this chapter, we refer only to the CICS Client for DOS.

This sample configuration (see Figure 145) consists of an IBM CICS Client for DOS V1.0 [1] connecting to a CICS/6000 server through the TCP/IP transport protocol provided by IBM TCP/IP for DOS V2.1.1 or later [2] on the client workstation and TCP/IP for AIX/6000 on the server.

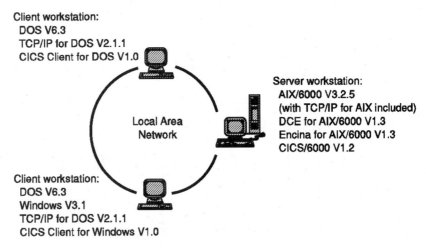

Figure 145. TCP/IP Configuration: CICS/6000-Clients for DOS and Windows-TCP/IP for DOS

Although we use CICS/6000 V1.2 as the CICS on Open Systems server in this sample configuration, you could use CICS for HP 9000 or CICS for DEC OSF/1 AXP.

We used a token-ring network for this configuration, but you can use other physical links, for example, Ethernet, FDDI, X.25, or asynchronous connections.

We used a domain nameserver for this configuration. If you intend to use the configuration without a domain nameserver, refer to Chapter 12, "CICS/6000 • CICS Client for OS/2 Using TCP/IP for OS/2," on page 179.

We installed the server and the client workstation on the same LAN. However, your server and client workstation can be on separate LANs or even on a WAN.

---

[1] Hereafter referred to as CICS Client for DOS.
[2] Hereafter referred to as TCP/IP for DOS.

Software Checklist

The levels of software used in the sample configuration are not necessarily the latest levels available. You should check the relevant products for levels of compatible software.

The software required on the server is:

- ❑ AIX/6000 V3.2.5 (TCP/IP for AIX/6000 included)
- ❑ DCE for AIX/6000 V1.3
- ❑ Encina for AIX/6000 V1.3
- ❑ CICS/6000 V1.2

The software required on the client workstation is:

- ❑ DOS V6.3
- ❑ Windows V3.1
- ❑ IBM TCP/IP for DOS V2.1.1
- ❑ IBM CICS Client for DOS V1.0

Notes:

1. CICS Client for DOS can run under any of the following DOS operating systems:
   - Microsoft or IBM PC DOS 3.3, DOS 4.0, DOS 5.0, or later
   - DOS J 4.0 or later
   - DOS H 4.0 or later
   - DOS T 4.0 or later
   - DOS J 5.0/V or later
   - DOS H 5.0/V or later
   - DOS T 5.0/V or later

2. A DOS client can also run in the "DOS box" of OS/2.

Definitions Checklist

Before you configure the products, we recommend that you acquire definitions for the parameters listed below. Reference keys are assigned to definitions that must contain the same value in more than one product. For example, HOSTNAME has the reference key **1**. These reference keys are used in later sections of this chapter.

- ❑ TCP/IP for AIX/6000

Definitions Checklist

- HOSTNAME **1**
- Internet ADDRESS **2**
- Network MASK **3**
- NAMESERVER Internet ADDRESS **4**
- DOMAIN Name **5**
- TCP/IP service name **6**
- Port number **7**
- Protocol type (TCP only)

❑ CICS/6000 V1.2

- Listener Identifier
- Protocol type (TCP only)
- TCP adapter address **2**
- TCP service name **6**

❑ TCP/IP for DOS

- Hostname
- IP address
- Subnet Mask **3**
- Domain nameserver address (DNSA) **4**
- Domain name **5**

❑ CICSCLI.INI for CICS Client for DOS. These entries are defined in the CICSCLI.INI initialization file, generally found in the CICSCLI\BIN subdirectory:

- Server
- Protocol
- Netname (hostname) **1**
- Netname (IP address) **2**
- Port **7**
- Driver
- DriverName

Matching Definitions

In this sample configuration a number of definitions must match. Table 16 shows definitions that must be the same. The last column (Example) shows values we used in our configuration (see "Sample Definitions" on page 195).

Table 16. Matching Definitions: CICS/6000-Clients for DOS and Windows-TCP/IP for DOS

	TCP/IP for AIX/6000	CICS/6000	TCP/IP for DOS	CICSCLI.INI	Example
1	HOSTNAME	-	-	Netname (hostname)	giant
2	Internet ADDRESS	TCP adapter address	-	Netname (IP address)	192.113.36.200
3	Network MASK	-	Subnet Mask	-	255.255.255.0
4	NAMESERVER Internet ADDRESS	-	DNSA	-	192.113.36.250
5	DOMAIN Name	-	Domain name	-	sanjose.ibm.com
6	TCP/IP service name	TCP service name	-	-	cicstcp
7	Port number	-	-	Port	2345

Sample Definitions

In this section, we present examples of the definitions mentioned in "Definitions Checklist" on page 193 . The values highlighted in the figures refer to the Example column of Table 16.

TCP/IP for AIX/6000

In this section we present the TCP/IP for AIX/6000 definitions, for the server.

We assume that your server is already running CICS/6000 V 1.2 and, as a prerequisite for CICS/6000, TCP/IP for AIX/6000 is already configured and started.

We highly recommend that you not change the TCP/IP for AIX/6000 definitions except for those covered on this section. For example, if you change the internet address of your server, you must reconfigure DCE, as the DCE Security Service maintains a degree of its integrity through the use of internet addresses.

Authorization

During the configuration on the server, you must be logged in in AIX as privileged user **root**.

TCP/IP for AIX/6000 Definitions

To obtain the TCP/IP for AIX/6000 definitions, enter the command:

 # smit mktcpip

Figure 146 on page 196 shows the definitions. Press F3 or F10 to quit this screen without making any changes.

```
                     Minimum Configuration & Startup

  To Delete existing configuration data, please use Further Configuration menus


  Type or select values in entry fields.
  Press Enter AFTER making all desired changes.
                                                    [Entry Fields]
  * HOSTNAME                                        [giant]
  * Internet ADDRESS (dotted decimal)               [192.113.36.200]
    Network MASK (dotted decimal)                   [255.255.255.0]
  * Network INTERFACE                                tr0
    NAMESERVER
          Internet ADDRESS (dotted decimal)         [192.113.36.250]
          DOMAIN Name                               [sanjose.ibm.com]
    Default GATEWAY Address                         []
    (dotted decimal or symbolic name)
    RING Speed                                       4
    START Now                                        no


  F1=Help             F2=Refresh          F3=Cancel           F4=List
  F5=Reset            F6=Command          F7=Edit             F8=Image
  F9=Shell            F10=Exit            Enter=Do
```

Figure 146. TCP/IP for AIX/6000 Definitions: CICS/6000-Clients for DOS and Windows-TCP/IP for DOS

Sample Definitions

TCP Service Definition for CICS/6000

> **Note**
>
> The default port number for CICS is **1435**. If you use this port number, you do not require this TCP service definition. However, you must ensure that no other TCP/IP service occupies this port.

You can add a TCP service entry by editing the **/etc/services** file:

 # vi /etc/services

Figure 147 shows the TCP service entry used for this sample. The port number 2345 **7** must be unique in this file.

```
:::

cicstcp      2345/tcp

:::
```

Figure 147. TCP Service Entry: CICS/6000-Clients for DOS and Windows-TCP/IP for DOS

CICS/6000

In this section we present the CICS/6000 definitions for the server.

To enable your CICS/6000 server for your CICS Clients, you must have a listener definition on your CICS/6000 server.

> **Note**
>
> If the default CICS port number **1435** is used, the default listener definition will be used, and you will not require this listener definition. However, you must ensure that the Protocol type in the default listener definition is TCP. The default listener identifier is ".".

You can add a listener definition using this command:

 # smit cicsaddld

When prompted to select a Model Listener Identifier, press Enter. The default listener definition will be used.

Figure 148 shows the CICS/6000 listener definition required for this sample configuration.

Sample Definitions

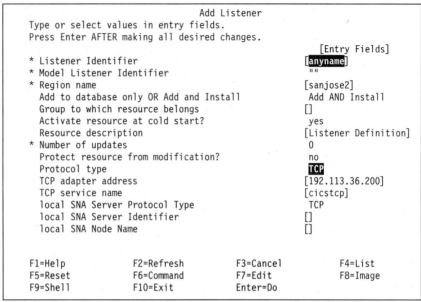

Figure 148. CICS/6000 Listener Definition: CICS/6000-Clients for DOS and Windows-TCP/IP for DOS

Notes:

1. We recommend that you use Add AND Install to make the listener definition available for the client workstation immediately.

2. If you do not specify a TCP adapter address, connection requests will be accepted on any installed and enabled adapter.

3. If you do not specify a TCP service name, the default ("") will be used, and therefore the default CICS port number (1435) will be used.

TCP/IP for DOS

In this section we describe the TCP/IP definitions required by the client workstation. We assume that your client workstation is running DOS and is physically connected to the same LAN as the server.

TCP/IP for DOS Installation

To install TCP/IP for DOS, insert the diskette labeled Diskette B-1 and then enter the command:

C:\>A:\INSTALL

When you are asked whether you would like to update your CONFIG.SYS and AUTOEXEC.BAT files, we recommend that you select *Yes*. Three new entries appear in the CONFIG.SYS file as shown in Figure 149.

```
C:\>type config.sys

  :::

DEVICE = C:\TCPDOS\BIN\PROTMAN.DOS /I:\TCPDOS\ETC
DEVICE = C:\TCPDOS\BIN\DOSTCP.SYS
DEVICE = C:\TCPDOS\BIN\IBMTOK.DOS

  :::

C:\>
```

Figure 149. CONFIG.SYS Entries

Four new entries appear in the AUTOEXEC.BAT file as shown in the Figure 150 on page 199.

```
C:\>type autoexec.bat

C:\TCPDOS\BIN\NETBIND

  :::

SET ETC=C:\TCPDOS\ETC
PATH=C:\DOS;C:\TCPDOS\BIN
CALL TCPSTART

  :::

C:\>
```

Figure 150. AUTOEXEC.BAT Entries

TCP/IP for DOS Network

To configure the TCP/IP for DOS Network, follow these steps:

1. Enter the command: **C:\>CUSTOM**
2. Select **Configure** in the configuration panel
3. Select **NDIS Interfaces**

- Set **IP address** to **192.113.36.78**.
- Set **Subnet mask** to **255.255.255.0** 3.
- Toggle **Enable interface** to be **[X]**.

4. Select **OK**.

Figure 151 on page 200 shows the TCP/IP for DOS network configuration definitions panel.

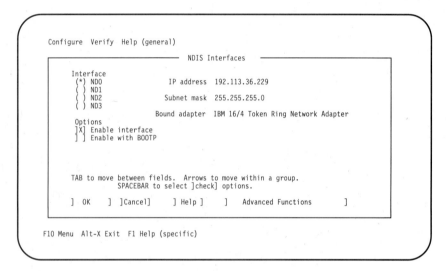

Figure 151. TCP/IP for DOS Network Configuration Definitions Panel

TCP/IP for DOS Name Resolution

To define the name resolution on TCP/IP for DOS using a domain name server, follow these steps:

1. Select **Configure** in the configuration panel
2. Select **Name Resolution**
   - Set **Host name** to **dwarf**.
   - Set **Domain name** to **sanjose.ibm.com** 5.
   - Set **DNSA** to be **192.113.36.250** 4.

   Note: 192.113.36.250 is the IP address of the domain name server, which should be already available on your network.
3. Select **OK**.

Figure 152 on page 201 shows the TCP/IP for DOS Name Resolution panel.

```
Configure  Verify  Help (general)
                  ─── Name ─Resolution ───
    Host name  (this computer's name)
      dwarf
    Domain name
      sanjose.ibm.com

         Domain name server addresses
      1  192.113.36.250
      2
      3
      4
      5

                 TAB to move between fields.
                ]  OK  ]      ]Cancel]        ] Help ]


or disclosure restricted by GSA ADP Schedule Contract with IBM Corp.
F10 Menu  Alt-X Exit  F1 Help (specific)
```

Figure 152. TCP/IP for DOS Name Resolution Definitions Panel

TCP/IP for DOS Startup

There are two ways to start TCP/IP for DOS. One is to enter CALL TCPSTART in the AUTOEXEC.BAT file (which enables TCP/IP for DOS to start automatically when you power on the machine); the other is to enter TCPSTART from an OS/2 window.

CICSCLI.INI

The CICSCLI.INI file is found in the \BIN subdirectory. Figure 153 on page 202 shows the definitions required for the sample configuration.

```
        Server              = CICSTCP

    (either)
        Netname             = giant              ▉1
    (or)
        Netname             = 192.113.36.200     ▉2

        Protocol            = TCPIP
        Port                = 2345               ▉7
        Driver              = TCPIP

    (for CICS Client for DOS)
        DriverName          = CCLIBMIP
    (for CICS Client for Windows)
        DriverName          = CCLWINIP
```

Figure 153. CICSCLI.INI Definitions: CICS/6000-Clients for DOS and Windows-TCP/IP for DOS

Notes:

1. The value of **Protocol** identifies the communication protocol to be used between the client and the server. This value must match the value you have assigned to **Driver**. This value can be up to eight characters long, and it can be made meaningful to the end user.

2. Select either a Netname (host name) ▉1 or a Netname (IP address) ▉2. Do not specify both for a given server.

3. The device driver for CICS Client for DOS is **CCLIBMIP**. For CICS Client for Windows use **CCLWINIP**.

4. If the default CICS port number **1435** is used, the port in the CICSCLI.INI file does not need to be defined.

Testing Your Configuration

After you have installed and configured all relevant products for this sample configuration, we recommend you do the following:

Step 1. Start TCP/IP for AIX on the server.

Step 2. Start the CICS/6000 region on the server.
→ See *AIX CICS/6000 Installation and Configuration: A Guide to Implementation* for details.

Step 3. Start TCP/IP for DOS on the client workstation.

Step 4. Start CICS Client for DOS/Windows on the client workstation.
→ See "Starting and Stopping Your CICS Client" on page 321.

Step 5. Check the status of CICS Client for DOS/Windows.
Issue **CICSCLI /L**.
→ See "Checking the Status of Your CICS Client" on page 322.

Step 6. Start a 3270 emulator session.
Issue **CICSTERM /S=CICSTCP**.
→ See "Using CICSTERM Commands" on page 322.

Step 7. Run a simple ECI application.
→ See "Sample Implementation" on page 277.

Step 8. Problems?
→ See Chapter 21, "Problem Determination," on page 293.
→ See Appendix C, "Common Problems: Symptoms and Solutions," on page 339.

Step 9. Need further information?
→ See Appendix B, "Frequently Asked Questions," on page 331.

14

CICS for Windows NT • PC/TCP • Clients Using TCP/IP

This chapter covers the following topics:
- "Software Checklist" on page 206
- "Definitions Checklist" on page 207
- "Matching Definitions" on page 208
- "Sample Definitions" on page 209
  - TCP/IP for Windows NT
  - CICS for Windows NT
  - PC/TCP for DOS/Windows (detailed step-by-step example)
  - CICS Clients
- "Testing Your Configuration" on page 213

This sample configuration is suitable for CICS Client for DOS and CICS Client for Windows. To facilitate your reading of this chapter, we refer only to the CICS Client for Windows.

The configuration (see Figure 154) consists of an IBM CICS Client for Windows V1.0[1] connecting to a CICS for Windows NT server using the TCP/IP transport protocol provided by the PC/TCP for DOS/Windows V3.0 on the client and TCP/IP for Windows NT on the server.

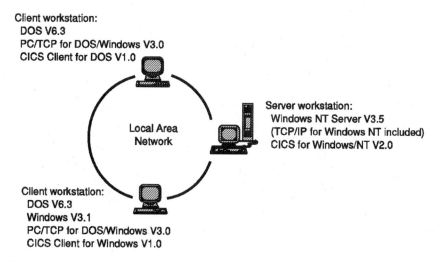

Figure 154. TCP/IP Configuration Using PC/TCP from FTP Inc.

We used a domain name server for this configuration.

Software Checklist

The levels of software used in the sample configuration are not necessarily the latest levels available. You should check the relevant products for levels of compatible software.

The software required on the server workstation is:

- ❑ Windows NT Server V3.5 (TCP/IP for Windows NT included)
- ❑ CICS for Windows NT V2.0 Multi-user

The software required on the client workstation is:

- ❑ PC DOS V6.3
- ❑ Windows V3.1

---

[1] Hereafter referred to as CICS Client for Windows.

- LAN Support Program Install V1.31 (optional)
- PC/TCP for DOS/Windows V3.0
- IBM CICS Client for Windows V1.0

Note: LAN Support Program Install V1.31 comes as part of OS/2 LAN Server V3.0. This product provides the IBM token-ring adapter driver support for PC/TCP for DOS/Windows.

Definitions Checklist

Before you configure the products for the sample configuration, we recommend that you acquire the definitions for the parameters listed below. Reference keys are assigned to definitions that must contain the same value in more than one product. For example, Host Name has the reference key **1**. These reference keys are used in later sections of this chapter.

- TCP/IP for Windows NT
    - Host Name **1**
    - IP Address **2**
    - Subnet Mask **3**
    - Domain Name Server **4**
    - Domain Name **5**
- CICS for Windows NT. The only parameter required is Maximum TCP/IP Systems.

> **Autoinstall**
>
> Connections and terminals from clients do not require additional definitions to be added to the CICS for Windows NT Connection and Session Table (TCS) or Terminal Control Table (TCT) because the definitions are automatically installed (this is known as autoinstall).

- PC/TCP for DOS/Windows
    - Hostname
    - IP Address
    - Router
    - Subnet Mask **3**
    - DNS Server Address **4**
    - Domain Name **5**
- CICSCLI.INI for CICS Client for Windows. These entries are defined in the CICSCLI.INI initialization file, generally found in the \CICSCLI\BIN subdirectory:

- Server
- Protocol
- Netname (host name) **1**
- Netname (IP address) **2**
- Port
- Driver
- DriverName

Matching Definitions

In this sample configuration a number of definitions must match. The Table 17 shows the definitions that must be the same. The last column (Example) shows the values we used in our configuration (see "Sample Definitions" on page 209).

Table 17. Matching Definitions: CICS for Windows NT-PC/TCP-Clients Using TCP/IP

	TCP/IP for Windows NT	CICS for Windows NT	PC/TCP for DOS/Windows	CICSCLI.INI	Example
1	Host Name	*	-	Netname (host name)	giant
2	IP Address	*	-	Netname (IP address)	192.113.36.200
3	Subnet Mask	-	Subnet Mask	-	255.255.255.0
4	Domain Name Server	-	DNS Server Address	-	192.113.36.250
5	Domain Name	-	Domain Name	-	sanjose.ibm.com

Note: Specifying * in the CICS for Windows NT SIT indicates that the equivalent values are defined for TCP/IP for Windows NT.

Enabling TCP/IP on the Windows NT Server

TCP/IP for Windows NT is supplied with Windows NT V3.5. After you have installed Windows NT, you must configure TCP/IP for Windows NT. Follow these steps:

1. Click on **Main** icon in the Windows NT desktop.
   The Main window is presented.
2. Click on the **Control Panel** icon.
   The Control Panel window is presented.
3. Click on the **Network** icon.
   The Network Setting window is presented.
4. In the **Installed Network Software:** list box, select **TCP/IP Protocol** and double-click on it.
   The TCP/IP Configuration window is presented.
   - Set **IP Address** to **192.113.36.200** 2.
   - Set **Subnet Mask** to **255.255.255.0** 3.
5. Click on **DNS...**.
   The DNS Configuration window is presented.
   - Set **Host Name** to **giant** 1.
   - Set **Domain Name** to **sanjose.ibm.com** 5.
   - Add **Domain Name Server - 192.113.36.250** 4.
6. Click on **OK** to return to the TCP/IP Configuration window.
7. Click on **OK** to return to the Network Setting window.
8. Click on **OK**.
9. Restart the Windows NT system.

Sample Definitions

In this section we present examples of the definitions listed in "Definitions Checklist" on page 207. The values highlighted in the figures refer to the Example column of Table 17.

CICS for Windows NT Definitions

For **Maximum TCP/IP Systems** you must specify a value of greater than zero in the SIT to enable TCP/IP support for CICS for Windows NT (see Figure 155).

The value specified for **Maximum TCP/IP Systems** determines the maximum number of remote systems with which the local system can concurrently communicate over TCP/IP. A remote system can be a CICS client or another CICS server.

Sample Definitions

```
   Update     Add    View    Delete                      Exit    Help

   FAASIT3              System Initialization Table-2
                                                          More : - +
       Group Name . . . . . . . . : FAASYS
   System Communications
       Local System ID. . . . . . : CICS
       Local System Appl ID . . . : CICSWNT
       Default Remote System ID . :
   NETBIOS Support
       NETBIOS Listener Adapter . : 0          (0, 1 or B)
       Maximum NETBIOS Systems. . :  0         (0-254)
   TCP/IP Support
       TCP/IP Local Host Name . . : *
       TCP/IP Local Host Port . . : *          (* or 1-65535)
       Maximum TCP/IP Systems . . :  5         (0-255)

   Enter F1=Help F3=Exit F7=Bkwd F8=Fwd F10=Actions F12=Cancel
```

Figure 155. TCP/IP Definitions: CICS for Windows NT Server

LAN Support Program

You must install the LAN Support Program (LSP) if the driver of your token-ring adapter card is not supplied with PC/TCP for DOS/Windows.

To install LSP for your client workstation, refer to "LAN Support Program" on page 238 .

PC/TCP for DOS/Windows

In this section we describe the PC/TCP for DOS/Windows definitions required for the client workstation.

Follow these steps to install PC/TCP for DOS/Windows on your client workstation:

1. Place Disk 1 in the disk drive, or put the CD-ROM into the player.
2. Windows or DOS:

Sample Definitions

- To install PC/TCP for DOS: at the DOS prompt, type the drive letter and **install**. Press Enter.
- To install PC/TCP for Windows: from the Program Manager File menu, select **Run**; then type the drive letter and **setup**. Select **OK**.

PC/TCP for DOS/Windows IP Configuration

To configure PC/TCP for DOS/Windows, on the IP Configuration window (see Figure 156 on page 211):

- Set **IP Address** to **192.113.36.78**.
- Set **Subnet Mask** to **255.255.255.0**.
- Set **Router(s)** to **192.113.36.78**.

Note: The router for communicating with other hosts in the same LAN is the host itself.

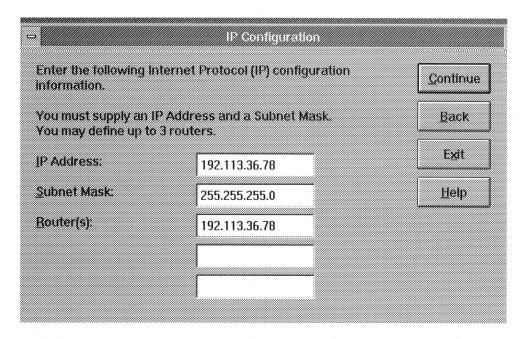

Figure 156. PC/TCP for DOS/Windows IP Configuration

PC/TCP for DOS/Windows DNS Configuration

To configure the domain name system (DNS), on the DNS Configuration window (see Figure 157 on page 212):

- Set **Hostname** to **dwarf**.

Sample Definitions

- Set **Domain Name** to **sanjose.ibm.com** 5.
- Set **DNS Server Address(es)** to **192.113.36.250** 4..

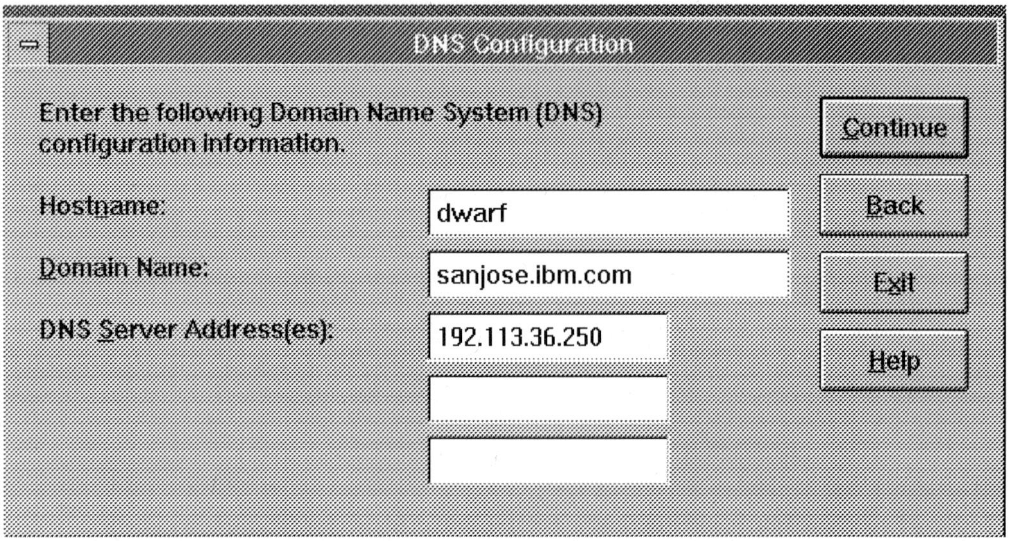

Figure 157. PC/TCP for DOS/Windows DNS Configuration

CICSCLI.INI

The CICSCLI.INI file is found in the CICS Client for Windows BIN subdirectory, generally in the \CICSCLI\BIN directory. Figure 158 shows the definitions required for this sample configuration.

```
   :::
Server           = CICSNT
Protocol         = TCPIP

(either)
  Netname        = giant            ❶
(or)
  Netname        = 192.113.36.200   ❷

   :::

Port             = 1435
Driver           = TCPIP

(for CICS Client for DOS)
  DriverName     = CCLFTPIP
(for CICS Client for Windows)
  DriverName     = CCLWINIP
```

Figure 158. CICSCLI.INI Definitions: CICS for Windows NT-PC/TCP-Clients Using TCP/IP

Notes:

1. A separate **Server** definition is required for each server to which the client needs to connect. You can make this value meaningful to the end user, for example, CICSNT.

2. The value of **Protocol** identifies the communication protocol to be used between the client and the server. This value must match the value you have assigned to **Driver**. You can make this value meaningful to the end user, for example, TCPIP.

3. Select either a Netname (host name) ❶ or a Netname (IP address) ❷. Do not specify both for a given server.

4. The default CICS port number **1435** is used in this sample configuration. If you intend to use another port number, you must add an entry for it in the \winnt35\system32\drivers\etc\services file on the server machine and specify the port number to the TCP/IP Local Host Port in the CICS for Windows NT SIT (see Figure 155 on page 210).

5. The device driver for DOS is **CCLFTPIP**; for Windows, it is **CCLWINIP**.

Testing Your Configuration

After you have installed and configured all relevant products for this sample configuration, we recommend that you do the following:

This sample configuration is suitable for CICS Client for DOS and CICS Client for Windows. To facilitate your reading of this chapter, we refer only to the CICS Client for Windows.

The configuration (see Figure 159) consists of an IBM CICS Client for Windows V1.0[1] connecting to a CICS for Windows NT server using the TCP/IP transport protocol provided by Novell's LAN WorkPlace V4.2 on the client and TCP/IP for Windows NT on the server.

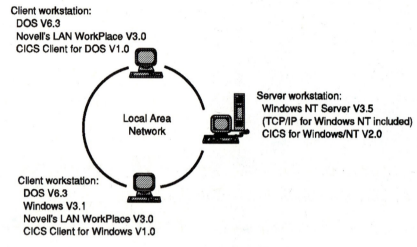

Figure 159. Configuration Using Novell's LAN WorkPlace

We used a domain name server for this configuration.

Software Checklist

The levels of software used in the sample configuration are not necessarily the latest levels available. You should check the relevant products for levels of compatible software.

The software required on the server workstation is:

- Windows NT Server V3.5 (TCP/IP for Windows NT included)
- CICS for Windows NT V2.0 Multi-user

The software required on the client workstation is:

- PC DOS V6.3
- Windows V3.1

---

[1] Hereafter referred to as CICS Client for Windows.

- Novell's LAN WorkPlace V3.0
- IBM CICS Client for Windows V1.0

Definitions Checklist

Before you configure the products for the sample configuration, we recommend that you acquire the definitions for the parameters listed below. Reference keys are assigned to definitions that must contain the same value in more than one product. For example, Host Name has the reference key **1**. These reference keys are used in later sections of this chapter.

- TCP/IP for Windows NT
    - Host Name **1**
    - IP Address **2**
    - Subnet Mask **3**
    - Domain Name Server **4**
    - Domain Name **5**
- CICS for Windows NT. The only parameter required is Maximum TCP/IP Systems.

Autoinstall

Connections and terminals from clients do not require additional definitions to be added to the CICS for Windows NT Connection and Session Table (TCS) or Terminal Control Table (TCT) because the definitions are automatically installed (this is known as autoinstall).

- LAN WorkPlace
    - Hostname
    - IP Address
    - Router
    - Subnet Mask **3**
    - DNS Server Address **4**
    - Domain Name **5**
- CICSCLI.INI for CICS Client for Windows. These entries are defined in the CICSCLI.INI initialization file, generally found in the \CICSCLI\BIN subdirectory:
    - Server
    - Protocol
    - Netname (host name) **1**
    - Netname (IP address) **2**

Matching Definitions

> Port
> Driver
> DriverName

Matching Definitions

In this sample configuration a number of definitions must match. Table 18 shows the definitions that must be the same. The last column (Example) shows the values we used in our configuration (see "Sample Definitions" on page 218).

Table 18. Matching Definitions: CICS for Windows NT-LAN WorkPlace-TCP/IP

	TCP/IP for Windows NT	CICS for Windows NT	LAN WorkPlace	CICSCLI.INI	Example
1	Host Name	*	-	Netname (host name)	giant
2	IP Address	*	-	Netname (IP address)	192.113.36.200
3	Subnet Mask	-	Subnet Mask	-	255.255.255.0
4	Domain Name Server	-	DNS Server Address	-	192.113.36.250
5	Domain Name	-	Domain Name	-	sanjose.ibm.com

Note: Specifying * in the CICS for Windows NT SIT indicates that the equivalent values are defined for TCP/IP for Windows NT.

Enabling TCP/IP on the Windows NT Server

For instructions on enabling TCP/IP on your server, refer to "Enabling TCP/IP on the Windows NT Server" on page 208.

Sample Definitions

In this section we present examples of the definitions listed in "Definitions Checklist" on page 217. The values highlighted in the figures refer to the Examples column of Table 18.

CICS for Windows NT Definitions

For **Maximum TCP/IP Systems** you must specify a value greater than zero in the SIT to enable TCP/IP support for CICS for Windows NT. Refer to "CICS for Windows NT Definitions" on page 209 for more information.

LAN WorkPlace

In this section we describe in detail the installation and configuration of LAN WorkPlace for the client workstation.

Installation and Configuration

You are asked to provide configuration information during the installation of LAN WorkPlace. Because the install program requires at least 512KB of conventional memory, we recommend that you check the amount of memory in your system before installation.

To install LAN WorkPlace for your client workstation, follow these steps:

1. Place Disk 1 in the disk drive.
2. At the DOS prompt, type the drive letter and **install**. Press Enter.
3. Prompt: Select the components you wish to install
   Response: Press Y to select the **LAN WorkPlace V4.2 Windows Applications**

   Note: For CICS Client for DOS, you do not have to select this option.
4. Prompt: Destination Drive Selection
   Response: Press Enter to select the default drive, **C:**
5. Prompt: Select the target directory
   Response: Press Enter to select the default directory, **C:\NET**
6. Prompt: Does your workstation boot from a file server?
   Response: Select **No**
7. Prompt: Do you want INSTALL to update your system files?
   Response: Select **Yes** (recommended)

   Note: The INSTALL program may update or create the following files:

Sample Definitions

- AUTOEXEC.BAT
- CONFIG.SYS
- \WINDOWS\SYSTEM.INI
- \WINDOWS\WIN.INI
- \WINDOWS\PROGMAN.INI
- \NET\NWCLIENT\NET.CFG (or \NWCLIENT\NET.CFG).

8. Prompt: Select the driver you wish to install
   Response: Select **IBM Token-Ring Network Adapter/A** for this sample configuration

9. Prompt: NET.CFG settings for the ODI driver TOKEN/(SLOT)Slot
   Response: Press Enter, then select the number of the slot of the token-ring adapter

10. Prompt: Are TCP/IP parameters provided automatically by a BOOTP server?
    Response: Select **No**.

11. Prompt: Enter the IP address for your workstation
    Response: Type **192.113.36.78**

12. Prompt: Does your network have subnets?
    Response: Select **Yes**

13. Prompt: Enter the Subnetwork mask
    Response: Type **255.255.255.0** 3

14. Prompt: Does your network use an IP router?
    Response: Select **Yes**

15. Prompt: Enter the router IP address
    Response: Type **192.113.36.78**

    Note: The router to connect to other hosts on the same LAN is the host itself.

16. Prompt: Does your network have a Domain Name Server?
    Response: Select **Yes**

17. Prompt: Enter the network domain name
    Response: Type **sanjose.ibm.com** 4

18. Prompt: Enter the Domain Name Server IP address
    Response: Type **192.113.36.250** 5

19. Prompt: Enter the username to use with the R-utilities (rcp,rsh,...)
    Response: Enter an appropriate value, for example, guido.

    Note: The username is required by LAN WorkPlace, not by CICS Clients. It is usually the account name on the remote host providing the R-utilities.

20. Prompt: Select the FRAME
    Response: Select **TOKEN-RING_SNAP MSB** (or **TOKEN-RING_SNAP LSB**)

21. Follow the instructions, finish the installation, and then restart your client workstation.

NET.CFG Configuration File

The LAN WorkPlace installation program provides the minimum NET.CFG settings required to run the LAN WorkPlace software. You can customize this file to enable optional LAN WorkPlace features and accommodate specialized network features.

The LAN WorkPlace software uses three sections of the NET.CFG file:

- **Link Driver** - configures ODI drivers. You can set up multiple drivers if you have more than one network adapter or want to run Serial Line IP (SLIP)/Point-to-Point Protocol (PPP) to use LAN WorkPlace over a COM port serial link.
- **Link Support** - determines the sizes of the Link Support Layer memory pool and buffers. You can change these values to suit your network configuration and application usage.
- **Protocol TCP/IP** - contains settings used by the LAN WorkPlace TCP/IP Transport software. You can modify this section to support optional features.

Figure 160 on page 221 shows a sample NET.CFG file.

```
Link Driver TOKEN
        Frame TOKEN-RING_SNAP MSB
        MAX FRAME SIZE 4208
        SLOT 2

Protocol TCPIP
        PATH LANG_CFG           C:\NET\LANG
        PATH SCRIPT             C:\NET\SCRIPT
        PATH PROFILE            C:\NET\PROFILE
        PATH LWP_CFG            C:\NET\HSTACC
        PATH TCP_CFG            C:\NET\TCP
        ip_router               192.113.36.78
        ip_netmask              255.255.255.0
        ip_address              192.113.36.78

Link Support
        Buffers 4 4202
        MemPool 4096
```

Figure 160. LAN WorkPlace Configuration File: NET.CFG

CICSCLI.INI

The CICSCLI.INI file is found in the CICS Client for Windows BIN subdirectory, generally in the \CICSCLI\BIN directory. Figure 161 on page 222 shows the definitions required for this sample configuration.

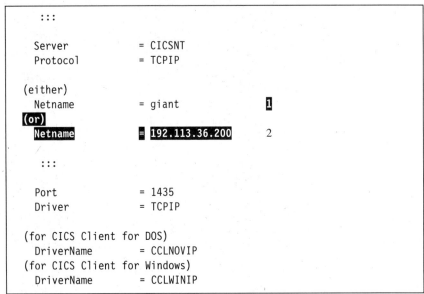

```
   :::

   Server              = CICSNT
   Protocol            = TCPIP

   (either)
   Netname             = giant                  1
   (or)
   Netname             = 192.113.36.200         2

   :::

   Port                = 1435
   Driver              = TCPIP

   (for CICS Client for DOS)
   DriverName          = CCLNOVIP
   (for CICS Client for Windows)
   DriverName          = CCLWINIP
```

Figure 161. CICSCLI.INI Definitions: CICS for Windows NT-LAN Work-Place-TCP/IP

Notes:

1. A separate **Server** definition is required for each server to which the client needs to connect. You can make this value meaningful to the end user, for example, CICSNT.

2. The value of **Protocol** identifies the communication protocol to be used between the client and the server. This value must match the value you have assigned to **Driver**. You can make this value meaningful to the end user, for example, TCPIP.

3. Select either a Netname (host name) 1 or a Netname (IP address) 2. Do not specify both for a given server.

4. The default CICS port number **1435** is used in this sample configuration. If you intend to use another port number, you must add an entry for it in the \winnt35\system32\drivers\etc\services file on the server machine and specify the port number to the TCP/IP Local Host Port in the CICS for Windows NT SIT.

5. The device driver for DOS is **CCLNOVIP**; for Windows, it is **CCLWINIP**.

Testing Your Configuration

After you have installed and configured all relevant products for this sample configuration, we recommend that you do the following:

Step 1. Start the CICS for Windows NT on the server.

Step 2. Start the LAN WorkPlace on the client workstation.

Step 3. Start the CICS Client for DOS/Windows on the client workstation.
→ See "Starting and Stopping Your CICS Client" on page 321.

Step 4. Check the status of the CICS Client for DOS/Windows. Issue **CICSCLI /L**.
→ See "Checking the Status of Your CICS Client" on page 322.

Step 5. Start a 3270 emulator session. Issue **CICSTERM /S=CICSNT**.
→ See "Using CICSTERM Commands" on page 322.

Step 6. Run a simple ECI application.
→ See "Sample Implementation" on page 277.

Step 7. Problems?
→ See Chapter 21, "Problem Determination," on page 293.
→ See Appendix C, "Common Problems: Symptoms and Solutions," on page 339.

Step 8. Need further information?
→ See Appendix B, "Frequently Asked Questions," on page 331.

Testing Your Configuration

16
CICS for OS/2 • CICS Client for OS/2 Using NetBIOS

This chapter covers the following topics:
- "Software Checklist" on page 226
- "Definitions Checklist" on page 227
- "Matching Definitions" on page 228
- "Enabling NetBIOS Support" on page 228
- "Sample Definitions" on page 229
  - CICS for OS/2
  - IBM CICS Client for OS/2
- "Testing Your Configuration" on page 231

Software Checklist

This sample configuration (see Figure 162) consists of an IBM CICS Client for OS/2 [1] connecting to an IBM CICS for OS/2 server using the NetBIOS transport protocol provided by Network Transport Services/2 (NTS/2).

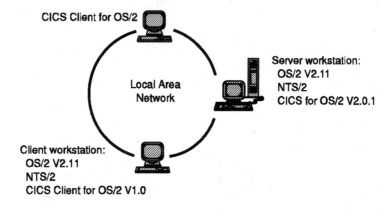

Figure 162. NetBIOS Configuration

Software Checklist

The levels of software used in the sample configuration are not necessarily the latest levels available. You should check the relevant products for levels of compatible software.

The software required on the server is:

- ❑ OS/2 operating system V2.11
- ❑ Network Transport Services/2
- ❑ CICS for OS/2 V2.0.1 Multi-user

The software required on the client workstation is:

- ❑ OS/2 operating system V2.11
- ❑ Network Transport Services/2
- ❑ CICS Client for OS/2 V1.0

---

[1] Hereafter referred to as CICS Client for OS/2.

Definitions Checklist

You must enable NetBIOS support for both the server and the client workstation. See "Enabling NetBIOS Support" on page 228.

Before you configure CICS for OS/2 and CICS Client for OS/2 for the sample configuration, we recommend that you acquire the definitions for the parameters listed below. Reference keys are assigned to definitions that must contain the same value in more than one product. For example, Local System Appl ID has the reference key **1**. These reference keys are used in subsequent sections of this chapter.

- CICS for OS/2
  - Local System Appl ID **1**
  - NetBIOS Listener Adapter **2**
  - Maximum NetBIOS Systems

> **Autoinstall**
>
> Connections and terminals from clients do not require additional definitions to be added to the CICS for OS/2 Connection and Session Table (TCS) or Terminal Control Table (TCT) because the definitions are automatically installed (this is known as autoinstall).

- CICSCLI.INI for CICS Client for OS/2. These entries are defined in the CICSCLI.INI initialization file, generally found in the \CICSCLI\BIN subdirectory:
  - Server
  - Protocol
  - Netname **1**
  - Adapter **2**
  - Driver
  - DriverName

Matching Definitions

In this sample configuration a number of definitions must match. Table 19 shows the definitions that must be the same. The last column (Example) shows values we used in our configuration (see "Sample Definitions" on page 229)..

Table 19. Matching Definitions: CICS for OS/2-CICS Client for OS/2 Using NetBIOS

	CICS for OS/2 Multi-user	CICSCLI.INI	Example
1	Local System Appl ID	Netname	CICSSRV1
2	NETBIOS Listener Adapter	Adapter	0

Enabling NetBIOS Support

You must perform the following steps on the server and the client workstation to enable NetBIOS support:

1. Change to the IBMCOM directory from an OS/2 command line.
2. Type: LAPS.
   The LAN Adapter and Protocol Support initial window is presented.
3. Click on **Configure**.
   The initial Configuration window is presented.
4. Select **Configure LAN transports** and click on **Continue**.
   The Configure Workstation window is presented (see Figure 163 on page 229).
5. Select your network adapter and NetBIOS protocol.

   — Note
   If you are not sure how to configure NetBIOS for your workstation, click on **Help** for further guidance.

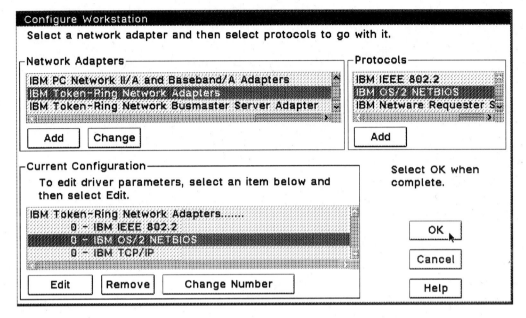

Figure 163. Enabling NetBIOS Support: NTS/2

Sample Definitions

In this section we present examples of the definitions listed in "Definitions Checklist" on page 227. The values highlighted in the figures refer to the Example column of Table 19 on page 228.

CICS for OS/2

You must provide three values in the SIT to enable NetBIOS support for CICS for OS/2 (see Figure 164 on page 230):

- Local System Appl ID
- NETBIOS Listener Adapter
- Maximum NETBIOS Systems.

The **Local System Appl ID** can be up to eight characters long. This field will be used for the NetBIOS Listener name on the LAN. If not specified, the default is CICSOS2. The Local System Appl ID must be unique within the LAN to ensure that clients attach to the correct server.

Sample Definitions

NETBIOS Listener Adapter is required for NetBIOS connections. CICS for OS/2 supports the use of two LAN adapters. Enter in this field the number of the LAN adapters to be used for inbound communications. The default is zero. If two LAN adapters are installed in your server workstation, enter B (both) to enable both adapters for inbound communication.

The value specified for **Maximum NETBIOS Systems** determines the maximum number of remote systems with which the local system can concurrently communicate over NetBIOS. A remote system can be a CICS client or another CICS server.

```
       Update     Add      View      Delete                    Exit

       FAASIT3                System Initialization Table-2
                                                                More :
          Group Name . . . . . . . . : FAASYS

       System Communications
          Local System ID. . . . . . : CICS
          Local System Appl ID . . . : CICSSRV1   ■1
          Default Remote System ID . :
       NETBIOS Support
          NETBIOS Listener Adapter . : 0        ■2    (0, 1 or B)
          Maximum NETBIOS Systems. . :   5             (0-254)
       TCP/IP Support
          TCP/IP Local Host Name . . : *
          TCP/IP Local Host Port . . : *              (* or 1-65535)
          Maximum TCP/IP Systems . . :   0             (0-255)
       PNA Support
          Load PNA Support . . . . . : N              (Y or N)
          PNA Model Terminal . . . . : MPNA

       Enter F1=Help F3=Exit F7=Bkwd F8=Fwd F10=Actions F12=Cancel
```

Figure 164. NetBIOS Definitions: CICS for OS/2 Server

CICSCLI.INI for CICS Client for OS/2

The CICSCLI.INI file is generally found in the \CICSCLI\BIN subdirectory. Figure 165 on page 231 lists the definitions required for this sample configuration.

```
   :::
   Server         = CICSNETB
   Protocol       = NETBIOS
   NetName        = CICSSRV1        ￼1
   Adapter        = 0               ￼2

   :::

   Driver         = NETBIOS
   DriverName     = CCLIBMNB
```

Figure 165. CICSCLI.INI Definitions: CICS for OS/2-CICS Client for OS/2 Using NetBIOS

Notes:

1. A separate **Server** definition is required for each server to which the client needs to connect. You can make this value meaningful to the end user, for example, CICSNETB.

2. The value of **Protocol** identifies the communication protocol to be used between the client and the server. This value must match the value you have assigned to **Driver**. You can make this value meaningful to the end user, for example, NETBIOS.

3. The **Netname** should match the Local System Appl ID of your CICS for OS/2 server.

4. The **Adapter** specifies the LAN adapter number you are using on the client workstation. The default is zero.

5. **Driver** must be the same as **Protocol**.

6. The device driver for all clients using NetBIOS to connect to a server is **CCLIBMNB**.

Testing Your Configuration

After you have installed and configured all relevant products for this sample configuration, we recommend that you do the following:

Step 1. Start the CICS server.

Step 2. Start the CICS Client for OS/2.
Issue **CICSCLI /S=CICSNETB**
→ See "Starting and Stopping Your CICS Client" on page 321.

Step 3. Check the status of the CICS Client for OS/2.
Issue **CICSCLI /L**
→ See "Checking the Status of Your CICS Client" on page 322.

Step 4. Start a 3270 emulator session.
Issue **CICSTERM /S=CICSNETB**

Step 5. Problems?
→ See Chapter 21, "Problem Determination," on page 293.
→ See Appendix C, "Common Problems: Symptoms and Solutions," on page 339.

Step 6. Need further information?
→ See Appendix B, "Frequently Asked Questions," on page 331.

17

CICS for OS/2 • CICS Client for DOS/Windows • NetBIOS

This chapter covers the following topics:

- "Software Checklist" on page 234
- "Definitions Checklist" on page 235
- "Matching Definitions" on page 236
- "Sample Definitions" on page 237
  - ➢ Network Transport Services/2 (NTS/2)
  - ➢ CICS for OS/2 V2.0.1
  - ➢ LAN Support Program (detailed step-by-step example)
  - ➢ CICS Client
- "Testing Your Configuration" on page 244

This sample configuration is suitable for CICS Client for DOS and CICS Client for Windows. To facilitate your reading of this chapter, we refer only to the CICS Client for DOS.

The configuration (see Figure 166) consists of an IBM CICS Client for DOS V1.0[1] connecting to a CICS for OS/2 server using the NetBIOS protocol provided by the LAN Support Program on the client and Network Transport Services/2 (NTS/2) on the server.

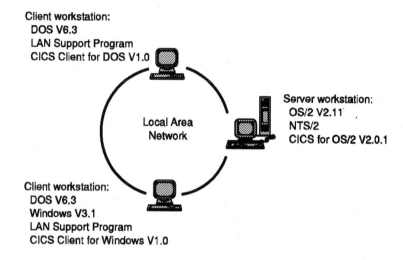

Figure 166. NetBIOS Configuration: CICS for OS/2-CICS Client for DOS/Windows-NetBIOS

Although the sample uses CICS for OS/2 V2.0.1 as the server, you also could use CICS OS/2 V2.0.

Software Checklist

The levels of software used in the sample configuration are not necessarily the latest levels available. You should check the relevant products for levels of compatible software.

The software required on the server workstation is:

- ❑ OS/2 V2.11 operating system
- ❑ Network Transport Services/2
- ❑ CICS for OS/2 V2.0.1 Multi-user

The software required on the client workstation is:

---

[1] Hereafter referred to as CICS Client for DOS.

- ❑ DOS V6.3
- ❑ Windows V3.1
- ❑ LAN Support Program V1.31
- ❑ IBM CICS Client for DOS V1.0

Note: LAN Support Program V1.31 comes as part of OS/2 LAN Server V3.0. Details on how to install and configure this product are given in "LAN Support Program" on page 238.

Definitions Checklist

Before you configure the products for the sample configuration, we recommend that you acquire the definitions for the parameters listed below. Reference keys are assigned to definitions that must contain the same value in more than one product. For example, Local System Appl ID has the reference key **1**. These reference keys are used in later sections of this chapter.

- ❑ CICS for OS/2
  - ➢ Local System Appl ID **1**
  - ➢ NetBIOS Listener Adapter **2**
  - ➢ Maximum NetBIOS Systems

  ---- **Autoinstall** ----
  Connections and terminals from clients do not require additional definitions to be added to the CICS for OS/2 TCS or TCT because the definitions are automatically installed (this is known as autoinstall).

- ❑ CICSCLI.INI for CICS Client for DOS. These entries are defined in the CICSCLI.INI initialization file, generally found in the \CICSCLI\BIN subdirectory:
  - ➢ Server
  - ➢ Protocol
  - ➢ Netname **1**
  - ➢ Adapter **2**
  - ➢ Driver
  - ➢ DriverName

Matching Definitions

In this sample configuration a number of definitions must match. The Table 20 shows the definitions that must be the same. The last column (Example) shows the values we used in our configuration (see "Sample Definitions" on page 237). .

Table 20. Matching Definitions: CICS for OS/2-CICS Client for DOS/Windows-NetBIOS

	CICS for OS/2 Multi-user	CICSCLI.INI	Example
1	Local System Appl ID	Netname	ALSKIX
2	NETBIOS Listener Adapter	Adapter	0

Enabling NetBIOS

You must perform the following steps on the server workstation to enable NetBIOS support:

1. Change to the IBMCOM directory from an OS/2 command line.
2. Type: LAPS.
   The LAN Adapter and Protocol Support initial window is presented.
3. Click on **Configure**.
   The initial Configuration window is presented.
4. Select **Configure LAN transports** and click on **Continue**.
   The Configure Workstation window is presented (see Figure 167 on page 237).
5. Select your network adapter and NetBIOS protocol.

   ---- Note ----
   If you are not sure how to configure NetBIOS for your workstation, click on **Help** for further guidance.

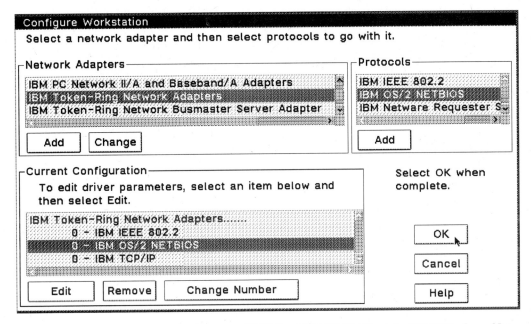

Figure 167. Enabling NetBIOS Support: CICS for OS/2-CICS Client for DOS/Windows-NetBIOS

Sample Definitions

In this section we present examples of the definitions listed in "Definitions Checklist" on page 235. The values highlighted in the figures refer to the Example column of Table 20 on page 236.

CICS for OS/2

You must provide three values in the SIT to enable NetBIOS support for CICS for OS/2 (see Figure 168 on page 238):

- Local System Appl ID
- NETBIOS Listener Adapter
- Maximum NETBIOS Systems

The **Local System Appl ID** can be up to eight characters long. This field will be used for the NetBIOS Listener name on the LAN. If not specified, the default is CICSOS2. The Local System Appl ID must be unique within the LAN to ensure that clients attach to the correct server.

Sample Definitions

NETBIOS Listener Adapter is required for NetBIOS connections. CICS for OS/2 supports the use of two LAN adapters. Enter in this field the number of the LAN adapters to be used for inbound communication. The default is zero. If two LAN adapters are installed in your server workstation, enter B (both) to enable both adapters for inbound communication.

The value specified for **Maximum NETBIOS Systems** determines the maximum number of remote systems with which the local system can concurrently communicate over NetBIOS. A remote system can be a CICS client or another CICS server.

```
   Update     Add       View      Delete                    Exit

   FAASIT3               System Initialization Table-2
                                                           More :
     Group Name . . . . . . . . : FAASYS

   System Communications
     Local System ID. . . . . . : CICS
     Local System Appl ID . . . : ALSKIX   1
     Default Remote System ID . :
   NETBIOS Support
     NETBIOS Listener Adapter . : 0       2   (0, 1 or B)
     Maximum NETBIOS Systems. . :     5           (0-254)
   TCP/IP Support
     TCP/IP Local Host Name . . : *
     TCP/IP Local Host Port . . : *           (* or 1-65535)
     Maximum TCP/IP Systems . . :     0           (0-255)
   PNA Support
     Load PNA Support . . . . . : N           (Y or N)
     PNA Model Terminal . . . . : MPNA

   Enter F1=Help F3=Exit F7=Bkwd F8=Fwd F10=Actions F12=Cancel
```

Figure 168. NetBIOS Definitions: CICS for OS/2-CICS Client for DOS/Windows-NetBIOS

LAN Support Program

For DOS, NetBIOS can be provided by the IBM LAN Support Program (LSP), which is part of OS/2 LAN Server V3.0. This product consists of a number of device drivers and supporting files to enable an application program to communicate with an adapter.[1] Some adapters require a Network Device Interface Specification (NDIS) MAC driver in addition to the LSP.

The IBM token-ring adapters, with the exception of the IBM Token-Ring Network 16/4 Adapter II, can function as either non-NDIS or NDIS adapters. The IBM Token-Ring Network 16/4 Adapter II is an NDIS adapter only.

The DOS NDIS MAC driver, for example, IBMTOK.DOS, is found on a diskette shipped with the adapter.

You can use several methods to install the NetBIOS protocol for DOS. The following steps describe one such method and include how to install a DOS NDIS MAC driver (IBMTOK.DOS):

1. Insert the diskette called **LAN Support Program Install**, which is supplied with IBM OS/2 LAN Server V3.0.
2. Enter a:\DXMAID to start the Installation Aid. [2]
3. Proceed to the Environment Information panel, as shown in Figure 169 on page 240.
4. Toggle the second option to **No** if an existing configuration does not exist.
5. For this sample configuration the 802.2 interface support is not required. However, some communication products require the 802.2 interface support, for example, APPC Networking Services for Windows V1.0, in which case you should toggle this option to **Yes**.
6. Press Enter to proceed to the Process Adapter Option Diskette panel (Figure 170 on page 240).

---

[1] A complete list of IBM and non-IBM adapters supported by the LAN Support Program can be found in the *OS/2 LAN Server: LAN Support Program User's Guide V3.0*
[2] To use this Installation Aid, you must have 282KB of free memory. If the Installation Aid is not used and configuration is completed manually, approximately 80KB of free memory are required.

Sample Definitions

```
                    LAN Support Program Installation Aid
 Press Tab to move between fields. Make changes as needed to the information
 below; then, press Enter.
 ┌──────────────────────── Environment Information ────────────────────────┐
 │ Use the Space bar to toggle between choices:                            │
 │                                                                         │
 │     Configuration for this computer?                          Yes       │
 │     Use existing configuration information?                   No        │
 │     Do you have adapter option diskettes?                     Yes       │
 │     Are you configuring for two adapters?                     No        │
 │     Do you need 802.2 interface support?                      No        │
 │                                                                         │
 │ Type changes as needed to the drive and directory information below:    │
 │                                                                         │
 │     Source for the LSP                              A:     \            │
 │     Target for new configuration                    C:     \lsp         │
 └─────────────────────────────────────────────────────────────────────────┘
     Enter      F1=Help      F3=Exit      F7=Previous panel
```

Figure 169. Environment Information: LAN Support Program

On the Process Adapter Option Diskette panel enter the path (without file name) of the DOS NDIS file, as shown in Figure 170. This action copies the IBMTOK.DOS and IBMTOK.NIF files from the Adapter Option Diskette.

```
                    LAN Support Program Installation Aid
 Type changes as needed to the information below. Insert the adapter option
 diskette in the drive; then, press Enter. Press Esc if you do not want to
 process an adapter option diskette.
 ┌──────────────────────── Process Adapter Option Diskette ───────────────┐
 │ Adapter option diskette drive, and directory for DOS NDIS files:        │
 │                                                                         │
 │          A: \ibm\tr164\ndis                                             │
 │                                                                         │
 └─────────────────────────────────────────────────────────────────────────┘
     Esc=Cancel     Enter      F1=Help      F3=Exit
```

Figure 170. Process Adapter Option Diskette: LAN Support Program

Press Enter to get to the Current Configuration panel (Figure 171 on page 241).

On the Current Configuration panel press **F4=Install** to install the Primary Adapter and Protocol. Once installed, the workstation will require rebooting.

```
              LAN Support Program Installation Aid
  Press Tab to select Adapter or Protocol Window. Use up and down arrow keys
  to move cursor; press Space bar to select or to clear selection.
                      Current Configuration
  ┌─────────────────── Primary Adapter Window ───────────────────┐
  │ IBM Token-Ring Network Adapters with NDIS support (IBMTOK.DOS) │
  └──────────────────────────────────────────────────────────────┘
  ┌─────────────────────── Protocol Window ──────────────────────┐
  │ IBM DOS NETBIOS Protocol for NDIS (DXMJOMOD.SYS)             │
  └──────────────────────────────────────────────────────────────┘
  ┌───────────────── Selections for Adapter Window ──────────────┐
  │                                                    More -+   │
  │ ]X] IBM Token-Ring Network Adapters with NDIS support (IBMTOK.DOS) │
  │ ] ] SMCDOSJP_MOD                                              │
  │ ] ] SMCDOSAT_MOD                                              │
  │ ] ] SMCDOSMC_MOD                                              │
  └──────────────────────────────────────────────────────────────┘
  Enter=Other adapter      F1=Help    F3=Exit    F4=Install
  F5=View/Change parameters           F9=Restart installation
```

Figure 171. Current Configuration Panel: LAN Support Program

During rebooting the messages shown in Figure 172 confirm that NetBIOS support is active.

```
        Starting PC DOS...
           ::
        IBM Local Area Network Support Program Version 1.31
           ::
        IBM DOS NETBEUI 2.01
        MS DOS LAN Manager Netbind v1.1
           ::
```

Figure 172. NetBIOS Active Confirmation: DOS System Bootup

After installing DOS V6.3 (with no options) and the LSP, the CONFIG.SYS file appears as shown in Figure 173 on page 242.

Sample Definitions

```
------ Top of file ------
DEVICE=C:\DOS\HIMEM.SYS
DOS=HIGH
DEVICE=C:\DOS\SETVER.EXE
FILES=30
BUFFERS=10
DEVICE=\LSP\PROTMAN.DOS /I:\LSP
DEVICE=\LSP\IBMTOK.DOS
DEVICE=\LSP\DXMA0MOD.SYS 001
DEVICE=\LSP\DXMJ0MOD.SYS
------ Bottom of file ------
```

Figure 173. CONFIG.SYS File: DOS Workstation

Notes:

1. The /I: parameter is used to enable PROTMAN.DOS to locate the PROTOCOL.INI file.

2. IBMTOK.DOS is the NDIS MAC driver.

3. DXMA0MOD.SYS is the interrupt arbitrator device driver and has one parameter that defines the language in which load-time messages are displayed. For example, 001=U.S. English, 081=Japanese.

4. DXMJ0MOD.SYS enables communication between an NDIS MAC driver and an application program that uses the NetBIOS interface. Associated with DXMJ0MOD.SYS is **PROTMAN.DOS**, the NDIS protocol manager.

5. If you use non-NDIS Token-Ring Network Adapter support device drivers, you will see **DXMCnMOD.SYS** to support the adapter and the **DXMT0MOD.SYS** device driver to enable NetBIOS support. The CONFIG.SYS would contain the following statements:

    ```
    DEVICE=\LSP\DXMA0MOD.SYS 001
    DEVICE=\LSP\DXMC0MOD.SYS
    DEVICE=\LSP\DXMT0MOD.SYS
    ```

6. Many different parameters can be appended to these device drivers. Some may improve the performance of your setup. See *OS/2 LAN Server: LAN Support Program User's Guide V3.0* for more information.

AUTOEXEC.BAT

If you are configuring an NDIS adapter, the AUTOEXEC.BAT file is updated with the following line:

```
\LSP\NETBIND
```

This is the NDIS protocol binding utility file and must be executed by the AUTOEXEC.BAT file before any network activity is started.

PROTOCOL.INI

The PROTOCOL.INI file contains a number of parameter bindings dependent upon the device driver or NDIS MAC driver installed. This file is found in the LSP directory.

CICSCLI.INI

The CICSCLI.INI file is generally found in the CICS Client for DOS \BIN subdirectory. Figure 174 shows the definitions required for this sample configuration.

```
    :::

    Server         = CICSOS2
    Protocol       = NETBIOS
    Netname        = ALSKIX              1
    Adapter        = 0                   2

    :::

    Driver         = NETBIOS
    DriverName     = CCLIBMNB
```

Figure 174. CICSCLI.INI Definitions: CICS for OS/2-CICS Client for DOS/Windows-NetBIOS

Notes:

1. A separate **Server** definition is required for each server to which the client needs to connect. You can make this value meaningful to the end user, for example, CICSOS2.

2. The value of **Protocol** identifies the communication protocol to be used between the client and the server. This value must match the value you have assigned to **Driver**. You can make this value meaningful to the end user, for example, NETBIOS.

3. The **Netname** should match the Local System Appl ID of your CICS for OS/2 server.

4. The **Adapter** specifies the LAN adapter number you are using on the client workstation. The default is zero.
5. **Driver** must be the same as **Protocol**.
6. The device driver for all clients using NetBIOS to connect to a server is **CCLIBMNB**.

Testing Your Configuration

After you have installed and configured all relevant products for this sample configuration, we recommend that you do the following:

Step 1. Start the CICS server.

Step 2. Start the CICS Client for DOS.
Issue **CICSCLI /S=CICSOS2**.
→ See "Starting and Stopping Your CICS Client" on page 321.

Step 3. Check the status of the CICS Client for DOS.
Issue **CICSCLI /L**.
→ See "Checking the Status of Your CICS Client" on page 322.

Step 4. Start a 3270 emulator session.
Issue **CICSTERM /S=CICSOS2**.

Step 5. Problems?
→ See Chapter 21, "Problem Determination," on page 293.
→ See Appendix C, "Common Problems: Symptoms and Solutions," on page 339.

Step 6. Need further information?
→ See Appendix B, "Frequently Asked Questions," on page 331.

18
CICS 3270 Client Printer Configurations

This chapter covers the following topics:

- "Method 1: Client Printer Attached to a CICS for OS/2 Server" on page 246
- "Method 2: Client Printer Attached to a CICS for OS/2 Server Running User Exit 21" on page 248
- "User Exit 21" on page 249
- "Method 3: Client Printer Attached to a CICS/6000 Server" on page 253

CICS 3270 Client printer support provides the ability to define a printer terminal on the client workstation. This support enables your CICS applications running on the server to direct output to the client-attached printers (see Figure 175 on page 246).

The printer support uses CICS 3270 emulation functions. See Table 1 on page 8 for CICS servers that currently support CICS 3270 emulation and, hence, CICS 3270 client printer support.

In this chapter we describe three methods of configuring client printers:

1. Method 1 - Client printer attached to a CICS for OS/2 server
2. Method 2 - Client printer attached to a CICS for OS/2 server running user exit 21
3. Method 3 - Client printer attached to a CICS/6000 server

First we discuss methods 1 and 2 for attaching a client printer to a CICS for OS/2 server and explain why method 2 is the recommended approach. Then we discuss method 3.

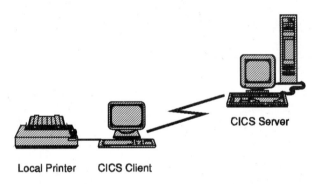

Figure 175. Printer Configuration

Method 1: Client Printer Attached to a CICS for OS/2 Server

To attach a CICS Client printer to a CICS for OS/2 server you must carefully specify the definitions on both products. You can use either TCP/IP or NetBIOS.

CICS for OS/2 Definitions

Figure 176 on page 247 shows the TCT definition required on the CICS for OS/2 server.

```
     Update    Add    View     Delete                          Exit

     FAATCT2                 Terminal Control Table-1
                                                              More : +
     Terminal Name. . . . . . . . : T1IP
     Group Name . . . . . . . . . : ALSKIX
     Network Name . . . . . . . . :
     Terminal Type. . . . . . . . : P      (V=3270 Terminal, J=3270J Terminal
                                            P=3270 printer,  Q=3270J Printer
                                            S=Sequential,    A=3270 3151-PC

     Model  . . . . . . . . . . . : N      (Y or N)

     Associated Printer . . . . . :

     Printer Close Mode . . . . . :        (T=end of task,
                                            F=end of file, or space)

     Initial Transaction Required : N      (Y or N)
     Remote System. . . . . . . . : CT00
     Remote Terminal Name . . . . :
     Description. . . . . . . . . : CLIENT PRINTER DEFINITION

     Enter F1=Help F3=Exit        F8=Fwd F10=Actions F12=Cancel
```

Figure 176. Client Printer TCT Definition (Method 1): CICS for OS/2

Note: On page 2 of the TCT you must specify Autoconnect=No.

CICS Client CICSCLI.INI Definition

For this configuration there are no special parameters to define in the CICSCLI.INI file. Before issuing the CICSPRNT command you can check whether your NetBIOS or TCP/IP connection is working by issuing a CICSTERM command.

CICS Client CICSPRNT Command

To start your CICS Client printer emulator, issue the following command:

```
─ CICSPRNT command ─────────────────────────────
     cicsprnt /s=<servername> /n=<netname> /f=<output_filename>

For example:
     cicsprnt /s=CICSOS2 /n=T1IP /f=c:\print.fil
```

Where:

s=\<servername> The name of the server you want to start your printer emulator.

n=\<netname> Must match the terminal name as defined in the CICS for OS/2 TCT (see Figure 176 on page 247). The value for /n is case sensitive.

f=\<output_filename> Specifies the file to which print requests are appended.

Method 1 is unlikely to work because, when the CICS Client definition is autoinstalled on the CICS for OS/2 server, you cannot guarantee that your Remote System name (see Figure 176 on page 247) will be **CT00** (if you are using a TCP/IP connection, or **CL00** if you are using NetBIOS). To guarantee that you will always use the same Remote System ID, you must prepare, compile, and link user exit 21 (TCS Autoinstall) on the CICS for OS/2 server.

Method 2: Client Printer Attached to a CICS for OS/2 Server Running User Exit 21

Method 2 uses the CICS for OS/2 user exit 21 (TCS Autoinstall). We recommend that you use this method to guarantee that your Remote System name does not vary during client autoinstall.

User Exit 21

Within the CICS for OS/2 user exit 21 you define the RemoteApplid you expect to receive from a CICS Clients autoinstall request, and the corresponding RemoteSystemID you want the client to use. For example:

User Exit 21 Assignment

```
if (strnicmp(pParms->Exp21RemoteApplid,"Prt1TCP",7) == 0)
  {
    strcpy(pParms ->Exp21RemoteSystemId,"P1IP");
```

Notes:

1. **RemoteApplid** matches the **Client=applid** parameter in the CICSCLI.INI file. The applid in this configuration is **Prt1TCP**.
2. **RemoteSystemId** matches the **Remote System** defined in the CICS for OS/2 TCT. This configuration uses **P1IP**.

CICS for OS/2 Definitions

Figure 177 shows the TCT definition required on the CICS for OS/2 server.

Method 2: Client Printer Attached to a CICS for OS/2 Server Running User Exit 21

```
     Update    Add      View       Delete                      Exit

   FAATCT2                   Terminal Control Table-1
                                                              More : +
   Terminal Name. . . . . . . . : T1IP
   Group Name . . . . . . . . . : ALSKIX
   Network Name . . . . . . . . :
   Terminal Type. . . . . . . . : P      (V=3270 Terminal, J=3270J Terminal
                                          P=3270 printer,  Q=3270J Printer
                                          S=Sequential,    A=3270 3151-PC


   Model  . . . . . . . . . . . : N      (Y or N)

   Associated Printer . . . . . :

   Printer Close Mode . . . . . :        (T=end of task,
                                          F=end of file, or space)


   Initial Transaction Required : N      (Y or N)
   Remote System. . . . . . . . : P1IP
   Remote Terminal Name . . . . :
   Description. . . . . . . . . : Client Printer via User Exit 21

   Enter F1=Help F3=Exit         F8=Fwd F10=Actions F12=Cancel
```

Figure 177. Client Printer TCT Definition (Method 2): CICS for OS/2

Where:

Terminal Name	Matches the name on your CICSPRNT /N=xxxx command
Terminal Type	Set to P for printer (J for DBCS printer)
Remote System	Matches the RemoteSystemID parameter in user exit 21
Remote Terminal Name	If left blank, this field assumes the Terminal Name entry. In this example, T1IP.
Autoconnect=No	On page 2 of the TCT you must specify Autoconnect=No.

CICS Client CICSCLI.INI Definition

The CICSCLI.INI file requires the following definition:

Method 2: Client Printer Attached to a CICS for OS/2 Server Running User Exit 21

```
Client = Prt1TCP
    :::
```

Note: The **Prt1TCP** applid supplied on the Client keyword must match the RemoteApplid specified in the user exit.

CICS Client CICSPRNT Command

To start your CICS Client printer emulator, issue the following command:

```
┌─ CICSPRNT command ─────────────────────────────────────
│       cicsprnt /s=<servername> /n=<netname> /f=<output_filename>
│
│ For example:
│       cicsprnt /s=CICSOS2 /n=T1IP /f=c:\print.fil
```

Where:

s=<servername>   The name of the server you want to start your printer emulator.

n=<netname>   Must match the terminal name as defined in the CICS for OS/2 TCT (see Figure 177 on page 250). The value of /n is case sensitive.

f=<output_filename>   Specifies the file to which print requests are appended.

Testing Your Printer Configuration

Before attaching your printer, you can check that your configuration is correct by running a simple program, such as the the **WHATTIME** program, which issues the following commands:

```
─ WHATTIME program ─────────────────────────────
   :::
   exec cics asktime      abstime(WS-TIME);

   exec cics formattime abstime(WS-TIME)
                          time(OK-TIME)
                          timesep;

   exec cics send text    from(OK-TIME)
                          length(length of OK-TIME)
                          print;

   exec cics return;
   :::
```

From a CICS for OS/2 terminal (client or local), you can issue the following command:

```
ceci start transid(TIME) termid(T1IP)
```

Notes:

1. Transid(TIME) runs the WHATTIME program.
2. Termid(T1IP) is the client printer terminal installed.
3. The output of the EXEC CICS SEND TEXT PRINT command will be appended to the **print.fil** output file as specified on the **CICSPRNT** command.

Matching Definitions

Table 21 on page 252 summarizes the printer definitions that must match.

Table 21. Matching Definitions: CICS 3270 Client Printer Configurations

CICSCLI.INI	User Exit 21	CICS for OS/2	CICSPRNT	Example
Client=applid	RemoteApplid	-	-	Prt1TCP
-	RemoteSystemID	Remote System	-	P1IP
-	-	Terminal Name	Netname	T1IP

Multiple Printers

Using Method 2 you must have one CICS for OS/2 TCT definition for each printer you want to install. You may want to have multiple client printers, but not want to define multiple TCT entries. To resolve this issue, in addition to user exit 21, you can use user exit 22 (Terminal Definition Autoinstall). By specifying a modelname rather than a netname on the CICSPRNT command, you can select a model within user exit 22 to match a model on the CICS for OS/2 server. Thus, you can predefine the remote terminal name and the remote system name of the printer.

Method 3: Client Printer Attached to a CICS/6000 Server

Whereas CICS for OS/2 references a termid defined in the TCT, CICS/6000 requires a netname to be specified on the CICSPRNT command. This netname can be up to eight characters long.

CICS/6000 Definitions

Here is the TCT definition, PRIN, used to define a CICS Client printer on a CICS/6000 server:

Method 3: Client Printer Attached to a CICS/6000 Server

CICS/6000 Definition

```
PRIN:
GroupName=""
ActivateOnStartup=yes
ResourceDescription="CICS Client Printer"
AmendCounter=0
Permanent=no
OutService=no
RemoteSysId=""
RemoteName=""
TSLKeyList=1
RSLKeyList=none
ModelId=""
NumLines=64
NumColumns=132
CanStartATIs=yes
CanStartTTIs=no
UCTranFlag=no
TCTUALen=0
NetName="printer6"
Katakana=no
IsPrinter=yes
IsShippable=yes
TermType=145
TermSubType=10
Priority=0
Validation=no
Highlight=no
Foreground=no
ExtDS=no
ProgramSymbols=no
Outline=no
SOSI=no
ERRLastLine=no
ERRIntensify=yes
ERRColor=no
ERRHilight=no
DevType=""
TerminalProtection=none
```

CICS Client CICSCLI.INI Definition

For this configuration there are no special parameters to define in the CICSCLI.INI file. Before issuing the CICSPRNT command you can check whether your TCP/IP connection is working by issuing a CICSTERM command.

CICS Client CICSPRNT Command

To start your CICS Client printer emulator, issue the following command:

```
── CICSPRNT command ─────────────────────────────
     cicsprnt /s=<servername> /n=<netname> /f=<output_filename>

For example:
     cicsprnt /s=CICS6000 /n=printer6 /f=c:\print.fil
```

Where:

s=<servername> The name of the server you want to start your printer emulator.

n=<netname> Must match the NetName parameter as defined in the CICS/6000 TCT. The value for /n is case sensitive.

f=<output_filename> Specifies the file to which print requests are appended.

Testing Your Configuration

Before attaching your printer, you can check that your configuration is correct by running a simple program, such as the **WHATTIME** program, which issues the following commands:

```
── WHATTIME program ─────────────────────────────
    exec cics asktime    abstime(WS-TIME)

    exec cics formattime abstime(WS-TIME)
                         time(OK-TIME)
                         timesep;

    exec cics send text  from(OK-TIME)
                         length(length of OK-TIME)
                         print;

    exec cics return;
```

From a CICS/6000 terminal (client or local), you can issue the following command:

```
    ceci start transid(TIME) termid(PRIN)
```

Notes:

1. Transid(TIME) runs the WHATTIME program.

Method 3: Client Printer Attached to a CICS/6000 Server

2. Termid(PRIN) is the client printer terminal installed.
3. The output of the EXEC CICS SEND TEXT PRINT command will be appended to the **print.fil** output file as specified on the **CICSPRNT** command.

19

External Call Interface

This chapter covers the following topics:

- "ECI Model" on page 258
- "Program Link Calls" on page 258
- "Status Information Calls" on page 265
- "Reply Solicitation Calls" on page 268
- "Managing Logical Units of Work" on page 269
- "Multiple Asynchronous Calls Accessing Multiple CICS Servers" on page 273
- "ECI Asynchronous Implementation with Callback" on page 274
- "Sample Implementation" on page 277
- "Further Information" on page 281

ECI Model

The ECI enables a non-CICS client application to call a CICS program as a subroutine. The client application communicates with the server CICS program using the COMMAREA. The COMMAREA is passed to the CICS server on the ECI call. The CICS program typically populates the COMMAREA with data accessed from files or databases, and the data is then returned to the client for manipulation or display. Figure 178 shows the CICS ECI model.

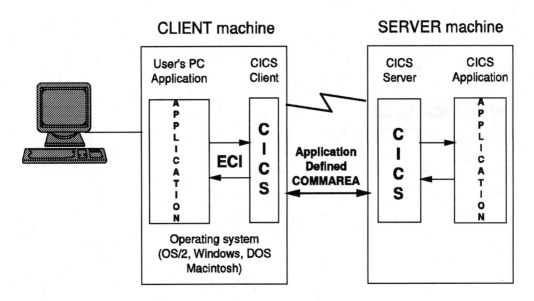

Figure 178. CICS ECI Model

Program Link Calls

A client running a non-CICS application program issuing an ECI program link call causes a CICS program to be executed on the CICS server (see Figure 17). This call from an ECI application is similar to a CICS program issuing an EXEC CICS LINK command.

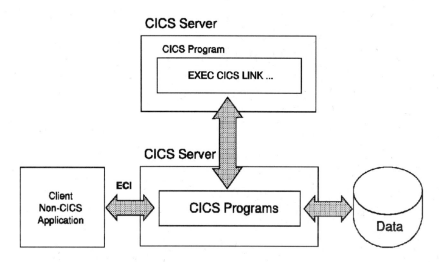

Figure 179. CICS ECI Program Link Calls

There are two types of ECI program link calls: synchronous and asynchronous.

Synchronous Program Link Calls

When the client application issues a synchronous program link call, the client application waits until the called program has finished.

Figure 180 on page 260 shows a simple example of a synchronous ECI program flow.

Program Link Calls

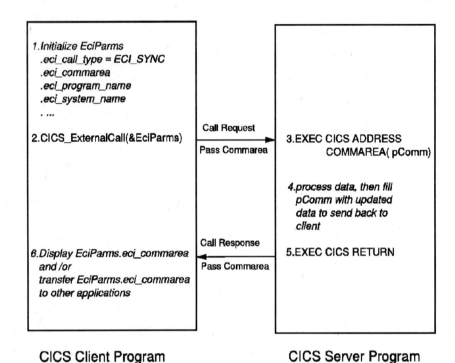

Figure 180. Synchronous ECI Program Flow

Notes:

- **EciParms** is a pointer to the ECI parameter block. The parameter block fields are used as input and output or to describe the function to be performed for the ECI calls. *The parameter block must be set to nulls before use.*

- **eci_call_type** is the parameter in the ECI parameter block for controlling the type of ECI call.

- **eci_commarea** is the COMMAREA for use by a called program or for returned status information. It carries the data that the ECI client program sends to the server CICS program. If no COMMAREA is required, supply a null pointer and set the length (specified in eci_commarea_length) to zero. If the code page of the application is different from the code page of the server, data conversion must be performed at the server. To do this, you must use CICS-supplied resource conversion capabilities, such as the DFH-CNV macro definitions (see "Data Conversion: ASCII to EBCDIC" on page 326).

- **eci_program_name** is the name of the server CICS program to be called.

Program Link Calls

- **eci_system_name** is the name of a CICS server.
- **CICS_ExternalCall** provides most of the function of the ECI. It is the ECI call not only used for ECI program link calls, but also for ECI status information calls and ECI reply solicitation calls (see "Sample Program Functions" on page 277).
- **EXEC CICS ADDRESS COMMAREA(pComm)** is a CICS command to obtain the COMMAREA passed from the client program. The pComm is the pointer to the COMMAREA.
- **EXEC CICS RETURN** commits the server transaction and ends the CICS server program. The COMMAREA is automatically sent to the client program.
- Your client program can display the updated data in the **eci_commarea** or transfer the data to another application on the client workstation, for example, a spreadsheet program.

Figure 181 on page 262 shows a simple example of a synchronous ECI program in COBOL. The associated CICS server program obtains the current date and time of the CICS region populating the COMMAREA with the information (See "Sample ECI and EPI Source Code" on page 351). We use the same server program for all of the examples in this chapter.

```
****************************************************************
* Variable definitions                                          *
****************************************************************
  01 WS-AREA.
     02 COMMAREA        VALUE LOW-VALUES   PIC X(18).


****************************************************************
* Copybooks                                                     *
****************************************************************
  COPY CICS_ECI.

****************************************************************
* Procedure Division                                            *
****************************************************************
  PROCEDURE DIVISION.

****************************************************************
* Issue a CICS_Externalcall for an ECI_SYNC                     *
****************************************************************

       MOVE LOW-VALUES TO ECI-PARMS

       SET  ECI-SYNC           TO TRUE
       MOVE 'EC01'             TO ECI-PROGRAM-NAME
       MOVE 'GUIDO'            TO ECI-USERID
       MOVE 'GUIDO'            TO ECI-PASSWORD
       MOVE 'CICSTCP'          TO ECI-SYSTEM-NAME
       SET  ECI-COMMAREA       TO ADDRESS OF COMMAREA
       MOVE LENGTH OF COMMAREA TO ECI-COMMAREA-LENGTH
       MOVE 0                  TO ECI-TIMEOUT
       SET  ECI-NO-EXTEND      TO TRUE
       SET  ECI-VERSION-1      TO TRUE


       CALL '_CICS_ExternalCall'
            USING BY REFERENCE ECI-PARMS.

       IF ECI-NO-ERROR
          DISPLAY 'CommArea returned:' COMMAREA
       END-IF


       EXIT.
```

Figure 181. Sample Synchronous ECI Program in COBOL

Asynchronous Program Link Calls

When the client application issues an asynchronous program link call, it gets back control without reference to the completion of the called program. The application can ask to be notified later when the information is available. It must use a reply solicitation call to determine the outcome of the asynchronous request. The ECI asynchronous program link call is available in all environments except DOS.

Figure 182 shows a simple example of an asynchronous ECI program flow.

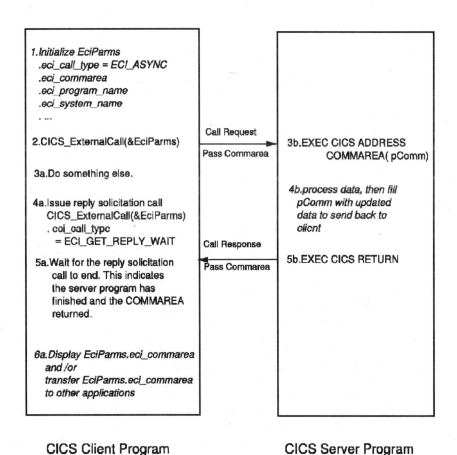

Figure 182. Asynchronous ECI Program Flow

Notes:

- After the ECI program has issued the asynchronous program link call, it gets back control immediately. The program can do something else while the server program is performing the client's request.

- The reply solicitation call is covered in "Reply Solicitation Calls" on page 268.

Figure 183 is a simple example of an asynchronous ECI program in C. The associated CICS server program obtains the current date and time of the CICS region populating the COMMAREA with the information (see Appendix, "Sample ECI and EPI Source Code," on page 351).

```c
/***************************************************************************/
/* HEADER FILES                                                            */
/***************************************************************************/

  :::

#include <cics_eci.h>

  :::

/***************************************************************************/
/* Global Variables                                                        */
/***************************************************************************/
   ECI_PARMS         EciParms;

/***************************************************************************/
/***************************************************************************/
/* main() - Sample Entry Point                                             */
/***************************************************************************/
/***************************************************************************/
int main(void)
{
  EciAsync();

  /* Do something else */

  EciGetReply();

} /* main */

/***************************************************************************/
/* EciASync                                                                */
/***************************************************************************/
/* Issue a CICS_Externalcall for an ECI_ASYNC                              */
/*                                                                         */
/***************************************************************************/
void EciAsync (void)
{
   short           Rc;
   char            CommArea [18];

   /* the beginning of this asynchronous ECI program link call */
   memset (CommArea, '\0', 18);
   memset (&EciParms, 0, sizeof (ECI_PARMS));

   memcpy(&EciParms.eci_program_name, "EC01",     4);
   memcpy(&EciParms.eci_userid,       "GUIDO",    8);
   memcpy(&EciParms.eci_password,     "GUIDO",    8);
   memcpy(&EciParms.eci_system_name,  "CICSTCP",  8);
```

Figure 183. (Part 1 of 2) Simple Example of an Asynchronous ECI Program in C

```
        EciParms.eci_call_type                  = ECI_ASYNC;
        EciParms.eci_version                    = ECI_VERSION_1;
        EciParms.eci_commarea                   = CommArea;
        EciParms.eci_commarea_length            = 18;
        EciParms.eci_extend_mode                = ECI_NO_EXTEND;
        EciParms.eci_luw_token                  = ECI_LUW_NEW;
        EciParms.eci_timeout                    = 0;

        Rc = CICS_ExternalCall (&EciParms);

        /* the end of this asynchronous ECI program link call */

} /* EciAsync */

/*************************************************************************/
/* EciGetReply                                                           */
/*************************************************************************/
/* Issue a CICS_Externalcall for an ECI_GET_REPLY                        */
/*                                                                       */
/*************************************************************************/
EciGetReply (void)
{
    short           Rc;
    char            CommArea [18];

    /* the beginning of this general ECI reply solicitation call */

    memset (CommArea, '\0', 18);
    memset (&EciParms, 0, sizeof (ECI_PARMS));

    EciParms.eci_version                        = ECI_VERSION_1;
    EciParms.eci_call_type                      = ECI_GET_REPLY_WAIT;
    memcpy(&EciParms.eci_userid,       "GUIDO",   8);
    memcpy(&EciParms.eci_password,     "GUIDO",   8);
    memcpy(&EciParms.eci_system_name,  "CICSTCP", 8);
    EciParms.eci_commarea                       = CommArea;
    EciParms.eci_commarea_length                = 18;
    EciParms.eci_extend_mode                    = ECI_NO_EXTEND;
    EciParms.eci_luw_token                      = ECI_LUW_NEW;
    EciParms.eci_timeout                        = 0;

    Rc = CICS_ExternalCall (&EciParms);

    if (Rc == ECI_NO_ERROR)
    {
        CommArea[17] = '\0';
        printf ("CommArea Returned: %s", CommArea);
    }

    /* the end of this general ECI reply solicitation call */
} /* EciGetReply */
```

Figure 183. (Part 2 of 2) Simple Example of an Asynchronous ECI Program in C

Status Information Calls

ECI status information calls retrieve status information about the type of system on which the application is running. Status information is supplied in the ECI status block, which is passed across the inter-

Status Information Calls

face in the **eci_commarea** parameter.

The following status information is held in the ECI status block:

- The type of connection (whether the ECI program is locally connected to a CICS server, a CICS client, or nothing).
- The state of the CICS server (available, unavailable, or unknown).
- The state of the CICS client (available, not applicable, or unknown).

The status information calls allow you to perform three tasks:

- Inquire about the type of system on which the application is running and its connection with a given server. For this task you must provide a COMMAREA in which the status is returned.
- Set up a request to be notified when the status changes from some specified value. For this task you must provide a COMMAREA in which the specified status is described. When the status is different from the status specified, you are notified of the new status. Only asynchronous calls can be used for this purpose.
- Cancel a request for notification of status change. For this task a COMMAREA is not required.

There are two types of status information calls: synchronous and asynchronous.

Synchronous

When the client application makes a synchronous status information call, it waits until the information is made available.

Figure 184 on page 267 shows an example of a synchronous status information call.

```
/*********************************************************************/
/* HEADER FILES                                                      */
/*********************************************************************/

  :::

#include <cics_eci.h>

  :::

/*********************************************************************/
/* Global Variables                                                  */
/*********************************************************************/
    ECI_PARMS          EciParms;

int main(void)
{
    short              Rc;
    char               CommArea [ECI_STATUS_LENGTH];

    :::

    memset (CommArea, '\0', ECI_STATUS_LENGTH);
    memset (&EciParms, 0, sizeof (ECI_PARMS));

    EciParms.eci_version                      = ECI_VERSION_1;
    EciParms.eci_call_type                    = ECI_STATE_SYNC;
    memcpy(&EciParms.eci_userid,       "GUIDO",    8);
    memcpy(&EciParms.eci_password,     "GUIDO",    8);
    memcpy(&EciParms.eci_system_name,  "CICSTCP",  8);
    EciParms.eci_commarea                     = CommArea;
    EciParms.eci_commarea_length              = ECI_STATUS_LENGTH;
    EciParms.eci_extend_mode                  = ECI_STATE_IMMEDIATE;
    EciParms.eci_luw_token                    = ECI_LUW_NEW;
    EciParms.eci_timeout                      = 0;

    Rc = CICS_ExternalCall (&EciParms);

    /* You can use those status information returned in CommArea. */

} /* main */
```

Figure 184. Sample Synchronous Status Information Call

Note: When you issue a synchronous status information call, you must set the **eci_call_type** parameter to ECI_STATE_SYNC. For more detail about synchronous status information calls, see *CICS Family: Client/Server Programming*.

Asynchronous

When the client application makes an asynchronous status information call, it gets back control while the information is being retrieved. The application can ask to be notified later when the information is available. It must use a reply solicitation call to determine the outcome of the asynchronous request. Asynchronous status information calls are available in all environments except DOS. See *CICS Family: Client/Server Programming* for more detail about asynchronous status information calls.

Reply Solicitation Calls

Reply solicitation calls get back information after asynchronous program link or asynchronous status information calls.

After an asynchronous program link call or asynchronous status information call, it is the responsibility of the calling application to solicit the reply. All calls return any outstanding reply that meets the selection criteria specified in the call.

An application that uses the asynchronous method of calling may have several program link and status information calls outstanding at any time. The **eci_message_qualifier** parameter in the ECI parameter block can be used on an asynchronous call to provide a user-defined identifier for the call. The use of different identifiers for different asynchronous calls within a single application is the programmer's responsibility.

Reply solicitation calls can be general or specific. General reply solicitation calls retrieve any piece of outstanding information. When a general reply solicitation call is made, the ECI uses the **eci_message_qualifier** field to return the name of the call to which the reply belongs. There are two types of general reply solicitation calls:

- **ECI_GET_REPLY**
  Provides a call to return information appropriate to any outstanding reply for any asynchronous request. If there is no such reply, ECI_ERR_NO_REPLY is returned.

- **ECI_GET_REPLY_WAIT**
  Provides a call to return information appropriate to any outstanding reply for any asynchronous request. If there is no such reply, the application waits until there is.

Specific reply solicitation calls retrieve information for a named asynchronous request. When a specific reply solicitation call is made, you must supply a value in the **eci_message_qualifier** field to identify the asynchronous call about which information is being sought. There are two types of specific reply solicitation calls:

- **ECI_GET_SPECIFIC_REPLY**
  Provides a call to return information appropriate to any outstanding reply that matches the **eci_message_qualifier** input. If there is no such reply, ECI_ERR_NO_REPLY is returned.

❏ **ECI_GET_SPECIFIC_REPLY_WAIT**
Provides a call to return information appropriate to any outstanding reply that matches the **eci_message_qualifier** input. If there is no such reply, the application waits until there is.

See *CICS Family: Client/Server Programming* for more information about reply solicitation calls.

Managing Logical Units of Work

Logical unit of work (LUW) is introduced for managing the recoverable resources in the CICS region. An LUW is the only processing in the server that is required to establish a set of updates to recoverable resources. When an LUW ends normally, all changes are committed. When an LUW ends abnormally, for instance, because a program abends, all changes by the program and by other programs that belong to the same LUW are backed out. An ECI application is often concerned with updating recoverable resources on the server, and the application programmer must understand the facilities that the ECI provides for managing LUWs.

ECI Facilities

The **eci_luw_token** integer field in the ECI parameter block is used to identify the LUW to which an ECI call belongs. It must be set to zero at the start of an LUW (regardless of whether the LUW is going to be extended). If the LUW is to be extended, the ECI updates the **eci_luw_token** field with a valid value on the first call of the LUW. That value should be used as input to all later calls related to the same LUW.

If the return code of an ECI call is not ECI_NO_ERROR, and the call was continuing or ending an existing LUW, the **eci_luw_token** field is used as output to report the condition of the LUW. If the field is set to zero, the LUW has ended, and its updates have been backed out. If the field is set to nonzero, it is the same as the input value, the LUW is continuing, and its updates are still pending.

The **eci_extend_mode** integer field in the ECI parameter block is also used to manage the LUWs when an application issues ECI program link calls. This field is used to determine whether an LUW is terminated at the end of the program link call.

When an application makes a program link call, the values for the **eci_extend_mode** field can be as follows:

- **ECI_NO_EXTEND**
  - If the input **eci_luw_token** field is zero, this is the only call for an LUW.
  - If the input **eci_luw_token** field is not zero, this is the last call for the specified LUW.
  - In either case, changes to recoverable resources are committed by a CICS end-of-task syncpoint, and the LUW ends.
- **ECI_EXTENDED**
  - If the input **eci_luw_token** field is zero, this is the first call for an LUW that is to be continued.
  - If the input **eci_luw_token** field is not zero, this call is intended to continue the specified LUW.
  - In either case, the LUW continues after the called program completes successfully, and changes to recoverable resources remain uncommitted.
- **ECI_COMMIT**
  Terminate the current LUW, identified by the input **eci_luw_token** field and commit all changes made to recoverable resources.
- **ECI_BACKOUT**
  Terminate the LUW identified by the input **eci_luw_token** field and back out all changes made to recoverable resources.

Single Program Link Call within One LUW

The changes to recoverable resources in an LUW could be affected by a single program link call. In this case, the application calls a program that is the only program of an LUW. The input parameters are set up as follows:

- **eci_extend_mode** = ECI_NO_EXTEND
- **eci_luw_token** = zero
- Other required parameters

If this program ends normally, the LUW ends normally, and all changes to the recoverable resources are committed. If this program ends abnormally, the LUW ends abnormally, and all changes to the recoverable resources are backed out.

Sequence of Program Link Calls within One LUW

The changes to recoverable resources in an LUW could be affected by a sequence of program link calls.

Figure 185 on page 272 shows an example of a sequence of program link calls within the same LUW. The application issues ECI calls to PROG_1 and PROG_2 and can then choose to end through:

- Option1 - calls PROG_3 then ends by specifying ECI_NO_EXTEND

Managing Logical Units of Work

- Option2 - commits changes by PROG_1 and PROG_2 without calling PROG_3 and then ends
- Option3 - backs out changes by PROG_1 and PROG_2 without calling PROG_3 and then ends

```
\   :::

/* The first program link call - PROG_1
    set    eci_extend_mode   :   ECI_EXTENDED
           eci_luw_token     :   zero
           eci_program_name  :   PROG_1
    call   CICS_ExternalCall( parameters block )
*/

/* After the first call, save the token assigned to
   eci_luw_token by the server, for example, my_token.
   The token is used for all later calls within the
   same LUW.
*/

/* The next program link call - PROG_2
    set    eci_extend_mode   :   ECI_EXTENDED
           eci_luw_token     :   my_token
           eci_program_name  :   PROG_2
    call   CICS_ExternalCall( parameters block )
*/

/* Option 1 choose to call PROG_3 then end.
    set    eci_extend_mode   :   ECI_NO_EXTEND
           eci_luw_token     :   my_token
           eci_program_name  :   PROG_3
    call   CICS_ExternalCall( parameters block )
*/

/* Option 2 choose to commit changes without calling PROG_3.
    set    eci_extend_mode   :   ECI_COMMIT
           eci_luw_token     :   my_token
           eci_program_name  :   null
    call   CICS_ExternalCall( parameters block )
*/

/* Option 3 choose to back out changes without calling PROG_3.
    set    eci_extend_mode   :   ECI_BACKOUT
           eci_luw_token     :   my_token
           eci_program_name  :   null
    call   CICS_ExternalCall( parameters block )
*/
```

Figure 185. Sequence of Program Link Calls in the Same LUW

On a successful return from the first call for an LUW, the **eci_luw_token** field in the parameter block contains a token that should be used for all later calls related to the same LUW. All program link calls for the same LUW will be sent to the same server.

Warning: Be careful when extending an LUW across multiple program link calls that may span a long time (for example, over user think time). The LUW holds various locks and other CICS resources on the server, and this may cause delays for other users who are waiting for those same locks and resources.

When an LUW ends, the CICS server attempts to commit the changes. If any of the program link calls in the sequence fails, all changes made by all of the previous calls will be backed out.

An asynchronous call is outstanding until a reply solicitation call has processed the reply, and only one program link call per LUW can be outstanding at any time. Never issue a program link call for the same LUW before you issue a reply solicitation call for the last asynchronous program link call.

Multiple Asynchronous Calls Accessing Multiple CICS Servers

An application can have multiple asynchronous calls accessing resources on multiple CICS servers at the same time. For example, an application has three LUW tokens. The asynchronous calls of those tokens belong to different LUWs and can therefore be processed at the same time.

Table 22 shows, for each asynchronous call, an associated message qualifier, the CICS program it will call, and the name of the CICS server where the called program resides.

Table 22. Multiple Asynchronous Calls Accessing Multiple Servers				
LUW Token	Asynchronous Call	Message Qualifier	CICS Program	CICS Server
TOKEN_A	CALL_ASYNC_A1	MSG_Q_A1	PROGRAM_P11	SERVER_S1
	CALL_ASYNC_A2	MSG_Q_A2	PROGRAM_P12	SERVER_S1
	CALL_ASYNC_A3	MSG_Q_A3	PROGRAM_P13	SERVER_S1
TOKEN_B	CALL_ASYNC_B1	MSG_Q_B1	PROGRAM_P13	SERVER_S1
TOKEN_C	CALL_ASYNC_C1	MSG_Q_C1	PROGRAM_P21	SERVER_S2

Figure 186 shows the application using multiple asynchronous program calls.

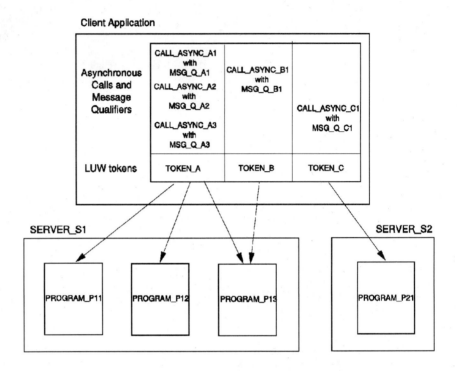

Figure 186. Multiple Asynchronous Calls Accessing Multiple Servers

ECI Asynchronous Implementation with Callback

After an asynchronous call has been made, the application can ask to be notified later (called back) when the information is available. Using this style of ECI programming allows you to do other processing while waiting for the response from the server.

For asynchronous implementation with callback, you must provide a callback routine in your application. A point to the callback routine is assigned to **eci_callback** in the ECI parameter block. If the return code of the ECI asynchronous call is ECI_NO_ERROR, the callback routine will be called automatically after the server program has finished.

Figure 187 on page 275 is an example of an asynchronous program link call with callback. This application uses the **eci_luw_token**, **eci_extend_mode**, and **eci_message_qualifier** fields.

```
/****************************************************************************/
/* HEADER FILES                                                             */
/****************************************************************************/
#include <os2.h>
#include <stdio.h>
#include <stdarg.h>
#include <string.h>
#include <cics_eci.h>

#define MESS_QU_1      1
#define MESS_QU_2      2

/****************************************************************************/
/* Global Variables                                                         */
/****************************************************************************/
   int             GlobalCallBackTracker_1;
   int             GlobalCallBackTracker_2;

/****************************************************************************/
/*  Function Prototypes                                                     */
/****************************************************************************/
int              main            (void);
void CICSEXIT    CallBackProc_1  (cics_ushort_t idx);
void CICSEXIT    CallBackProc_2  (cics_ushort_t idx);

/****************************************************************************/
/****************************************************************************/
/* main() - Sample Entry Point                                              */
/****************************************************************************/
/****************************************************************************/
int main(void)
{
   short           Rc_1, Rc_2, Rc_r;
   char            CommArea [18];
   ECI_PARMS       EciParms;
   int             my_token;

   /* begin of the first asynchronous program link call */
   GlobalCallBackTracker_1 = 0;
   memset (CommArea, '\0', 18);
   memset (&EciParms, 0, sizeof (ECI_PARMS));

   memcpy(&EciParms.eci_program_name, "ECO1",    4);
   memcpy(&EciParms.eci_userid,       "GUIDO",   8);
   memcpy(&EciParms.eci_password,     "GUIDO",   8);
   memcpy(&EciParms.eci_system_name,  "CICSTCP", 8);
   EciParms.eci_call_type          = ECI_ASYNC;
   EciParms.eci_version            = ECI_VERSION_1;
   EciParms.eci_commarea           = CommArea;
   EciParms.eci_commarea_length    = 18;
   EciParms.eci_extend_mode        = ECI_EXTENDED;
```

Figure 187. (Part 1 of 3) Example of an Asynchronous Program Link Call with Callback

ECI Asynchronous Implementation with Callback

```
    EciParms.eci_luw_token            = ECI_LUW_NEW;
    EciParms.eci_timeout              = 0;
    EciParms.eci_message_qualifier    = MESS_QU_1;
    EciParms.eci_callback = (CICS_EciNotify_t)CallBackProc_1;

    Rc_1 = CICS_ExternalCall (&EciParms);

    my_token = EciParms.eci_luw_token;

    if( Rc_1 == ECI_NO_ERROR )
    {
        while ( !GlobalCallBackTracker_1) {}

        EciParms.eci_call_type            = ECI_GET_SPECIFIC_REPLY;
        EciParms.eci_message_qualifier    = MESS_QU_1;

        Rc_r = CICS_ExternalCall (&EciParms);

        if (Rc_r == ECI_NO_ERROR)
        {
            CommArea[17] = '\0';
            printf ( "1: CommArea Returned: %s\n", CommArea);
        }
    }
    /* end of the first asynchronous program link call     */

    /* begin of the second asynchronous program link call */
    GlobalCallBackTracker_2 = 0;
    memcpy(&EciParms.eci_program_name, "ECO1",    4);
    EciParms.eci_extend_mode          = ECI_NO_EXTEND;
    EciParms.eci_luw_token            = my_token;
    EciParms.eci_message_qualifier    = MESS_QU_2;
    EciParms.eci_callback = (CICS_EciNotify_t)CallBackProc_2;
    /* other parameters keep the same as last call         */

    Rc_2 = CICS_ExternalCall (&EciParms);

    if( Rc_2 == ECI_NO_ERROR )
    {
        while ( !GlobalCallBackTracker_2) {}

        EciParms.eci_call_type            = ECI_GET_SPECIFIC_REPLY;
        EciParms.eci_message_qualifier    = MESS_QU_2;

        Rc_r = CICS_ExternalCall (&EciParms);

        if (Rc_r == ECI_NO_ERROR)
        {
            CommArea[17] = '\0';
            printf ( "2: CommArea Returned: %s\n", CommArea);
        }
    }
    /* end of the second asynchronous program link call    */

} /* main */
```

Figure 187. (Part 2 of 3) Example of an Asynchronous Program Link Call with Callback

```
/************************************************************************/
/* CallBackProc                                                        */
/************************************************************************/
/* This is the function that was registered on the asynchronous call.  */
/* It gets called when there is a reply ready.                         */
/************************************************************************/
void CICSEXIT CallBackProc_1 (cics_ushort_t idx)
{
   GlobalCallBackTracker_1 = 1;
} /* CallBackProc_1 */
void CICSEXIT CallBackProc_2 (cics_ushort_t idx)
{
   GlobalCallBackTracker_2 = 1;
} /* CallBackProc_2 */
```

Figure 187. (Part 3 of 3) Example of an Asynchronous Program Link Call with Callback

Sample Implementation

In this section we present a sample ECI client/server implementation. The sample programs that we used are provided with the CICS Client product. They are available in two programming languages, COBOL and C. We installed the C version of the sample program on the client workstation and the CICS server.

The program name on the client workstation is ECIC01.C. It can be found in the \CICSCLI\SAMPLES\C directory.

— **Note:** —————————————————————
ECIC01 is a sample application that demonstrates how to use the ECI. It does not demonstrate all of the techniques required for a large application. It is simply an example of the form of an ECI application; it is not a template, and you should not use it as the foundation for your next mission-critical application.

This sample requires that the EC01 transaction be installed on your server. The EC01 transaction requires that the EC01 program also be installed. The source program, EC01.CCS, can be found in the CICS-CLI\SAMPLES\SERVER subdirectory.

Sample Program Functions

The sample programs perform the following functions:

1. The client program first issues a **status information call** to check the status of both the client and the server.
2. A **synchronous ECI call** is issued to link to the EC01 server program. The COMMAREA sent to the server program does not contain any data.

Sample Implementation

3. The EC01 server program returns the COMMAREA with the current date and time of the CICS region. The same date and time also are displayed in the message log of the server (or written to the CSMT transient data queue if the server is a CICS/6000 system).
4. The sample program on the workstation obtains the date and time from the COMMAREA and displays them in the ECI Test Window.
5. After completion of the synchronous ECI call, an **asynchronous ECI call** is issued to start the EC01 server program.
6. The EC01 server program performs the same functions as for the synchronous call (it does not distinguish between the two calls).
7. The client program issues a **reply solicitation call** when it has been notified that the reply from the CICS server is available.
8. After the reply solicitation call gets back the COMMAREA, the contents of the COMMAREA are displayed in the ECI Test Window, and the program terminates normally.

Note: The client and server programs do not need to be written in the same language. For example, your workstation program could be written in COBOL, and your server program, in C.

Client Sample Program Modification

Before you compile and link-edit the client sample program, ECIC01, you must provide the name of your server, your userid, and your password in the Global Variables section of the program.

For example, in Figure 188 on page 278, your CICS/6000 server is called CICSTCP (defined in the CICSLI.INI file), and you use the default user ID, CICSUSER. Providing a password is optional for the default user ID, CICSUSER.

```
/****************************************************************
/* Global Variables
/****************************************************************

   :::

   ECI_PARM   EciParms;
   char       Server[9] = "CICSTCP";    /* FILL IN YOUR SERVER HERE */
   char       UserID[9] = "CICSUSER";   /* FILL IN YOUR USER ID HERE */
   char       PassWd[9] = "";           /* FILL IN YOUR PASSWORD HERE */

   :::
```

Figure 188. Modification for Client Sample Program

Portability and Compatibility Considerations

The sample ECI programs provided with the CICS Client product are portable to other CICS server platforms without any modification, with one exception. If you want to execute this sample program in a CICS/6000 server environment, you must make the following modification: Replace the CICS command EXEC CICS WRITE OPERATOR..., with the following CICS command:

```
EXEC CICS WRITEQ TD
           QUEUE("CSMT")
           FROM(MESSAGE)
           LENGTH(LENGTH OF MESSAGE)
           RESP(RESPCODE);
```

This modification is required because CICS/6000 does not support the WRITE OPERATOR command.

Running the Sample Program

Before you can run the sample program, ensure that you have:

- Compiled and link-edited the ECICO1 program without any errors on the CICS Client workstation and stored it in the \CICSCLI\BIN directory.
- Compiled and link-edited the EC01 program without any errors on the CICS server platform and stored it in an appropriate library or directory.
- Defined the EC01 program in the processing program table (PPT) of the CICS server, or in the program definition (PD) if it is for a CICS/6000 server. (This definition is not required if the server is a CICS for OS/2 or a CICS for Windows NT system.)
- Predefined the CSMT transient data queue during installation of the CICS/6000 system, if the server is a CICS/6000. If you intend to use a different transient data queue, it must be defined in the transient data definition (TDD), either intrapartition or extrapartition.
- Started the CICS server and the communication software layer.

To run the sample application, follow these steps:

1. From an OS/2 command line on the client workstation, select the CICSCLI\BIN directory.
2. Enter the command: ECICO1.
   The **ECI Test Window** is presented.

3. Click on **GO**.
   A drop-down list is presented.
4. Select **Go...** from the drop-down list to start the execution of the ECICO1 program on the client workstation.
   For every function that the program executes, a message is written to the **ECI Test Window**. Figure 189 shows an example of the ECI Test Window after the sample program has been executed.

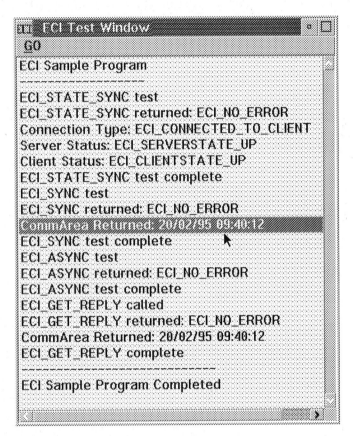

Figure 189. ECI Test Window: Sample Program Messages

5. To stop program execution, click on **GO**. From the drop-down list, select **Quit** to close the ECI Test Window.

You can check the successful completion of the sample program as follows:

- On the client workstation
  The date and the time of the sample program execution must appear twice (once for the synchronous and once for the asynchronous call) in a message in the ECI Test Window (see Figure 189 on page 280)
- On the server
  Check the message log or the CSMT transient data queue for the date and time message of the sample program execution. If the messages have been written, the sample programs have executed successfully.

Further Information

For further information on programming with the ECI, see *CICS Family: Client/Server Programming*.

Further Information

20

External Presentation Interface

This chapter covers the following topics:

- "EPI Model" on page 284
- "Application Flow" on page 284
    - EPI Initialization
    - EPI Starting Transaction
    - EPI Events Processing
    - EPI Termination
- "Sample Implementation" on page 288
- "Further Information" on page 292

EPI Model

The EPI allows a non-CICS application program to be viewed as one or more 3270 terminals by the CICS server system to which it is connected. The CICS application sends and receives 3270 data streams to and from the client application, as though it were conversing with a 3270 terminal.

The client application captures the data streams and typically displays them with a non-3270 presentation product, such as GUI or multimedia software. Figure 190 shows the EPI model.

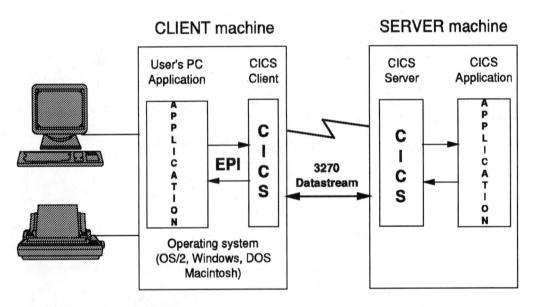

Figure 190. CICS EPI Model

Application Flow

To simplify our explanation of the EPI program flow, we have divided the flow into four parts: initialization, starting transaction, events processing, and termination.

Initialization

Figure 191 shows the EPI initialization.

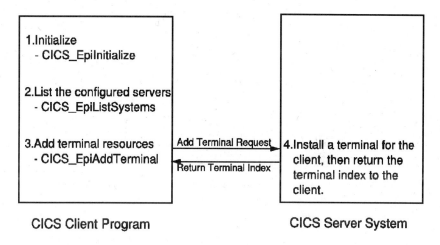

Figure 191. EPI Initialization

The CICS_EpiInitialize call initializes the EPI for this program. Until this call is made, no other EPI function is allowed.

The CICS_EpiListSystems call checks which CICS servers are configured for use.

The CICS_EpiAddTerminal call sends a request to the server to install a terminal for the client program. It returns a terminal index, which is used as the identifier of this terminal in this EPI program.

After EPI initialization, the server CICS system will look like a 3270 terminal to the client program.

Starting Transaction

Figure 192 on page 286 shows the EPI starting transaction.

Application Flow

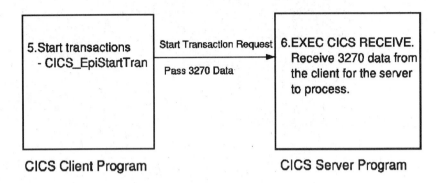

Figure 192. EPI Starting Transaction

The CICS_EpiStartTran call starts a transaction from the previously defined terminal resource. To the CICS server it appears as if a terminal user had typed a transaction code on the screen and pressed Enter (or AID).

The EXEC CICS RECEIVE command in the server program receives the 3270 data sent from the client EPI program. Typically, the CICS server program contains this command at the beginning the program, especially in pseudoconversational mode, although it is not mandatory.

Events Processing

Figure 193 on page 287 shows the EPI events processing. Generally, this part is the main body of the EPI program.

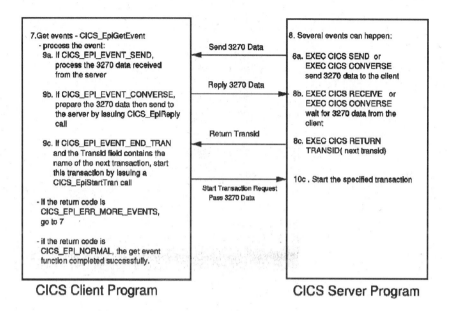

Figure 193. EPI Events Processing

Events occur in the previously defined terminal resource because of actions in the CICS server. The client EPI program cannot predict when those events will occur, but it is responsible for collecting and processing the events as appropriate.

The CICS_EpiGetEvent call collects the events that have occurred and the associated data.

The CICS_EPI_EVENT_SEND event indicates that, as the result of an EXEC CICS SEND or an EXEC CICS CONVERSE, a transaction has sent some 3270 data to the client program. The client program can process the data, for example, to display it with a GUI.

The CICS_EPI_EVENT_CONVERSE event indicates that, as a result of an EXEC CICS RECEIVE or an EXEC CICS CONVERSE, a transaction is expecting a reply. The client program should issue a CICS_EpiReply call to return some 3270 data to the CICS server.

The CICS_EPI_EVENT_END_TRAN event indicates that a transaction has ended as the result of an EXEC CICS RETURN or that the transaction has abended. If in pseudoconversational mode, the TransId field contains the name of the next transaction required. The client program should issue a CICS_EpiStartTran call to start the specified transaction.

The CICS_EPI_ERR_MORE_EVENTS return code indicates that more events are outstanding against this terminal resource. The client program should issue the CICS_EpiGetEvent call again to collect the events that have occurred, and then process the events in the same way that it processed the previous event.

The CICS_EPI_NORMAL return code indicates that the CICS_EpiGetEvent function completed successfully and that the client program can start another transaction or delete the terminal.

Termination

Figure 194 shows the EPI termination.

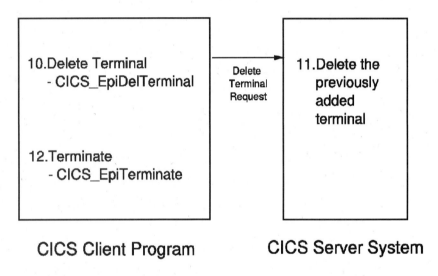

Figure 194. EPI Termination

The CICS_EpiDelTerminal call sends a request to the CICS server to release the terminal resource that has been defined previously.

The CICS_EpiTerminate call is issued to terminate the EPI.

Sample Implementation

In this section we present a sample EPI client/server implementation. The sample programs that we used in this scenario are provided with the CICS Client product. They are available in two programming languages, COBOL and C. On the client workstation, we installed the C version of the sample program. The program name is EPC01.C. It can be found in the \CICSCLI\SAMPLES\C directory. On the server platform, we installed the COBOL version of the sample program provided by CICS Client for OS/2. The program name is EP01.CCP. It can be found in the \CICSCLI\SAMPLES\SERVER directory.

Sample Program Functions

The sample programs perform the following functions:

1. The client program sends a request to the server program to install a terminal and obtain the terminal index of the installed terminal.
2. The client program also requests the server program to start the EP01 transaction and sends a message: *"Hello Server"*.
3. The server program receives the message from the client and writes the message text to the message log (or to the CSMT transient data queue, if it is a CICS/6000 server).
4. The server program sends the following message text to the client: *Greetings from the transaction EP01*.
5. The client program receives the message from the server and displays it in the EPI Test Window.
6. The client program then sends the following message text to the server: *"This is my reply"*.
7. The server program receives the reply message and sends it to the message log or the CSMT destination.

> **Note:**
> EPICO1 is a sample application that demonstrates how to use most of the EP1 functions. It does not demonstrate all of the techniques required for a large application. It is simply an example of the form of an EPI application; it is not a template, and you should not use it as the foundation for your next mission-critical application.

Portability and Compatibility Considerations

The sample programs provided with the CICS Client product are portable to other CICS server platforms without any modification, with one exception. If you want to execute the sample program in a CICS/6000 server environment, you must make the following modification: Replace the CICS command, EXEC CICS WRITE OPERATOR..., with the following command:

Sample Implementation

```
EXEC CICS WRITEQ TD
          QUEUE("CSMT")
          FROM(MESSAGE)
          LENGTH(LENGTH OF MESSAGE)
          RESP(RESPCODE);
```

This modification is required because CICS/6000 does not support the WRITE OPERATOR command.

Running the Sample Program

Before you can run the sample program, make sure you have completed the following steps:

- Compiled and link-edited the EPCO1 program without any errors on the CICS Client workstation and stored it in the CICSCLI\BIN directory.
- Compiled and link-edited the EP01 program without any errors on the CICS server platform and stored it in an appropriate library or directory.
- Defined the EP01 program in the PPT of the CICS server, or in the PD if it is for a CICS/6000 server. (This definition is not required if the server is a CICS for OS/2 system or a CICS for Windows NT system.)
- The transaction EP01 has been defined in the PCT (or in the TD for a CICS/6000) of the CICS server system.
- Predefined the CSMT transient data destination during installation of the CICS/6000 system, if the server is a CICS/6000. If you intend to use a different transient data queue, it must be defined in the TDD, either intrapartition or extrapartition.
- Started the CICS server and the communication software layer.

To run the sample application, follow these steps:

1. From an OS/2 command line on the client workstation, select the CICSCLI\BIN directory.
2. Enter the command: EPICO1.
   The **EPI Test Window** is presented.
3. Click on **GO**.
   A drop-down list is presented.
4. Select **Go...** from the drop-down list to start the execution of the EPICO1 program on the client workstation.
   For every function that the program executes, a message is written to the **EPI Test Window**. Figure 195 on page 291 shows an example of the EPI Test Window after the sample program has been executed.

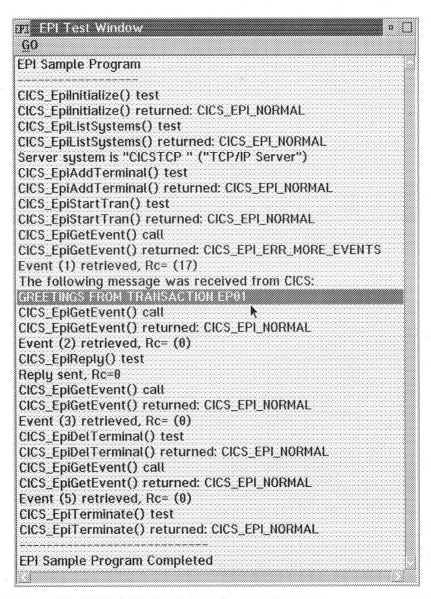

Figure 195. EPI Test Window Sample Program Messages

5. To stop the sample program execution, click on **GO**. From the drop-down list, select **Quit** to close the EPI Test Window.

You can check the successful completion of the sample program as follows:

- On the client workstation
  The *GREETINGS FROM TRANSACTION EP01* message must appear in the EPI Test Window.
- On the server
  Check the message log or the CSMT transient data queue for the following messages:
  Hello Server and
  This is my reply

If these messages have been written, the sample programs have executed successfully.

Further Information

For further information on programming with the EPI, see *CICS Family: Client/Server Programming*.

21

Problem Determination

— **This chapter covers the following:** —
- "Tools" on page 294
- "Sources of Information" on page 295
- "CICS Client Environment" on page 296
- "CICS Server Environment" on page 299
- "Communications Environment" on page 302
- "CICS Client Trace Analysis" on page 305
- "Common Errors in a CICS Client Environment" on page 312
- "Common Errors in a CICS Server Environment" on page 313

This chapter will help you determine the cause of and resolve common problems that you might encounter when you install a CICS Client and connect it to a CICS server.

To resolve problems with your CICS system, you usually start with a symptom (or a set of symptoms) and trace it back to its cause. We call this process problem determination.

We focus on those problem determination aspects that are pertinent to resolving problems in a client-server environment, an environment comprising:

- Client workstation
  - CICS Client product
  - Communication software
- Physical communication link
  - LAN
  - SDLC or coaxial connection
- Server environment
  - CICS Server product
  - Communication software

Other areas of problem determination, such as performance problems, are outside the scope of this chapter and therefore are not covered.

Tools

In this section we list the tools and techniques that are available and can help you with problem determination and trouble shooting in a CICS intercommunication environment. In general, several different products are involved when a connection between a CICS Client and a CICS server is established. Therefore, you must consider those products involved in such a connection in the problem determination process. All of these products provide functions that help you with problem determination. Whenever appropriate, we include information about the problem determination aids provided with the products.

The most important functions and facilities available for problem determination in a CICS and communications environment are:

- On the Client workstation
  - Trace
  - Error message log
- On the Server
  - Traces
    - Auxiliary
    - Internal
  - Dumps
  - CICS message logs

- Statistics information
- Monitoring information
- Execution diagnostic facility (EDF)
- CICS-supplied transactions, CEBR and CECI
- Independent software vendor (ISV) tools
☐ Communications
  - Trace for
    - APPC connections
    - TCP/IP connections
    - NetBIOS connections
  - Dumps
  - Tools and utilities
    - First Failure Support Technology/2 (FFST/2)
    - Tools for the TCP/IP environment
    - Tools for the APPC environment

In a CICS Client and CICS server environment, the tools you use for problem determination depend on the type of error that you have to resolve. In "Communications Environment" on page 302 we briefly explain the most important functions and facilities for problem determination related to a CICS intercommunication environment.

Sources of Information

Collecting problem determination information should be the first activity that you perform when an error has been detected. You must gather and correlate information from several sources. In a communications environment, where many clients may be connected to several servers, you must obtain information from both the client and the server sides. To facilitate problem determination, try to reduce your environment to only one client workstation and one server to narrow down the range of possibilities that may cause the error.

The most common sources of information for problem determination are:

☐ On the client workstation
  - Description of what you or the end user attempted to do
  - Description of your environment setup
    - Software levels of products
    - Installation and customization parameters in effect at time of failure (for example, the client's .INI file or the .NDF file of CM/2)
  - Trace information
  - Messages written to the CICS Client error log (CICSCLI.LOG)
  - Messages issued by the applications (for example, an ECI return code)

❑ On the server
  ➢ Description of your server environment setup
    - Software levels of products
    - Installation and customization parameters in effect at time of failure (for example, of the CM/2 .NDF file)
  ➢ Trace information (auxiliary, internal)
  ➢ Dumps
  ➢ Messages written to the CICS message log

If you cannot resolve your problem and require help, your service organization will request the information listed above to further investigate the problem.

Preliminary Checks

Before you begin the problem determination process, it is worth considering some fundamental questions to see whether there is an obvious cause of the problem or a preferred area to start your investigation. The questions to consider at this stage include:

❑ Are there any messages explaining the failure (on the client workstation and/or server)?

❑ Has the connection run successfully before?

❑ Are specific parts of the network affected by the problem?

❑ Can you reproduce the error?

As you go through the questions, make note of anything that is relevant to the problem. Even if your observations do not, at first, suggest a cause, they could be useful later in a more detailed problem determination exercise.

If the cause of the problem is not obvious, we suggest that you check your definitions in the following sequence:

1. Client workstation
2. Server
3. Communications

CICS Client Environment

In a CICS Client environment, two sources of information are available for problem determination: the CICS Client trace and the CICS Client error log. Because the CICS Client is not a full-function CICS system, the trace and error logs are the only functions available for problem determination. However, these two functions provide sufficient information to diagnose problems related to the CICS Client environment.

CICS Client Environment

The **trace function** is the most useful problem determination tool for communication problems. (See "CICS Server Trace" on page 300 for a brief description of the trace function.) Traces typically are not used in development and testing of individual application programs, except when all other methods have failed. You are more likely to need them during a system test or when you establish communication links. You can use the trace function to help with problem determination or to collect detailed information on the execution of a certain function or transaction. A trace can show you how the execution of a particular activity is affected by, or interacts with, the execution of other tasks in a CICS system, for example. It is also a source of detailed information on the time taken to perform certain activities, because each trace entry has a time stamp attached to it.

In this section we describe how to set up and run a trace in a CICS Client environment and how to access the information written to the CICS Client error log.

Starting and Stopping CICS Client Trace

To start the CICS Client trace, enter the CICSCLI command with the /d option (or click on the equivalent icon, if you have created one). For example:

CICSCLI /d=*nnn* [=*nnn*] is optional.

where *nnn* is the maximum size in bytes of the data areas to be traced. The default value is 64.

If you need to trace the client activities immediately from startup, you can specify both the start option (/s) and the option to enable tracing (/d) in the same CICSCLI command. For example, the following command starts the connection to a server with the name CICSSNA, enables the trace function, and sets the maximum data area size to be traced to 128 bytes:

CICSCLI /s=CICSSNA /d=128

To stop the CICS Client trace, enter the CICSCLI command with the /o option (or click on the equivalent icon), thus:

CICSCLI /o

The trace also is automatically stopped if you stop the client by using the CICSCLI /x command.

> **Note**
>
> For the CICS Client for Macintosh you start and stop the Client trace by using the **Start Trace** and **Stop Trace** radio buttons on the CICS Client for Macintosh Administration Utility (see "CICS Client for Macintosh Operation" on page 323).

CICS Client Trace File

You can specify the name of the CICS Client trace file in the **Tracefile** parameter in the CICSCLI.INI file. The default for this name is **CICSCLI.TRC** in the current directory. You can change the file name and the directory in which it is placed by editing the CICSCLI.INI file. You must stop and restart the client for changes to take effect.

The Client trace file is a plain ASCII text file. It does not need any formatting before analysis. You can browse the client trace file with a standard text editor. The contents of the client trace file and how it is interpreted are discussed in Chapter "CICS Client Trace Analysis" on page 305.

CICS Client Error Processing

Any errors on the client workstation that are not caused by incorrect use of the CICS API are written to the CICS Client error log. The CICS Client error log is a plain ASCII text file. You can use a standard text editor to review the messages that have been written to it. You can specify the name of the error log in the **LogFile** parameter in the CICSCLI.INI file. The default for this name is **CICSCLI.LOG** in the current directory. All CICS Client error messages that are written to the CICS Client error log are described in the *CICS Client Messages* manual. Figure 196 on page 298 shows a sample CICS Client error log.

```
02/16/95 14:41:53 [4650] CCL4612 No sessions established between local LU SJA2051I and partner
LU USIBMSC.SCMCICSX
02/20/95 17:37:32 [4403] CCL4404 TCP/IP (to CICSTCP) unable to resolve name: Rc=2
```

Figure 196. Sample CICS Client Error Log

Errors resulting from incorrect use of the CICS API simply result in error return codes returned to the application. It is the responsibility of the application to notify the end user of the error and provide guidance on corrective actions.

Errors generated from within the client process are displayed in a pop-up window. You must click on **OK** in the pop-up window before the client can continue processing. There may be times when you do not want messages (client error and security) to appear in pop-up windows; for example, if you leave a CICS Client running unattended overnight.

You can disable the display of pop-up messages by entering the following CICSCLI command:

CICSCLI /n

When the display of pop-up messages is disabled, the messages are still written to the client error log.

You can re-enable the display of pop-up messages by entering the following CICSCLI command.

CICSCLI /e

You can specify the /n parameter together with the /s parameter.
The display of pop-up messages is enabled by default.

Figure 197 shows a sample CICS Client pop-up message window.

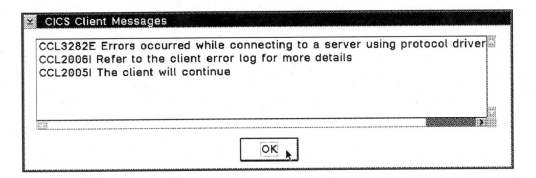

Figure 197. CICS Client Error Message Pop-up Window

CICS Server Environment

The most common functions used for problem determination in a CICS server environment are:

- CICS server traces
    - Internal
    - Auxiliary

- Message logs
- Dumps

We briefly describe the information that you can obtain by using these functions. For detailed information refer to the problem determination documentation of the individual CICS server product or contact your support organization for further guidance and assistance.

CICS Server Trace

A trace is a record of system and transaction activity that you can use to debug a problem in your CICS system. You can use a trace to trace the flow of execution through CICS code and through your application as well. You can see the functions that are being performed, the parameters being passed, and the values of important data fields at the time trace calls are made. A trace provides a history of the processing, which can reveal the cause of the problem and hence lead to its solution. Depending on the CICS server platform, you can direct the trace output to several different destinations.

The two most common destinations for your trace data are the **internal trace** table kept in main storage, and the **auxiliary trace** kept on a data set on disk. The internal trace table wraps when it is full. In practice, the internal trace table cannot be very big, so it is most useful for background tracing or when you do not need to capture an extensive set of trace entries. If you have to trace CICS system activities over a long period or need many entries over a short period of time, the auxiliary trace destination is more appropriate. Before you can look at the trace entries sent to either destination, however, you must format the trace output. Utilities are provided for this formatting.

Depending on the CICS family member, trace functions are implemented slightly differently; however, they all provide the same type of information.

If you need detailed information on how to set up and run a CICS trace in a specific CICS server environment, refer to the *Problem Determination Guide* of the relevant CICS library.

Note

Extensive use of the trace function can dramatically affect the performance of the CICS system. We recommend, therefore, that you use the trace function with care.

CICS Server Dumps

Dumps are an important source of detailed information about problems. Whether the result of an abnormal termination or a user request, dumps allow you to see a snapshot of what was happening inside CICS at the moment the dump was taken. However, because dumps provide only a snapshot, you may want to use them in conjunction with other sources of information, such as logs, traces, and statistics, that provide information relating to a longer period of time. A dump is produced when certain error conditions occur or when you explicitly request that CICS takes a dump. There are two different types of CICS dumps to help you with problem determination: the **transaction dump**, which contains transaction-related storage areas; and the CICS **system dump**, which shows the entire CICS region.

CICS Server Message Logs

Message log is a generic term for all messages that are displayed during the execution of a CICS server system. The messages include startup, shutdown, and any message displayed while the system is running, including error messages. Depending on the server platform, the messages are written to different destinations; however, they all provide basically the same information.

The CSMT log is one source of information for problem determination that you can easily access. When a transaction terminates abnormally or an error in the network occurs, a message is written to the CSMT log, a CICS transient data destination.

To view the CSMT log messages, you must either redirect them to a destination where they are immediately displayed or use a CICS-supplied transaction to display the contents of the CSMT log. In a mainframe environment, you can direct the messages to the MVS console to be displayed immediately. In a CICS for OS/2 environment, for example, you can use the browse transaction (CEBR) to browse temporary storage queues and transfer a transient data queue to temporary storage to look at its contents. The other CICS server products provide similar functions. Information from message logs should be used for initial analysis of an error. Consult the *Messages and Codes* manual of the relevant CICS server product or use online message information (for example, the CMAC transaction supplied by CICS/ESA, or the CHLP transaction provided by CICS for OS/2) for a detailed description of all messages issued.

Figure 198 shows a sample CICS for OS/2 message log containing messages issued during CICS for OS/2 startup.

Communications Environment

```
2-22-95 1:19:55p MAIN MAIN FAA0000I CICS for OS/2 Version 2.0.1
2-22-95 1:19:55p MAIN MAIN FAA0001I Service Level 00, UL00000, Released 27-Jan-95
2-22-95 1:19:59p MAIN MAIN FAA1660I Initialization for System CICS, ApplID CICSSRV1
  :::
  :::
  :::
2-22-95 1:20:01p MAIN MAIN FAA5706I Internal trace function enabled
2-22-95 1:20:02p MAIN MAIN FAA5570I NetBIOS Listener starting for CICSSRV1 on adapter 0
2-22-95 1:20:12p MAIN MAIN FAA5780I TCP/IP Listener starting
2-22-95 1:20:12p MAIN MAIN FAA5781I Hostname:'GIANT'(9.113.36.31) Listen ANY Port:1435
  :::
  :::
  :::
```

Figure 198. CICS for OS/2 Message Log

The highlighted messages show useful information from the CICS server that you may need for problem determination:

Message ID	*Explanation*
FAA0000I	Shows the service level of the product
FAA1660I	Shows the Appl ID for this CICS server
FAA5570I	Indicates that NetBIOS has been enabled and started for adapter 0
FAA5781I	Displays important TCP/IP information and shows that the TCP/IP support has been enabled for this server

Communications Environment

Even a small telecommunications network is a very complex system in which all components depend on one another. If one component fails and presents incorrect information to the other components, the latter may fail even more severely than the former. Sometimes the failure may be considerably delayed, and the error indicator may be lost before the error is detected. Thus, it is sometimes very difficult to analyze a problem in the communications part of a system.

The communication products themselves generate error messages. For an explanation of these messages, and for information on troubleshooting, refer to the documentation for the product providing communication support.

In this section we briefly describe the problem determination functions provided by various communication products:

❑ Trace

- APPC
  - VTAM (buffer trace)
  - CM/2
  - APPC NS/Windows
  - Novell NetWare for SAA
  - SNA service trace (Win/NT)
- TCP/IP
  - CM/2
- NetBIOS
  - CM/2
- ❑ CM/2 dump facility
- ❑ Other tools and utilities
  - FFST/2
  - Tools for the TCP/IP environment
  - Tools for the APPC environment

See the relevant documentation for each product if you want detailed information or consult your network administrator for assistance.

Communication Traces and Dumps

Among other functions, communication traces gather information related to the establishment of a session or connection, including details of all steps executed and the information (for example, flow of commands and return codes) exchanged between the two partners that try to establish a connection. This information is particularly useful to resolve errors that are caused by a mismatch of definitions on either the client or the server side of a connection.

VTAM Buffer Trace

You can use VTAM buffer tracing to record the flow of data between logical units in the CICS environment. The trace entries include the netname of the terminal (logical unit) to which they relate. For details on VTAM buffer tracing and other VTAM problem determination functions, see the appropriate manual in the VTAM library.

CM/2 Trace

CM/2 provides a broad range of problem determination functions covering different types of APIs, connections, and services. The trace selections for the CM/2 product include the following lists:

API   Contains APIs supported by CM/2, for example, APPC or EHLLAPI.

DLC Contains data link control (DLC) types that pass through CM/2. When CM/2 encounters DLC of the type you selected, it copies the data to a trace record. For example, if you select *IBMTRNET* from the DLC list, *IBMTRNET DLC* is traced every time it passes through CM/2.

Events Contains functions that are performed within CM/2. When CM/2 encounters the event you selected, it copies the data to a trace record. For example, if you selected *APPC SNDRCV* from the events list, a trace record is written every time APPC sends or receives data through the network.

CM/2 Dumps

The CM/2 dump service is a diagnostic tool that helps you identify the source of certain types of communication problems. You can use dump services to copy the data stored in a portion of memory being used by a communications component.

APPC NS/Windows Trace

The Networking Services for Windows application toolkit includes a powerful multiproduct trace facility. It is an effective tool for problem diagnosis and helps you quickly resolve both network and user problems. Refer to the NS/Windows documentation for details.

Other Tools and Utilities

In addition to the trace and dump functions described above, other diagnostic tools and techniques are available.

First Failure Support Technology/2

First Failure Support Technology/2 (FFST/2) is a software problem diagnosis tool for OS/2 system software and applications. It is designed to facilitate the capture of problem diagnosis information when a problem occurs. Unless you are an advanced user, your primary use of FFST/2 will be the system error log and the message log formatter. Refer to the *Problem Determination Guide* for a complete description of the tasks you can perform with FFST/2.

Tools for the TCP/IP Environment

In a TCP/IP environment, several utilities and commands are available to diagnose a communication problem:

PING — Tests your TCP/IP installation. Ping sends an Internet Control Message Protocol (ICMP) echo request to a specified destination and waits for an echo reply. The receiver echoes the frames it receives back to the originator. If the ping command completes successfully, you installed TCP/IP correctly.

NETSTAT — Helps obtain information about your own IP interfaces, for example, to list IP addresses and TCP/IP routing tables in use at your workstation.

IFCONFIG — Initializes an IP interface at your workstation and allows you to query its status. Helpful when you have to determine whether an IP interface is active.

ARP — Displays the IP-to-hardware address mapping table at your workstation. You can manually add a hardware address to your ARP table, for example, if you lose the connection to a router.

HOSTNAME — Displays the IP address of your workstation

NSLOOKUP — Displays the default server name and IP address

Tools for the APPC Environment

In an APPC environment, you can use the aping utility to test a connection. Aping exchanges data packets with a partner computer over APPC and times how long the data transfer takes. It can be used to get a first estimate of the session setup time between two computers and the throughput and turnaround time on that APPC session. Aping can be used to determine whether a session can be set up between two computers and displays extensive error information if session allocation fails. Aping consists of two transaction programs: APING, which runs on the client side, and APINGD, which runs on the server side.

CICS Client Trace Analysis

The CICS Client trace records detailed information on all actions taken during the execution of a particular activity. You can use the information obtained from running a trace in your problem determination activities, and to understand how the CICS Client performs a particular function, for example, establishing a connection to a CICS server.

Below we describe how to interpret a CICS Client trace.

CICS Client Trace Analysis

Sample CICS Client Trace

Figure 199 on page 306 shows the trace information recorded during the successful connection of a CICS Client for OS/2 to a CICS for OS/2 server using the NetBIOS protocol.

```
02/08/95 12:52:45 [ 2047] CCL2039 **** CICS Client for OS/2 - Service Trace Begins ****
02/08/95 12:52:45 [ 2051] CCL2048 Maximum trace data size set to 64
02/08/95 12:52:45 [ 2031] CCL2023 Client Response (SessId=00000039, Slot=0, ReqRc=0, AppRc=0)
02/08/95 12:53:42 [ 2036] CCL2028 Server Start request (SessId=0000003A)
9747:0010  636963736E657462                  cicsnetb         ....>...
02/08/95 12:53:42 [ 2060] CCL2045 Request directed to server "CICSNETB"
02/08/95 12:53:42 [ 3231] CCL3231 Comms Load request (Driver=CCLIBMNB)
02/08/95 12:53:42 [ 3253] CCL3233 Loading protocol driver (DLL=C:\CICSCLI\BIN\CCLIBMNB.DLL)
02/08/95 12:53:42 [ 3232] CCL3232 Comms Load completed (Driver=CCLIBMNB, DrvId=1, Rc=0)
02/08/95 12:53:43 [ 3235] CCL3249 Comms Open request (Server=CICSNETB, Driver=CCLIBMNB)
02/08/95 12:53:43 [ 4222] CCL4215 NetBIOS name added for adapter 0
007F:1F9B  43434C4F5332AB33 805A00080C352B06  CCLOS2.3.Z...5+. ..<!.....]....
02/08/95 12:53:47 [ 3236] CCL3236 Comms Open completed (Server=CICSNETB, LinkId=1, Rc=0)
02/08/95 12:53:48 [ 2031] CCL2023 Client Response (SessId=0000003A, Slot=0, ReqRc=0, AppRc=0)
02/08/95 12:53:48 [ 4208] CCL4216 NetBIOS connection established for session 0/8
007F:134A  434943535F434943 5352455331202020  ....CICS_CICSRES1  ....¤..........
02/08/95 12:53:48 [ 2054] CCL2055 Connection with server established (LinkId=1)
02/08/95 12:53:48 [ 3239] CCL3251 Comms Allocate request (LinkId=1, Tran="CCIN")
02/08/95 12:53:48 [ 3240] CCL3238 Comms Allocate completed (LinkId=1, ConvId=1, Rc=0)
02/08/95 12:53:48 [ 3116] CCL3113 CCIN install request: ApplId="*        ", Codepage=850
02/08/95 12:53:48 [ 3245] CCL3242 Comms Send request: Length=32 (ConvId=1)
007F:0CF8  002012FF0000000C 0101000000000002  . ..............  ................
007F:0D08  0000000803F8F5F0 0000000804010000  ..............850........
02/08/95 12:53:48 [ 3246] CCL3241 Comms Send completed (ConvId=1, Rc=0)
02/08/95 12:53:48 [ 3247] CCL3254 Comms Wait request (ConvId=1)
02/08/95 12:53:48 [ 4224] CCL4210 NetBIOS send data for session 0/8: Length=128
007F:1FF8  8132311400010000 81AB33805A000852  .21......3.Z..R a.......a...]..
007F:2008  2020202020202020 2020202000000000
007F:2018  0000000000000000 0000000000000000  ................  ................
007F:2028  0000000000000000 0000000000000000  ................  ................
02/08/95 12:53:48 [ 3248] CCL3243 Comms Wait completed (ConvId=1, Rc=0)
02/08/95 12:53:48 [ 4205] CCL4212 NetBIOS receive pdu for session 0/8: Type=0082
02/08/95 12:53:48 [ 4225] CCL4211 NetBIOS receive data for session 0/8: Length=127
007F:1386  00434C3031434943 53434C3031000000  .CL01CICSCL01... ..<.......<.....
007F:1396  0000000000000000 0000000000000000  ................  ................
007F:13A6  0000000000000000 0000000000000000  ................  ................
007F:13B6  0000000000000000 0000000000000000  ................  ................
02/08/95 12:53:48 [ 2057] CCL2058 Incoming conversation data (ConvId=1)
02/08/95 12:53:48 [ 3249] CCL3244 Comms Receive request (ConvId=1)
02/08/95 12:53:49 [ 3255] CCL3256 Comms Receive completed (last): Length=29 (ConvId=1, Reason=0, Rc=0)
007F:1FF8  001D12FF0000000C 0102000000000001
007F:2008  0000000D01C3C9C3 E2C3D3F0F1        .............    .....CICSCL01
02/08/95 12:53:49 [ 3117] CCL3114 CCIN install response: ApplId="CICSCL01", Codepage=, Rc=0
02/08/95 12:53:49 [ 3251] CCL3255 Comms Complete request (ConvId=1)
02/08/95 12:53:49 [ 3252] CCL3246 Comms Complete completed (ConvId=1, Rc=0)
02/08/95 12:53:49 [ 3241] CCL3252 Comms Deallocate request (ConvId=1)
02/08/95 12:53:49 [ 3242] CCL3239 Comms Deallocate completed (ConvId=1, Reason=0, Rc=0)
02/08/95 12:53:59 [ 2048] CCL2040 Service Trace Disable request (SessId=0000003B)
02/08/95 12:54:00 [ 2049] CCL2041 ***** CICS Client for OS/2 - Service Trace Ends *****
```

Figure 199. Sample CICS Client Trace

Message ID	*Explanation*
CCL2039	Start of trace message. The trace file is appended to each time a trace is started. You can delete the file when required. Check the date and time stamp to ensure that you are reading the correct trace.

CICS Client Trace Analysis

CCL2048 Maximum trace data size is at the default size of 64 bytes. You can modify this size by specifying the size value in the start command for the client trace (see "Starting and Stopping CICS Client Trace" on page 297).

CCL2045 CICSNETB is the name of the server as specified by the *Server=* keyword in the CICSCLI.INI file.

CCL3231 Shows the name of the protocol driver used for this session.

CCL3233 Shows the pathname of the directory from the protocol driver (CCLIBMNB) is used for all clients using IBM NetBIOS.

CCL4215 The NetBIOS adapter number used for this connection.

CCL4216 The name of the server to which a connection has been established. The name of the server is the Local System Appl ID specified in the SIT.

CCL3251 The client sends a CCIN transaction to the server to install its connection definition on the server.

CCL3238 Reply to message CCL3238, includes the conversation ID for this conversation.

CCL3113 The client sends a CCIN transaction to the server with Appl ID set to * to install its application. The Appl ID is specified in the CICSCLI.INI file as *Client=**. Specifying the Appl ID as *client=** requests the server to dynamically generate an Appl ID that is unique within the CICS server system.

CCL3114 This is the response to message CCL3114 with the dynamically generated Appl ID.

CCL2041 End of trace message.

ECI Application Error

The trace shown in Figure 200 on page 308 is an example of an ECI call from a CICS Client for OS/2 to a server program located on a CICS/ESA server. The transaction on the server terminates abnormally, and an error code and abnormal termination code are returned to the application.

CICS Client Trace Analysis

```
02/10/95 15:01:30 [2047] CCL2039 **** CICS Client for OS/2 - Service Trace Begins ****
02/10/95 15:01:30 [2051] CCL2048 Maximum trace data size set to 64
02/10/95 15:01:30 [2031] CCL2023 Client Response (SessId=000000B3, Slot=0, ReqRc=0, AppRc=0)
02/10/95 15:01:35 [2030] CCL2021 ECI request (SessId=000000B4, Slot=2, Type=516)
95B7:000E  0402464141444543 4943000000000000    ..FAADECIC...... ................
95B7:001E  0000000000000000 0000000000002020    ................ ..............
95B7:002E  202070021F001200 0000000000000000    p............... ................
95B7:003E  0000000000000000 0000000000000100    ................ ................
02/10/95 15:01:35 [2044] CCL2022 ECI COMMAREA Data: Length=18
95B7:007C  0000000000000000 0000000000000000    ................ ................
95B7:008C  0000                                 ..
02/10/95 15:01:35 [2060] CCL2045 Request directed to server 'CICSSNA '
02/10/95 15:01:35 [3239] CCL3251 Comms Allocate request (LinkId=2, Tran='CPMI')
02/10/95 15:01:35 [3240] CCL3238 Comms Allocate completed (LinkId=2, ConvId=1, Rc=0)
02/10/95 15:01:35 [3245] CCL3242 Comms Send request: Length=47 (ConvId=1)
007F:0D5A  002F12F20A850202 0102000001040E43    ./.............C ...2.e......
007F:0D6A  0E02000007E00000 00800100000B02C6    ................ .....\........F
007F:0D7A  C1C1C4C5C3C9C300 05040012000306             ........ AADECIC........
02/10/95 15:01:35 [3246] CCL3241 Comms Send completed (ConvId=1, Rc=0)
02/10/95 15:01:35 [3247] CCL3254 Comms Wait request (ConvId=1)
02/10/95 15:01:36 [4648] CCL4646 APPC send data: Length=47
9677:0000  002F12F20A850202 0102000001040E43    ./.............C ...2.e......
9677:0010  0E02000007E00000 00800100000B02C6    ................ .....\........F
9677:0020  C1C1C4C5C3C9C300 05040012000306             ........ AADECIC........
02/10/95 15:01:36 [3248] CCL3243 Comms Wait completed (ConvId=1, Rc=0)
02/10/95 15:01:36 [2057] CCL2058 Incoming conversation data (ConvId=1)
02/10/95 15:01:36 [3249] CCL3244 Comms Receive request (ConvId=1)
02/10/95 15:01:36 [4649] CCL4647 APPC receive data: Length=12
96D7:0000  000C12F208430E02 00000101              .....C......    ...2........
02/10/95 15:01:36 [3255] CCL3256 Comms Receive completed (last): Length=12 (ConvId=1, Reason=0, Rc=0)
96D7:0000  000C12F208430E02 00000101              .....C......    ...2........
02/10/95 15:01:36 [2031] CCL2023 Client Response (SessId=000000B4, Slot=2, ReqRc=0, AppRc=-7)
00B7:877E  0402464141444543 4943000000000000    ..FAADECIC...... ................
00B7:878E  0000000000000000 0000000000004145    ................ ..........AE....
00B7:879E  493070021F001200 0000000000000000    IOp............. ................
00B7:87AE  000000000000FFFF FFFF000000000100    ................ ................
02/10/95 15:01:49 [2048] CCL2040 Service Trace Disable request (SessId=000000B5)
02/10/95 15:01:49 [2049] CCL2041 ***** CICS Client for OS/2 - Service Trace Ends *****
```

Figure 200. CICS Client Trace Showing ECI Application Error

Message ID   *Explanation*

CCL2021   Shows the name of the program that is executed on the CICS server.

CCL2045   Contains the name of the server to the request is directed.

CCL3251   Shows the request is run under the CPMI mirror transaction on the CICS server. You can specify your own transaction ID within the ECI control block.

CCL2023   This message contains two important pieces of error information: **AppRc=-7** and an abend code, **AEI0**.

AppRc=-7 indicates that the transaction on the server (CPMI) has terminated abnormally. Refer to the layout of the ECI control block for a complete list of return

CICS Client Trace Analysis

codes. Depending on the programming language you use, you will find the layout of the ECI control block in one of the following directories:

- CICSCLI\COPYBOOK for COBOL (CICS_ECI.CBL)
- CICSCLI\PLIHDR for PL/I (CICS_ECI.INC)
- CICSCLI\INCLUDE for C (CICS_ECI.H).

Abend code AEI0 indicates that a program-not-found-condition caused the abnormal termination. Explanations of abnormal termination codes can be found in the *Messages and Codes* manual of the CICS server product.

Connecting to CICS for Windows NT Using NetBIOS

Figure 201 shows a trace of the unsuccessful attempt to connect a CICS Client for OS/2 to a CICS for Windows NT server.

```
02/15/95 08:46:07 [2047] CCL2039 **** CICS Client for OS/2 - Service Trace Begins ****
02/15/95 08:46:07 [2051] CCL2048 Maximum trace data size set to 64
02/15/95 08:46:07 [2031] CCL2023 Client Response (SessId=0000005C, Slot=0, ReqRc=0, AppRc=0)
02/15/95 08:46:10 [2039] CCL2029 Server Stop request (SessId=0000005D, Type=NORMAL)
96A7:0010   636963736E657462                  cicsnetb          ....>...
02/15/95 08:46:11 [2060] CCL2045 Request directed to server 'CICSNETB'
02/15/95 08:46:11 [2031] CCL2023 Client Response (SessId=0000005D, Slot=0, ReqRc=0, AppRc=2043)
02/15/95 08:46:25 [2036] CCL2028 Server Start request (SessId=0000005E)
96A7:0010   636963736E657462                  cicsnetb          ....>...
02/15/95 08:46:25 [2060] CCL2045 Request directed to server 'CICSNETB'
02/15/95 08:46:25 [3235] CCL3249 Comms Open request (Server=CICSNETB, Driver=CCLIBMNB)
02/15/95 08:46:25 [3236] CCL3236 Comms Open completed (Server=CICSNETB, LinkId=1, Rc=0)
02/15/95 08:46:25 [2031] CCL2023 Client Response (SessId=0000005E, Slot=0, ReqRc=0, AppRc=0)
02/15/95 08:46:34 [2035] CCL2027 Server Status request (SessId=0000005F, Space=87)
02/15/95 08:46:34 [2031] CCL2023 Client Response (SessId=0000005F, Slot=0, ReqRc=0, AppRc=0)
96A7:0010   0100434943534E45 5442004E45544249  ..CICSNETB.NETBI  ......+....+....
96A7:0020   4F53000043494353 4E54000000000000  OS..CICSNT...... !.......+.......
96A7:0030   0000000000000000 0000000000000000  ................ ................
96A7:0040   0000000000000000 0000000000000000  ................ ................
02/15/95 08:46:35 [4227] CCL4217 NetBIOS command failed for conversation 0/0: Cmd=0090, Rc=0014
02/15/95 08:46:35 [2055] CCL2056 Connection with server lost (LinkId=1)
02/15/95 08:46:35 [3237] CCL3250 Comms Close request (LinkId=1)
02/15/95 08:46:35 [3238] CCL3237 Comms Close completed (LinkId=1, Rc=0)
02/15/95 08:46:45 [2035] CCL2027 Server Status request (SessId=00000060, Space=87)
02/15/95 08:46:45 [2031] CCL2023 Client Response (SessId=00000060, Slot=0, ReqRc=0, AppRc=0)
96A7:0010   0100434943534E45 5442004E45544249  ..CICSNETB.NETBI  ......+....+....
96A7:0020   4F53000043494353 4E54000000000000  OS..CICSNT...... !.......+.......
96A7:0030   0000000000000000 0000000000000000  ................ ................
96A7:0040   0000000000000000 0000000000000000  ................ ................
02/15/95 08:47:01 [2048] CCL2040 Service Trace Disable request (SessId=00000061)
02/15/95 08:47:01 [2049] CCL2041 ***** CICS Client for OS/2 - Service Trace Ends *****
```

Figure 201. CICS Client Trace: Connecting to a CICS for Windows NT Server

In this trace, only the following message provides information related to the possible cause of the failure:

CCL4217   Shows that the NetBIOS command, Cmd=0090, has failed with a return code of Rc=0014.

Cmd=0090 is the CALL command used to open a connection with a server. Rc=0014 indicates a *Cannot find name called* condition. (Refer to the *LAN Technical Reference IEEE 802.2 and NetBIOS Application Program Interfaces* manual for an explanation of commands and return codes.) There are several possible reasons for this error. Because the client cannot determine why the server failed, you must look at server error logs and traces to diagnose the server problems. Check the following:

- Is the CICS server available?
- Is NetBIOS support enabled?
- Is the correct adapter number specified?
- Does the server have the correct Appl ID specified?
- Is the NetBIOS support customized correctly?

Installation and customization of the NetBIOS support in a CICS for Windows NT environment require special attention. The default support for NetBIOS in a CICS for Windows NT environment is set to Novell's IPX/SPX. If you require NetBIOS support, you must ensure that the customization is performed accordingly.

In a CICS for Windows NT environment, the default setting for NetBIOS support is set to Novell's emulation of NetBIOS over IPX. If you want to use the IBM NetBIOS support, you must customize your network settings accordingly:

1. Double-click on the **MAIN** icon in the Program Manager window.
   The Main window is displayed.
2. Double-click on the **Control Panel** icon.
   The Control Panel window is displayed.
3. Double-click on the **Network** icon.
   The Network Settings window is displayed.
4. Check the :Installed Network Software selection box. It must show the following two selections:
   - NetBEUI protocol
   - NetBIOS interface
5. Double-click on **NetBIOS Interface**
   The **NetBIOS Interface** window is displayed.
   Set the **Network Route** value to 0:Nbf->IbmTok->IbmTokMc1.
   Set the **Lana Number** to 0.
6. Click on **OK** and exit.

CICS Client Trace Analysis

Windows NT allows multiple physical adapters in a machine (as does OS/2). It also allows several logical adapters to use one physical adapter (which OS/2 does not support). When CICS manuals refer to adapters, the reference is to logical LAN adapters (Lana number) and not the physical adapters as in OS/2.

If you have installed Windows NT using the default parameters, you will have IPX (NWLINK IPX/SPX Compatible Transport) as your default transport on logical adapter 0. Hence, you cannot talk to a client unless the client also uses IPX. Alternatively, you could install NetBIOS Frames as your default transport on Lana 0.

Connecting to CICS/6000 Using TCP/IP

Figure 202 shows trace information recorded when we tried to connect to a CICS/6000 server over TCP/IP using an invalid port number. The port number specified in the CICSCLI.INI file was not defined in the services file of the server. Hence, the connection could not be established.

```
02/16/95 17:48:26 [2047] CCL2039 **** CICS Client for OS/2 - Service Trace Begins ****
02/16/95 17:48:26 [2051] CCL2048 Maximum trace data size set to 64
02/16/95 17:48:27 [2036] CCL2028 Server Start request (SessId=000001D1)
96A7:0010   6369637374637000                  cicstcp.        ........
02/16/95 17:48:27 [2060] CCL2045 Request directed to server 'CICSTCP '
02/16/95 17:48:27 [3231] CCL3231 Comms Load request (Driver=CCLIBMIP)
02/16/95 17:48:27 [3253] CCL3233 Loading protocol driver (DLL=C:\CICSCLI\BIN\CCLIBMIP.DLL)
02/16/95 17:48:27 [3232] CCL3232 Comms Load completed (Driver=CCLIBMIP, DrvId=1, Rc=0)
02/16/95 17:48:27 [3235] CCL3249 Comms Open request (Server=CICSTCP, Driver=CCLIBMIP)
02/16/95 17:48:27 [4408] CCL4413 TCP/IP (to CICSTCP) address=9.113.36.78, port=1345, socket=59
02/16/95 17:48:27 [3236] CCL3236 Comms Open completed (Server=CICSTCP, LinkId=1, Rc=0)
02/16/95 17:48:27 [2031] CCL2023 Client Response (SessId=000001D1, Slot=0, ReqRc=0, AppRc=0)
02/16/95 17:48:27 [2055] CCL2056 Connection with server lost (LinkId=1)
02/16/95 17:48:27 [3237] CCL3250 Comms Close request (LinkId=1)
02/16/95 17:48:28 [3238] CCL3237 Comms Close completed (LinkId=1, Rc=0)
02/16/95 17:48:31 [2035] CCL2027 Server Status request (SessId=000001D3, Space=87)
02/16/95 17:48:31 [2031] CCL2023 Client Response (SessId=000001D3, Slot=0, ReqRc=0, AppRc=0)
96A7:0010   0100434943535443 5000005443504950  ..CICSTCP..TCPIP  ........&....&.&
96A7:0020   0053000006261796B 616C000000000000  .S..baykal......  ...../',/%......
96A7:0030   0000000000000000 0000000000000000  ................  ................
96A7:0040   0000000000000000 0000000000000000  ................  ................
02/16/95 17:48:37 [2048] CCL2040 Service Trace Disable request (SessId=000001D4)
02/16/95 17:48:37 [2049] CCL2041 ***** CICS Client for OS/2 - Service Trace Ends *****
```

Figure 202. CICS Client Trace: Using an Invalid Port Number

Message ID   *Explanation*

CCL4413   Shows the port number used for this connection request.

CCL2056   Contains the error indication. You must check your definitions in the SIT on the server, the CICSCLI.INI file on the workstation, and the services file for the port number specified.

You must provide a valid port number or use the default value. Refer to "TCP/IP Port Selection" on page 328 for a description of how the port number is selected.

Common Errors in a CICS Client Environment

After you have customized the CICSCLI.INI file, you can test the client-server link by following these steps:

1. **For CICS Client for DOS only.** You must run the CICS-DOSC.BAT program before you can start the client.
2. On the client workstation, enter the *CICSCLI /s=servername* command (or click on the equivalent icon), where *servername* is the name of the server.

   Note: For CICS Client for Macintosh, use the CICS Client for Macintosh Administration Utility.
3. After a few moments, enter the *CICSCLI /l* command, or click on the equivalent icon to display information on the status of the server to which the client is connected or attempting to connect. Verify that the server is available.

If the connection to the server cannot be established, examine any messages in the CICS client error log to determine the cause of the problem. The CICS Client generates various messages associated with the use of the supported communication protocols and the associated products. These messages are written to the CICS client error log. Always consult the online message information for a list of these messages and their explanation. Common problems are:

- The wrong server was selected, or the server was not specified in the start command.
- The communication product was not started.
- The selection of TCP/IP Local Host Port was not consistent.
- The selection of NetBIOS Listener adapter was not consistent.
- The wrong protocol driver was used.
- The value for *Maximum servers* was set to 1 (default), and more than one server is accessed.
- CICSCTSR was not executed for CICS Client for DOS.

Refer to Appendix , "Common Problems: Symptoms and Solutions," on page 339 for more information on how to deal with these problems.

Common Errors in a CICS Server Environment

If a connection from a CICS Client to a CICS server cannot be established, several areas could cause the failure. Depending on the communication protocol, customization varies from very simple (in the case of TCP/IP or NetBIOS it may need no more than the server name), to rather complex (SNA and particularly Novell's Netware for SAA require many special settings). In general, SNA is more complex to set up than any other communication protocol, and errors are usually difficult to diagnose.

Common errors in a CICS server environment are:

- Definition mismatches between CM/2, CICS, and VTAM, regarding the following parameters:
    - Aliases in CM/2 definitions
    - Modename
    - LU name
- LU name already in use by another CICS client.
- The CCIN and CTIN transactions have not been defined.
- The CRSR transaction for transaction routing has not been defined.
- The CPMI mirror transaction has not been defined.
- Required resources have not been defined properly, for example:
    - Connections and sessions
    - Mirror transactions
    - Server programs
    - Conversion templates
- Server name is not unique.
- ISC not enabled in the SIT.
- NetBIOS communication is not enabled, or the value for Maximum NetBIOS systems (SIT) is too low.
- TCP/IP is not enabled, or the value for Maximum TCP/IP systems (SIT) is too low.

Hints and Tips

This appendix contains hints and tips that you may find useful while configuring and testing your network.

The following topics are covered:

- "Establishing a Connection Between CM/2 and CICS Mainframe" on page 316
- "Establishing a Connection Using APPC NS/Windows" on page 317
- "Automatic Start of CICS Client" on page 320
- "Starting CICS Client for DOS" on page 321
- "Starting and Stopping Your CICS Client" on page 321
- "Checking the Status of Your CICS Client" on page 322
- "Using CICSTERM Commands" on page 322
- "CICS Client for Macintosh Operation" on page 323
- "Data Conversion: ASCII to EBCDIC" on page 326
- "Using the Ping Utility to Verify TCP/IP Connections" on page 327
- "TCP/IP Port Selection" on page 328

Establishing a Connection Between CM/2 and CICS Mainframe

You can activate the connection between CM/2 and the CICS mainframe from either product.

From the CICS mainframe:

1. Issue **CEMT INQUIRE CONNECTION(xxxx),** where CONNECTION(xxxx) is the sysid pointing to the partner system.
2. If the status of the connection is **INS REL**, overtype the **REL** with **ACQ**.
3. If the status of the connection is **OUT REL**, overtype the **OUT REL** with **INS ACQ**.
4. You may have to wait a few seconds for the connection to become acquired.

```
┌─ CEMT INQ CONNECTION(C272) ─────────────────
  INQUIRE CONNECTION(C272)
  STATUS:  RESULTS - OVERTYPE TO MODIFY
    Con(C272) Net(SJA2072I)    Ins Acq    Xno
```

5. When the connection is INS ACQ, check the number of user sessions available.
   Issue the command **CEMT INQUIRE MODE(*) CONNECTION(xxxx)**.

```
┌─ CEMT INQ MODE CONNECTION(C272) ─────────────
  INQUIRE MODE CONNECTION(C272)
  STATUS:  RESULTS - OVERTYPE TO MODIFY
    Mod(SNASVCMG) Con(C272) Max(002) Ava(002) Act(002)
    Mod(LU62APPB) Con(C272) Max(008) Ava(008) Act(004)
```

6. Allocate requests from the CICS Client automatically acquire an LU6.2 user session if one is not available. In the example above, four LU6.2 user sessions are currently acquired, Act(004), and a total of eight LU6.2 user sessions, Ava(008), could be acquired, assuming you have set a maximum number of sessions to eight or more for the LU62APPB mode name within CM/2.

To have your CICS mainframe server automatically attempt to connect to an active client workstation running CM/2, set INSERVICE=YES and AUTOCONNECT=YES on both the CONNECTION and SESSIONS definitions.

From CM/2, using CM/2 Subsystem Management:

1. Select SNA Subsystem

2. Select LU6.2 Sessions

3. Select Establish and fill in the appropriate fields.

The recommended method is to add CNOS definitions to your .NDF file. This will enable your workstation to automatically connect to an active server system each time CM/2 is started. See "Change Number of Sessions" on page 45 for an example.

Establishing a Connection Using APPC NS/Windows

To establish a connection from your CICS Client for Windows using APPC Networking Services for Windows (hereafter referred to as APPC NS/Windows) to a CICS server using SNA, follow these steps:

1. Select the **IBM APPC Networking Services** icon.

2. Select the **Autostart Networking Services** icon (depicted by a rocket). Depending on your configuration, Networking Services may take several seconds to start. If APPC NS/Windows appears to hang permanently at this point, see "SNA" on page 341 . To automatically start Networking Services when Windows is started, drag the Autostart Networking Services icon into the Startup program group.

3. Select the **Advanced Operations** icon.

4. Select **Operation**.

5. From the pull-down menu, select **LU Control**. The Local LU Control window (see Figure 203 on page 318) displays the number of active link stations. In Figure 193 there is one active link station but no sessions to partner systems. If your Local LU Control window displays zero link stations, you can attempt to initialize your LU by selecting the **Initialize LU** button.

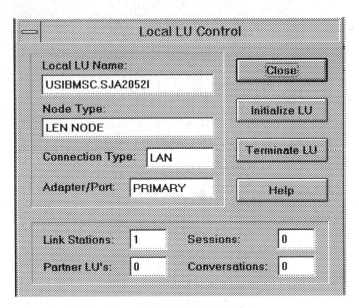

Figure 203. Local LU Control: APPC NS/Windows

6. Select **Close** to return to the Advanced Operations icon.
7. Select **Operation**.
8. From the pull-down menu, select **Connections**.
9. Figure 204 on page 319 shows the active link station, **CICSESA**. To acquire LU6.2 sessions to a partner system, select **Activate**.

Establishing a Connection Using APPC NS/Windows

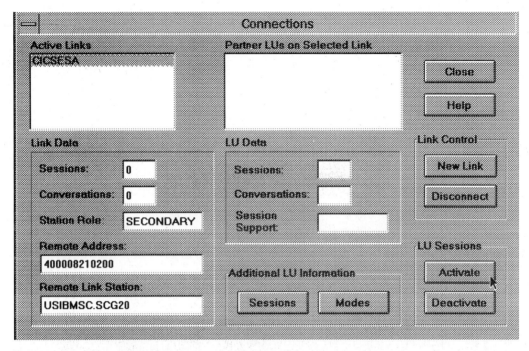

Figure 204. Connections Window Showing No Active LU Sessions

10. On the Activate LU Sessions window (see Figure 205) enter the applid (LU) of the partner CICS system, the minimum number of sessions you want to activate, and the name of your LU6.2 user modegroup.

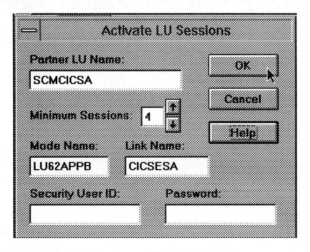

Figure 205. Activate LU Sessions: APPC NS/Windows

Appendix A. Hints and Tips 319

11. When the sessions between APPC NS/Windows and your partner CICS system are established, a Connections window similar to that shown in Figure 206 will appear. For further information on the active sessions, select the **Sessions** or **Modes** button within the Additional LU Information section of the window.

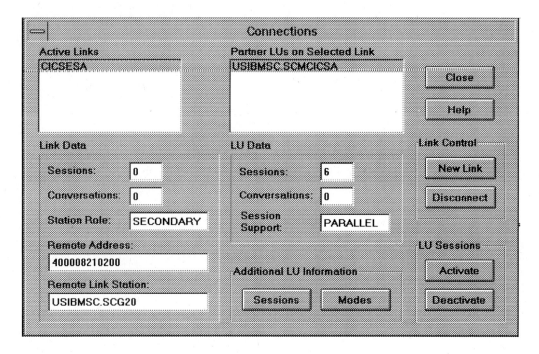

Figure 206. Connections Window Showing Active LU Sessions

12. For further information, refer to your APPC NS/Windows documentation.

Automatic Start of CICS Client

Before you can issue an ECI, EPI, or terminal emulation request, the client needs to be started. With the IBM CICS Clients V1.0 (with the exception of the CICS Client for DOS, see "Starting CICS Client for DOS" on page 321) the CICS Client is **automatically** started when the first ECI, EPI, or terminal emulation request is issued.

Starting CICS Client for DOS

Before you can start CICS Client for DOS, you must run CICSCTSR, the terminate and stay resident (TSR) program. The supplied program, CICSDOSC.BAT, runs CICSCTSR (which starts the DOS transport layer) and then starts the CICS Client for DOS automatically.

You may therefore want to add the following line to your AUTOEXEC.BAT file:

    CALL CICSDOSC

Starting and Stopping Your CICS Client

Depending on the CICS Client you are using, you can issue CICS Client commands from the installed icons or from a command line.

The basic CICS Client commands are:

CICSCLI /S	To start the CICS Client.
CICSCLI /S=<servername>	To start the CICS Client to a specified server.
CICSCLI /X	To stop the CICS Client and all connected servers after all outstanding units of work have completed.
CICSCLI /X=<servername>	To stop the session only with the specified server once all outstanding units of work have completed.
CICSCLI /I	To stop the CICS Client immediately, without waiting for outstanding units of work to complete.
CICSCLI /I=<servername>	To stop the CICS Client immediately with the specified server. without waiting for outstanding units of work to complete.

See the *CICS Clients: Administration* book for further information.

Checking the Status of Your CICS Client

You can check the status of all CICS Clients, except CICS Client for DOS, by clicking on the **Client Status** icon.

Alternatively, for all CICS Clients except CICS Client for Macintosh, you can issue the following command: **CICSCLI /L**.

Either method lists the servers connected to your client and their status. For example:

```
─── CICSCLI /L ───────────────────────────────────────────────
CCL8001I CICSCLI - CICS Client Control Program
CCL0002I (C) Copyright IBM Corporation 1994.  All rights reserved.
CCL8041I The CICS client is using the following servers:
CCL8042I Server 'CICSOS2' (using 'TCPIP' to 'Malawi') is connecting
CCL8042I Server 'CICSNT' (using 'NETBIOS' to 'Dozey') is unavailable
CCL8042I Server 'CICSESA' (using 'APPC' to 'Goliath') is available
CCL8042I Server 'CICSVSE' (using 'GATEWAY' to 'Rome') is stopping
```

Using CICSTERM Commands

Depending on the CICS Client you are using, you can issue CICS Client commands from the installed icons or from a command line.

The basic CICS Client CICSTERM commands are:

CICSTERM	Attempts to install a CICS Client terminal on the first server listed in your CICSCLI.INI file.
CICSTERM /S=\<servername\>	Starts a CICS Client terminal on the specified server.
CICSTERM /S	Lists the servers in your CICSCLI.INI file. You can then choose on which server you want to install a terminal. For example, on the CICS Client for OS/2:

```
─── CICSTERM /S ──────────────────────────────────────────────
CCL7001I CICSTERM - CICS Client 3270 Terminal Emulator
CCL0002I (C) Copyright IBM Corporation 1994.  All rights reserved.
CCL7040I Please choose the CICS server you require:
CCL7042I 1. ALSKIX   - CICS for OS/2 server, TCP/IP
CCL7042I 2. SIXPACK  - CICS/6000 server, TCP/IP
CCL7042I 3. DOZEY    - CICS for Windows NT, NetBIOS
CCL7041I Enter the number of the server or Esc to cancel
```

CICS Client for Macintosh Operation

The following commands are interchangeable (the result is the same):

```
CICSTERM /S[=servername]
CICSTERM -S[=servername]
CICSTERM /R[=servername]
CICSTERM -R[=servername]
```

See the *CICS Clients: Administration* book for further information on the CICSTERM command and associated parameters.

CICS Client for Macintosh Operation

This section provides a basic introduction to using the CICS Client for Macintosh Administration utility.

To start up the Administration utility, within the CICSCLI BIN folder select the **CICS Client Admin** icon.

Figure 207 shows the client in an inactive state. The **-F** parameter shows the location of the CICSCLI.INI file. You can select different initialization files by selecting the **File** option at the top of your screen.

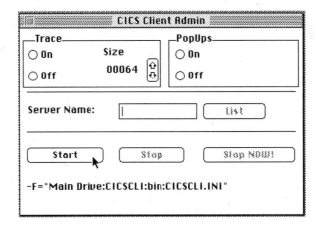

Figure 207. Inactive CICS Client for Macintosh

To start the CICS Client for Macintosh select **Start**. If you want to connect to a particular server, you must specify the server name (as assigned by **Server=** in your CICSCLI.INI file) in the **Server Name:** box.

Appendix A. Hints and Tips

Once the CICS Client for Macintosh is active, you can select **List** to inquire about the state of connections to servers (see Figure 208).

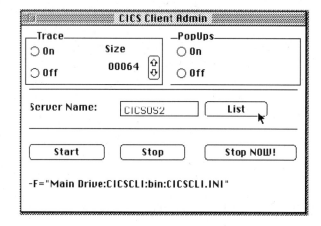

Figure 208. Selecting the List Option: CICS Client for Macintosh

Figure 209 shows that the CICS Client for Macintosh has one available TCP/IP connection to the CICSOS2 server.

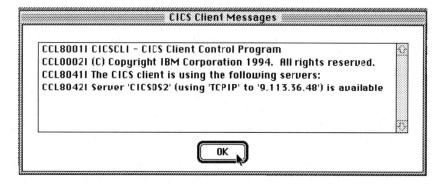

Figure 209. Connection Status List: CICS Client for Macintosh

Alternatively, you can select the **Client Status** icon from the CICSCLI BIN folder.

Here is a summary of the CICS Client for Macintosh Administration Utility features:

START <no Server Name>   Start the client only. Equivalent to the **CICSCLI /S** command.

CICS Client for Macintosh Operation

START with a Server Name	Start the client (if not already started) and attempt to connect to the specified server. Equivalent to the **CICSCLI /S=<servername>** command.
Stop <no Server Name>	Stop the client and shut down connections to servers once tasks are complete. Equivalent to the **CICSCLI /X** command.
Stop with a Server Name	Shut down the connection to the specified server once tasks are complete. The client will continue to be active. Equivalent to the **CICSCLI /X=<servername>** command.
Stop NOW! <no Server Name>	Stop the client immediately, terminating all connections to servers whether tasks are complete or not. Equivalent to the **CICSCLI /I** command.
Stop NOW! with a Server Name	Terminate the connection to the specified server immediately, whether tasks are complete or not. The client will continue to be active. Equivalent to the **CICSCLI /I=<servername>** command.
Trace On	Activates the trace utility for problem determination. Equivalent to the **CICSCLI /D=<data area size>** command.
Trace Off	Stops the trace utility. Equivalent to the **CICSCLI /O** command.
Size	The maximum size of data areas to be traced. This option is useful for checking data in large COMMAREAS.

Appendix A. Hints and Tips

PopUps On — Enable the display of error and security pop-up messages.
Equivalent to the **CICSCLI /E** command.

PopUps Off — Disable the display of error and security pop-up messages.
Equivalent to the **CICSCLI /N** command.

See the *CICS Clients: Administration* book for further information on using the CICS Client for Macintosh.

Data Conversion: ASCII to EBCDIC

When sending data within a COMMAREA on an ECI call from a CICS Client to an EBCDIC CICS server (for example, CICS/ESA), you may want to convert the data from ASCII to EBCDIC. For this conversion you need to assemble the **DFHCNV** macro on your server system.

The following example shows the coding required to convert the data from ASCII to EBCDIC:

```
┌── DFHCNV ─────────────────────────────────────────────────
         DFHCNV TYPE=INITIAL,CDEPAGE=(437,USRD)
*
* THIS TABLE IS NEEDED ON THE HOST FOR ASCII <-
> EBCDIC DATA CONVERSION
* FOR SNA BETWEEN CICS RUNNING UNDER MVS/ESA/VSE AND CICS CLIENTS.
*
         DFHCNV TYPE=ENTRY,RTYPE=PC,RNAME=EC01,USREXIT=NO
         DFHCNV TYPE=SELECT,OPTION=DEFAULT
         DFHCNV TYPE=FIELD,OFFSET=0,DATATYP=CHARACTER,DATALEN=32767,
 X
               LAST=YES

           :::

LABLN    DFHCNV TYPE=FINAL
         END    DFHCNVBA
```

Notes:

1. RTYPE=PC is for a program call. This definition includes ECI, which is basically a DPL call.

2. RNAME=EC01 is the name of the server program to be called.

3. OFFSET=0 indicates that all data from the start of the COMMAREA is to be converted.

4. DATATYP=CHARACTER is the type of data to be converted.
   5. DATALEN=32767 is the maximum number of bytes to be converted in this field.
   6. You can have multiple fields specifying different DATATYPs for each TYPE=ENTRY. Your last TYPE=FIELD must end with LAST=YES.

Using the Ping Utility to Verify TCP/IP Connections

You can verify the TCP/IP communication between the client and the server workstation using a utility called **ping**.

To **start** the ping utility, enter the following command:

ping 9.113.36.31

where 9.113.36.31 is the IP address of the server. If you are using a Domain Nameserver, you can specify the symbolic hostname rather than the IP address of the server.

To **stop** the ping utility, press the Ctrl-C keys simultaneously.

If you have installed TCP/IP correctly, you will see the messages shown in Figure 210.

```
# ping 9.113.36.31 56 3
PING 192.113.36.78: (192.113.36.78): 56 data bytes
64 bytes from 9.113.36.31: icmp_seq=0 ttl=255 time=3 ms
64 bytes from 9.113.36.31: icmp_seq=1 ttl=255 time=3 ms
64 bytes from 9.113.36.31: icmp_seq=2 ttl=255 time=3 ms

----9.113.36.31 PING Statistics----
3 packets transmitted, 3 packets received, 0% packet loss
round-trip min/avg/max = 3/3/3 ms
#
```

Figure 210. Messages Returned from Ping Utility

If the statistic messages show a value other than **0% packet loss**, it is likely that you did not install or customize TCP/IP correctly. Therefore:

- Check for TCP/IP definition errors.
- Check for TCP/IP definition mismatches.
- Check the network physical connection.

> **Note:**
> Depending on the platform, the implementation of the ping utility might be slightly different regarding the operation of the utility (icon or command) and the parameters that can be used. See the individual product documentation for details.

TCP/IP Port Selection

When a CICS Client wants to connect to a CICS server over TCP/IP, it must supply the hostname or the IP address of the machine on which the server resides. It also must supply a port number, which distinguishes one TCP/IP service from another.

TCP/IP architects a set of (well-known) port numbers that are reserved for specific applications and services. When using a CICS Client to connect to a CICS server, you only need to supply the hostname of the server because the default port number for CICS is predefined as port 1435. However, if another service is using this port number, you must define and use a different port number for CICS.

You can specify the port number in the CICSCLI.INI file. It is a numeric value in the range of 0 through 65535 defining the port number at the server to which the client should connect.

A setting of port=0 in the CICSCLI.INI file or the omission of this parameter indicates that the **Services** file in the TCPIP\etc directory should be used to locate the port number.

If no entry can be located in the services file, a value of 1435 is assumed. This is the port assigned by the TCP/IP architecture for CICS clients.

Figure 211 on page 329 summarizes the port selection process.

TCP/IP Port Selection

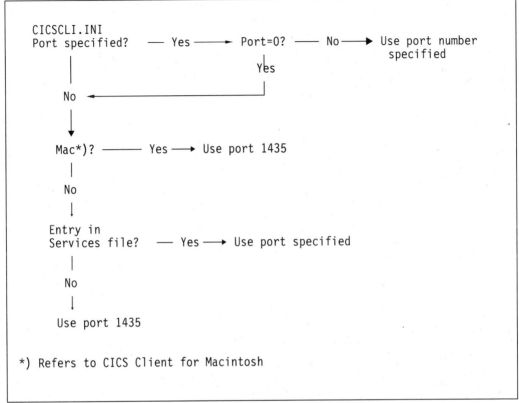

Figure 211. Port Selection Summary

Note: For CICS Client for Macintosh, no reference is made to a services file. If a value of 0 is entered, 1435 is assumed.

TCP/IP Port Selection

B

Frequently Asked Questions

This appendix covers frequently asked questions that arise during the process of installing and customizing a CICS Client and CICS server environment. The queries are related to the following topics:

- "Operating Environment" on page 331
- "Limitations" on page 333
- "Compatibility and Migration" on page 334
- "ECI" on page 336

Operating Environment

Q Does CICS Client for OS/2 run under OS/2 WARP V3?

A Yes, as documented in the announcement information for CICS Client. The OS/2 version required to run CICS Client is OS/2 Version 2.11 or higher.

Operating Environment

Q What is the minimum hardware requirement to run the CICS Client product?

A The CICS Client runs on any machine capable of running the appropriate operating system and other prerequisite software. CICS Client for DOS and CICS Client for Windows support any IBM-compatible PC, provided it will support the operating system and has sufficient memory for the required software components.

In the case of the CICS Client for OS/2, the requirement is for any machine that will support IBM OS/2 V2.0 or later. This implies a machine with an Intel 386SX or higher processor. The CICS Client for Macintosh requires any Apple machine containing the Motorola M68020 processor (or later), such as an Apple Classic or an Apple LC II.

Q How much disk space is required for the CICS Client?

A In addition to the base operating system and application programs, the following disk space is required for the client code:

Client	Disk space (MB)
CICS Client for DOS	0.9
CICS Client for OS/2	1.0
CICS Client for Windows	0.9
CICS Client for Macintosh	1.0

Q How much memory does the CICS Client for DOS require?

A The following gives an approximate summary of the memory requirements for the CICS Client for DOS and some advice on reducing those requirements to a minimum.

The CICS Client for DOS operates as a terminate-and-stay-resident (TSR) program. It is in two pieces: CICSCTSR.EXE, which is loaded once and stays resident, and CCLCLNT.EXE, which can be loaded and unloaded using the CICSCLI command program. CICSCTSR.EXE requires approximately 4K of memory, and CCLCLNT.EXE requires approximately 79K of memory.

Additional memory then will be required based on the contents of the client initialization file. The DOS memory pool must be allocated; the size of this pool is controlled by the **DosMemory** parameter in the **Client** section. The default is 48K. Each communications driver listed in a **Driver** section also must be loaded. The size of these drivers varies:

- CCLIBMNB.DLL requires approximately 14K of memory
- CCLIBMIP.DLL requires approximately 48K of memory
- CCLFTPIP.DLL requires approximately 49K of memory
- CCLNOVIP.DLL requires approximately 44K of memory

- CCLNOVSN.DLL requires approximately 20K of memory
- CCL400SN.DLL requires approximately 6K of memory

The client and any loaded communications drivers allocate any additional memory they require from the client's DOS memory pool. These requirements vary, but are typically based on the **MaxServers** and **MaxBufferSize** parameters in the **Client** section. To reduce memory requirements to a minimum, do the following:

- Remove all unwanted **Driver** sections from the initialization file.
- Reduce the **MaxServers** parameter to a minimum (the smallest possible value is 1).
- Reduce the **MaxBufferSize** parameter to a minimum (the smallest possible value is 4).
- Reduce the **DosMemory** parameter to a minimum (the smallest possible value is MaxBufferSize + 4, although more may be required if the "Free memory is exhausted" message is displayed).

Q Can a CICS Client connect to a CICS OS/2 V2 server?

A Yes. CICS Clients can connect to old CICS OS/2 V2.0 servers at the Version 2.0 functionality.

Q Why does CICS Client for DOS not support APPC NS/DOS?

A APPC is very large and uses virtually all of the memory below 640K. Because of this fact, few customers use this product.

Q Can I have CICS Client for OS/2 and CICS for OS/2 server running on the same workstation?

A Yes. This is a good way to test communications between your client and server without the need for additional hardware. Using a TCP/IP connection between the client and server should cause no problems. However, if you run CICS for OS/2 and CICS Client for OS/2 on the same workstation, even if they are not attempting to communicate with each other, you may run out of NetBIOS resources.

Limitations

Q How many clients can I attach to the server?

A The limitations are usually determined by the resources available at the server, for example, memory, power of processor, or communications hardware or software constraints. From a CICS server point of view, there is no limit to the number of clients that can be connected to it.

Q How many ECI transactions can I run concurrently?

A A single application on the CICS Client for OS/2, CICS Client for Windows, or CICS Client for Macintosh can have an unlimited number of concurrent ECI conversations with CICS servers. CICS Client for DOS is limited to 16 concurrent ECI conversations. The calls can be to the same or different servers and use different communications protocols. The communications protocols themselves may impose some limitations on the number of unique servers that can be concurrently accessed. Updates across multiple servers from the same application are not coordinated in the same LUW.

Q How many EPI transactions can I run concurrently?

A When using the EPI, a single client application can have up to 15 concurrent logical terminals connected to CICS servers. The terminals can be connected to the same or different servers and use different communication protocols.

Q How many terminal emulation sessions can I run concurrently?

A When using terminal emulation, a single client application can have up to 15 concurrent logical terminals connected to CICS servers. The terminals can be connected to the same or different servers and use different communication protocols.

Compatibility and Migration

Q What effort is required to migrate an application from a Distributed Feature client to the new CICS Client environment?

A Existing ECI and EPI applications that were written for the Distributed Feature clients of CICS OS/2 V2.0 are binary compatible and can be run without modification in a CICS Client environment. The source code for the applications requires minor changes before recompilation for the new CICS Clients. It is merely a question of changing a header file and link library names.
Note the following points:

- The header files are now called <cics_eci.h> and <cics_epi.h>. References to <faaecih.h> and <faaephi.h> must be changed.

Compatibility and Migration

- The CICS ECI entry point is now called CICS_ExternalCall(). Any calls to FaaExternalCall() must be changed.
- The correct link libraries are now called CCLDOS.LIB (for DOS), CCLWIN.LIB (for Windows) and CCLOS2.LIB or CCLOS232.LIB (for 16-bit and 32-bit applications, respectively). Attempts to link with FAACLIB.LIB will fail.
- Full 32-bit applications are supported for both ECI and EPI by linking with the CCLOS232.LIB. However, some of the client itself is still built as a 16-bit application, so care must be taken not to pass it data structures that span a 64K boundary. The IBM C Set++ compiler provides options and facilities to prevent infeasible data structures from being passed. This limitation should be removed in a future version of the client.

These notes apply to C language applications only; however, similar rules can be applied to COBOL applications.

Q Are client applications portable between members of the CICS Client family?

A Yes. ECI and EPI client applications are portable between members of the CICS Clients family, provided the application does not contain operating system specific calls.

Q What are the differences between a CICS for OS/2 server and a CICS for Windows NT server?

A CICS for Windows NT is a client-server implementation of CICS that enables desktop systems to interoperate with customer CICS applications executing on a Windows NT server, thereby enabling the applications to be integrated into the end-user working environment.

CICS for Windows NT is a port of CICS for OS/2 to the Windows NT environment. Table 23 lists the functional differences between the two CICS offerings.

Table 23. (Part 1 of 2) CICS for OS/2 and CICS for Windows NT: Functional Differences

	CICS for OS/2	CICS for Windows NT
PL/I	Supported	Not supported
Double-byte character set support	Supported	Not supported
Batch support for files	Supported	Not supported
File manager	Btrieve	Shared file system

Appendix B. Frequently Asked Questions

Table 23. (Part 2 of 2) CICS for OS/2 and CICS for Windows NT: Functional Differences

	CICS for OS/2	CICS for Windows NT
Performance monitoring support	Information passed to SPM/2. Performance Analyzer/2 available.	Information not provided
IBM 3151 ASCII terminal support	Support provided through: 1. PC serial connectors 2. RTIC card/PNA	Support provided only through PC serial connectors

ECI

Q What is the maximum COMMAREA size supported in an ECI application?

A The theoretical maximum length is 32767 bytes because the COMMAREA length is held in a half-word binary field. However, recommendations vary from 24KB to 32,500 bytes. The CICS family supports a maximum COMMAREA of 32,500 bytes; this limit assumes any-to-any connection. When you decide on the actual size of the COMMAREA, depending on the environment you are using, consider the following points:

- VTAM has a limit of 32KB on the physical buffer size.
- Function Management Header information (FMH5 and FMH43) must be shipped with the actual COMMAREA.
- You can send multiple ECI requests within the same unit of work.

Q Can ECI requests be routed from a CICS Client to a CICS server across a WAN without an intermediate CICS server on the LAN?

A Yes. An intermediate server is not required. The CICS Clients can communicate directly with any CICS server. The only problem is that not all servers support all communication transport protocols. For example, if you want to connect a CICS Client directly to a CICS/ESA server, you have to use SNA for your communications. Thus, CM/2 (OS/2), APPC NS/Windows (Windows), SNA.ps (Macintosh), or Novell Netware for SAA (DOS, Windows and OS/2) is required. If the protocol is TCP/IP, you can connect directly to a CICS for OS/2, CICS for Windows NT, or CICS for AIX V1.2 server.

Q When is data conversion required between the client and the server?

A If the code page of the ECI application differs from the code page of the server, data conversion for the COMMAREA must be performed at the server. You can use the CICS-supplied resource conversion capabilities, such as the DFHCNV macro definitions. For an example of how the DFHCNV macros are coded, see "Establishing a Connection Between CM/2 and CICS Mainframe" on page 316.

Q Should I use nulls or blanks in the eci_transid field of the ECI parameter list to use the default mirror transaction at the server?

A The eci_transid field must contain nulls if you want to use the default mirror transaction (CPMI) at the server. Blanks are considered as characters and will, if specified, result in an error condition (invalid transaction ID) at the server. Data conversion for the COMMAREA is not performed automatically if you do not use the default CPMI mirror transaction.

Q Which associated tools and products support ECI and EPI?

A A number of vendors support the ECI and EPI. Refer to "Associated Tools and Products" on page 23 for a list of vendors and vendor products.

C

Common Problems: Symptoms and Solutions

This appendix covers symptoms of and solutions to problems you may encounter while configuring your networks. The symptoms are discussed under the following headings:

- "Starting Clients and Terminals" on page 340
- "SNA" on page 341
- "TCP/IP" on page 344
- "NetBIOS" on page 345
- "ECI" on page 346
- "Documentation" on page 346

Starting Clients and Terminals

Q Why does my CICS Client for DOS fail to start?

A The CICS Client for DOS will not start if the CICSCTSR.EXE program has not been run first. For the CICS Client for DOS only, before you issue any client commands, you must run the terminate and stay resident (TSR) program, CICSCTSR.EXE, to enable the DOS transport layer. You only need to issue this program once; however, no harm is done if you run it multiple times. The supplied program CICSDOSC.BAT, runs CICSCTSR and then starts the client automatically. You may therefore want to add the following statement to your AUTOEXEC.BAT file:

CALL CICSDOSC

so that the program is run automatically during the startup of your workstation.

Q After running CICSCTSR, my ECI/EPI/3270 application still fails. Why?

A For the CICS Client for DOS only, the client must be started before you can run any ECI, EPI, or terminal emulation application. Use the supplied CICSDOSC.BAT batch file to start up the DOS transport layer (CICSCTSR) and the CICS Client for DOS automatically.

Q CICS Client for Macintosh: Selecting CICS Client Admin bleeps and fails to start the client. Why?

A The likely cause is that you have not installed the Apple Shared Library Manager. This software is required by the CICS Client for Macintosh and should be within the extensions folder.

Q CICS Client for Macintosh: error log reports CCL2067 Failure loading shared library manager. What does this mean?

A The likely cause is that you have not installed the Apple Shared Library Manager. This software is required by the CICS Client for Macintosh and should be within the extensions folder.

Q My CICS for OS/2 server reports "transaction CCIN failed." How can I resolve this?

A CCIN and CTIN are two transactions required on the CICS for OS/2 server to enable a CICS Client (or another CICS for OS/2 server) to attach using TCP/IP. For TCP/IP support you must have either CICS for OS/2 V2.0.1 or CICS for OS/2 V2.0 with CSD4 applied. Although the two products are basically identical, for the latter you must manually define the CCIN and CTIN in your PCT. Both transactions call the same program—FAATPPCI.

Q   The CICSTERM request goes to the wrong server. Why?

A   If you do not specify the /s or the /s=<server-name> option on the CICSTERM command, the CICSTERM request will be issued against the first server listed in your CICSCLI.INI file, even if it is not yet activated. The <server-name> should be as specified in the Server=<server-name> option on the CICSCLI.INI file.

Q   CICS Client printers attaching to a CICS for OS/2 server. How can I ensure I assign the same terminal identifier each time the client attaches to the server?

A   For the CICS for OS/2 server we recommend that you use user exit 21. This allows you to provide an applid (supplied by the Client= statement in your CICSCLI.INI file) to the user exit on the server, which can then assign a predetermined remote system identifier. Using this method you will always know the name of the client printer terminal to which to send data. See Chapter 18, "CICS 3270 Client Printer Configurations," on page 245 for examples and further information.

SNA

Q   CCIN not recognized. CTIN not recognized. What does this mean?

A   CCIN is a transaction that installs your CICS Client definition on the server. CTIN is a transaction that installs your client terminal definition on the server. These transactions must be available on your server if your server supports EPI. EPI implies CICS 3270 terminal emulation and CICS 3270 printer emulation. See Table 1 on page 8 to see which servers support EPI and, hence, CICS 3270 emulation.

Q   The CICSTERM for my CICS mainframe server fails. Why?

A   CICSTERM and CICSPRNT use CICS 3270 emulation. Most CICS mainframe servers do not support CICS 3270 emulation. See Table 1 on page 8 and the accompanying table notes to see which servers support CICS 3270 emulation.

Q   How do I establish my LU6.2 sessions between CM/2 and my CICS server?

A With CICS Client for OS/2, the sessions between CM/2 and the server must be established before the client is started. There are three ways to establish the sessions:

1. Acquire the connection from the CICS server. For example, on the CICS mainframe you could issue CEMT SET CONNECTION(xxxx) ACQUIRED, where CONNECTION(xxxx) is directed to your client workstation.

2. From CM/2, using CM/2 Subsystem Management:
   - Select SNA Subsystem
   - Select LU6.2 Sessions
   - Select Establish and fill in the appropriate fields

3. Use CNOS definitions in your .NDF file. This is the recommended method. For an example see "Change Number of Sessions" on page 45.

Q Why do my ATIs not work?

A Because of the different APPC implementations provided by products for handling inbound attaches, for CICS Clients using CM/2 and APPC Networking Services for Windows, you need to predefine the CRSR attach program to relay the information to the CICS Client. This predefinition will enable the CICS server to perform automatic transaction initiation (ATI) against the CICS Client terminals.

Note: CICS 3270 terminal emulation must be supported on your CICS server (see Table 1 on page 8).

For a CICS Client for OS/2 using CM/2, you must define the inbound attach transaction, CRSR, to use program CCLSNOTP.EXE. See "CRSR Transaction Program" on page 43 to see how to define CRSR within CM/2.

For a CICS Client for Windows using APPC Networking Services for Windows, you must define the CRSR to use program CCLSNWTP.EXE. See "Defining the Mode and CRSR Transaction Program" on page 59 to see how to define CRSR within APPC Networking Services for Windows.

For a CICS Client for Windows using NetWare, you do not need to define the CRSR because an exit is automatically driven when an inbound attach is received.

For a CICS Client for DOS using NetWare, you do not need to define CRSR because the CICS Client for DOS automatically polls for any inbound attach requests.

For a CICS Client for Macintosh using SNA•ps, you must define CRSR as an inbound attach transaction.

Q APPC Networking Services for Windows hangs during startup. Why?

A The hang may occur if your configuration requires a NODE ID and you have failed to specify one (or the correct one) in the NSD.INI file. The NODE ID must match the node id configured in VTAM. Otherwise, your workstation may be responsive after it attempts to connect to the server system. (See "Node ID Definition" on page 61 for an example.)

Q When I start APPC Networking Services for Windows I receive the message "Adapter Not Present." Why?

A You may get this message if you attempt to use APPC Networking Services for Windows with a token-ring network. You must configure your adapter before you can use APPC Networking Services for Windows. "LAN Support Program" on page 238 shows you how to configure your adapter using the LAN Support Program.

Q What does the FILE ERROR. CANNOT FIND NSWD.DDL message mean?

A Your CICS Client for Windows has attempted to use APPC Networking Services for Windows, but APPC Networking Services for Windows has not been started. You must start APPC Networking Services for Windows before you start the CICS Client for Windows. You can start APPC Networking Services for Windows automatically by copying the ***Autostart Networking Services*** icon to the STARTUP program group.

Q With APPC Networking Services for Windows I receive errors using my Dependent LU. Why?

A APPC Networking Services for Windows V1.0 only supports independent logical units (ILUs). Therefore, your LU defined within VTAM must be an ILU and not a dependent LU (DLU).

Q APPC Networking Services for Windows does not work under WIN-OS/2. Why?

A APPC Networking Services for Windows does not run under WIN-OS/2 because it uses Windows functions that currently are not supported with WIN-OS/2 (as supplied with OS/2 V2.11).

TCP/IP

Q My CICS Client for Windows cannot load the TCP/IP protocol driver. Why?

A You have probably received message CCL3229E in a pop-up window and message CCL3247 in the CICSCLI.LOG error log file. These messages indicate that you probably have specified the wrong device driver in the CICSCLI.INI file for your CICS Client for Windows. For all TCP/IP communications, your CICS Client for Windows should use the CCLWINIP driver. Any vendor offering a WINSOCK interface can use this TCP/IP driver.

Q CICS Client for OS/2 returns a CCL4401 TCP/IP not available message. Why?

A For your CICS Client for OS/2, ensure that TCP/IP is one of the protocols listed in your LAN Adapter and Protocol Support (LAPS) current configuration list. LAPS is part of Network Transport Services/2 (NTS/2). "Enabling NetBIOS Support" on page 228 describes how to enable NetBIOS support. You can use the same method to enable TCP/IP support.

Q What does the CCL4404 TCP/IP (to 'CICSTCP') unable to resolve name: RC=2 message mean?

A The server value, in this example, CICSTCP, could not be resolved by the TCP/IP protocol driver. Ensure that your nameserver and router address information is correct, and that any names and IP addresses in the TCP/IP etc\hosts file are correct.

Q The TCP/IP connection to my CICS for OS/2 server fails. What could be the problem?

A Check the following:
- Maximum TCP/IP Systems is greater than zero in the SIT of your CICS for OS/2.
- Both the client and server are using the same port number.
- CCIN and CTIN have been defined on your CICS for OS/2 (see the related CCIN symptom in "Starting Clients and Terminals" on page 340 for more information).

NetBIOS

Q I have only a few NetBIOS resources when running the CICS Client for OS/2 and CICS for OS/2 server on the same workstation. Why?

A It is likely that CICS for OS/2 has taken all of the NetBIOS resources for itself and left none for your CICS Client for OS/2. To avoid restricting the number of commands and sessions, reduce the values of n1, n2, and n3 in your \ibmlan\ibmlan.ini file. However, if you are using the LAN services program, leave sufficient resources for the LAN server/requester.

```
[networks]
    net1 = netbeui$, 0, LM10, n1,n2,n3
```

This file also should contain:

```
wrkheuristics=
    #18 must be 0
```

Q My NetBIOS connection fails. The trace reports:
CCL4217 NetBIOS command failed for conversation 0/0: Cmd=0090, Rc=0014

A This is a general return code returned by NetBIOS with no other clues as to what went wrong. Check your setup for the following:

- In your CICS for OS/2 or CICS for Windows NT server SIT definition, do you have **Maximum NETBIOS Systems** set to zero? If so, increase this number.

- If using CICS for Windows NT, have you configured your NetBIOS for the correct LAN type? For example, Novell or IBM? The default is Novell. See "Connecting to CICS for Windows NT Using NetBIOS" on page 309 for more information on this particular problem.

Q NetBIOS Listener Name exists elswhere on adapter 0. Why?

A If the application ID specified in the CICS for OS/2 SIT is not unique in the network, message FAA5573W will be displayed during startup of CICS for OS/2. This usually happens if you use the default value (CICSOS2) for the application ID.

To solve this problem, select **Continue** in the CICS for OS/2 console window and change the application ID according to your standards. You must shut down and restart CICS for OS/2 for the changes to take effect.

ECI

Q My ECI call request goes to the wrong server. Why?

A If you do not specify a server name in the eci-system-name value of your program's ECI parameter, the ECI call will be issued against the first server listed in your CICSCLI.INI file, even if it is not yet activated. For program flexibility, you may want to consider passing the server name parameter to the program during program initiation.

Q The stacksize for my COBOL ECI program is too small. How can I resolve this problem?

A You can increase your stacksize by creating a .DEF file. You should include a STACKSIZE 32768 statement. The .DEF file should be specified as the last parameter on the LINK command. The sample COBOL ECI program, ECICOBO1, within the \CICS-CLI\SAMPLES\COBOL directory contains a .DEF file that can be used as an example.

Q Why does ECI-CICS-TRACE-STATE and ECI-CICS-TRACE-FLAGS produce errors during compilation?

A These ECI fields, which are supported only by the CICS OS/2 V2.0 Distributed Feature Clients, are not available for the CICS Clients. Existing ECI applications containing these fields will continue to work on the CICS Client. However, if you want to recompile the ECI application using the modules supplied with the CICS Client, you must remove any statements containing ECI-CICS-TRACE-STATE or ECI-CICS-TRACE-FLAGS.

Documentation

Q Why can I not find the message number in the CICS Clients messages book?

A Check the following:
- The CICS Clients messages book is split into two sections. The first lists the messages seen by the end user at the terminal; the second lists messages for the CICS Client error log and the trace log.

    Note: The CICS Clients messages book is available as a softcopy only. The book is included in CICS Client for OS/2 and CICS Client for Windows products.

Documentation

- All CICS Client messages are prefixed by CCL. If the message number does not contain this prefix, you should find the product that is issuing the message. Here is a list of some CICS product prefixes:

CCL	CICS Clients
FAA	CICS for OS/2 and CICS for Windows NT
DFH	CICS mainframe
ERZ	CICS/6000
AEG	CICS/400

- If you have received a service update to your CICS Client ensure that you have updated your documentation component too.

Q Where is the online documentation?

A CICS Clients V1.0 provides full online documentation for the CICS Client for OS/2 and CICS Client for Windows. Ensure that you have chosen the documentation option during installation. All clients can view the end-user messages and the trace and log message files.

D. Programming Languages and Compilers

Your non-CICS applications can be written in C (or C++), COBOL, or PL/1, although not all of these languages are available in every environment. The non-CICS applications are portable between different CICS Client systems if they do not make operating-system-specific calls.

Table 24 shows the language compilers supported by the CICS Clients.

Table 24. Language Compilers Supported by CICS Clients

CLIENT	C (or C++)	COBOL	PL/1
DOS	Microsoft C 6.0	Micro Focus COBOL 3.0.54	Not supported
Windows	❏ Microsoft C 6.0 ❏ Microsoft Visual C++ 1.0 ❏ Other compatible compilers	Micro Focus COBOL 3.0.54	Not supported
OS/2	❏ Microsoft C 6.0 (16-bit) ❏ IBM C/2 1.1 ❏ IBM C Set/2 1.0 (32-bit) ❏ IBM C Set ++ 2.1 (32-bit) ❏ Other compatible compilers	Micro Focus COBOL/2 Level 2.5	IBM PL/1 for OS/2 1.1 Professional Edition
Macintosh	❏ Apple MPW C 3.31 ❏ Symantec C/C++ for MPW 6.01 ❏ Any C compilers that support the ASLM	Not supported	Not supported
Note: Later levels of these compilers are expected to be supported.			

E

Sample ECI and EPI Source Code

This appendix lists the source code of the programs that we used in "Sample Implementation" on page 277 and "Sample Implementation" on page 288.

Client Program for the ECI Sample

This section lists only the code relevant to the ECI calls.

Client Program for the ECI Sample

```c
/************************************************************************/
/*                                                                      */
/* MODULE NAME        ECIC01.C                                          */
/*                                                                      */
/* DESCRIPTIVE NAME   CICS External Call Interface                      */
/*                    OS/2 PM Sample - C Source                         */
/*                                                                      */
/* Statement:         (C) Copyright IBM Corporation 1994, 17H7627       */
/*                                                                      */
/* Status:            Version 1 Release 0                               */
/*                                                                      */
/* NOTES :-                                                             */
/*                                                                      */
/* You must fill in the name of your SERVER, USERID and PASSWORD        */
/* in the GLOBALS section below.                                        */
/*                                                                      */
/************************************************************************/

/************************************************************************/
/* HEADER FILES                                                         */
/************************************************************************/

  :::

#include <cics_eci.h>

  :::

/************************************************************************/
/* DEFINES                                                              */
/************************************************************************/
   #define ECI_SYNC_SIZE  18

/************************************************************************/
/* Global Variables                                                     */
/************************************************************************/
   ECI_PARMS      EciParms;
   char           Server[9] = "CICSTCP";      /* FILL IN YOUR SERVER HERE */
   char           UserID[9] = "CICSUSER";     /* FILL IN YOUR USER ID HERE */
   char           PassWd[9] = "";             /* FILL IN YOUR PASSWORD HERE */

/************************************************************************/
/************************************************************************/
/* main() - Sample Entry Point                                          */
/************************************************************************/
/************************************************************************/
int main(void)
{

  :::

} /* main */


/************************************************************************/
/* EciStateSync                                                         */
/************************************************************************/
/* Issue a CICS_Externalcall for an ECI_STATE_SYNC                      */
/*                                                                      */
/************************************************************************/
void EciStateSync (void)
```

```
{
   char            *Name = "ECI_STATE_SYNC";
   short           Rc;
   char            CommArea [ECI_STATUS_LENGTH];

    :::

   Print ("ECI Sample Program");
   Print ("------------------");

   Print ("%s test", Name);

   memset (CommArea, '\0', ECI_STATUS_LENGTH);
   memset (&EciParms, 0, sizeof (ECI_PARMS));

   EciParms.eci_version                         = ECI_VERSION_1;
   EciParms.eci_call_type                       = ECI_STATE_SYNC;
   memcpy(&EciParms.eci_userid,      UserID,    8);
   memcpy(&EciParms.eci_password,    PassWd,    8);
   memcpy(&EciParms.eci_system_name, Server,    8);
   EciParms.eci_commarea                        = CommArea;
   EciParms.eci_commarea_length                 = ECI_STATUS_LENGTH;
   EciParms.eci_extend_mode                     = ECI_STATE_IMMEDIATE;
   EciParms.eci_luw_token                       = ECI_LUW_NEW;
   EciParms.eci_timeout                         = 0;

   Rc = CICS_ExternalCall (&EciParms);

    :::

   Print ("%s test complete", Name);

} /* EciStateSync */

/****************************************************************************/
/* EciSync                                                                  */
/****************************************************************************/
/* Issue a CICS_Externalcall for an ECI_SYNC                                */
/*                                                                          */
/****************************************************************************/
void EciSync (void)
{
   char            *Name = "ECI_SYNC";
   short           Rc;
   char            CommArea [ECI_SYNC_SIZE];

   Print ("%s test", Name);

   memset (CommArea, '\0', ECI_SYNC_SIZE);
   memset (&EciParms, 0, sizeof (ECI_PARMS));

   EciParms.eci_version                         = ECI_VERSION_1;
   EciParms.eci_call_type                       = ECI_SYNC;
   memcpy(&EciParms.eci_program_name, "EC01",   4);
   memcpy(&EciParms.eci_userid,       UserID,   8);
   memcpy(&EciParms.eci_password,     PassWd,   8);
   memcpy(&EciParms.eci_system_name,  Server,   8);
   EciParms.eci_commarea                        = CommArea;
   EciParms.eci_commarea_length                 = ECI_SYNC_SIZE;
   EciParms.eci_extend_mode                     = ECI_NO_EXTEND;
   EciParms.eci_luw_token                       = ECI_LUW_NEW;
```

Client Program for the ECI Sample

```c
      EciParms.eci_timeout                     = 0;

      Rc = CICS_ExternalCall (&EciParms);
      Response(Name, Rc, EciParms.eci_abend_code);

      if (Rc == ECI_NO_ERROR)
      {
         CommArea[(ECI_SYNC_SIZE-1)] = '\0';
         Print ("CommArea Returned: %s", CommArea);
      } /* endif */

      Print ("%s test complete", Name);

} /* EciSync */

/*************************************************************************/
/* EciASync                                                              */
/*************************************************************************/
/* Issue a CICS_Externalcall for an ECI_ASYNC                            */
/*                                                                       */
/*************************************************************************/
void EciAsync (void)
{
   char           *Name = "ECI_ASYNC";
   short          Rc;
   char           CommArea [ECI_SYNC_SIZE];

   Print ("%s test", Name);

   memset (CommArea, '\0', ECI_SYNC_SIZE);
   memset (&EciParms, 0, sizeof (ECI_PARMS));

   EciParms.eci_version                        = ECI_VERSION_1;
   EciParms.eci_call_type                      = ECI_ASYNC;
   memcpy(&EciParms.eci_program_name, "ECO1",   4);
   memcpy(&EciParms.eci_userid,        UserID,  8);
   memcpy(&EciParms.eci_password,      PassWd,  8);
   memcpy(&EciParms.eci_system_name,   Server,  8);
   EciParms.eci_commarea                       = CommArea;
   EciParms.eci_commarea_length                = ECI_SYNC_SIZE;
   EciParms.eci_extend_mode                    = ECI_NO_EXTEND;
   EciParms.eci_luw_token                      = ECI_LUW_NEW;
   EciParms.eci_timeout                        = 0;
   EciParms.eci_callback = (CICS_EciNotify_t)CallBackProc;

   Rc = CICS_ExternalCall (&EciParms);

   Print ("%s test complete", Name);

} /* EciAsync */

/*************************************************************************/
/* EciGetReply                                                           */
/*************************************************************************/
/* Issue a CICS_Externalcall for an ECI_GET_REPLY                        */
/*                                                                       */
/*************************************************************************/
void EciGetReply (void)
{
   char           *Name = "ECI_GET_REPLY";
   short          Rc;
```

```
            char              CommArea [ECI_SYNC_SIZE];

            Print ("%s called", Name);

            memset (CommArea, '\0', ECI_SYNC_SIZE);
            memset (&EciParms, 0, sizeof (ECI_PARMS));

            EciParms.eci_version                           = ECI_VERSION_1;
            EciParms.eci_call_type                         = ECI_GET_REPLY;
            memcpy(&EciParms.eci_userid,       UserID,     8);
            memcpy(&EciParms.eci_password,     PassWd,     8);
            memcpy(&EciParms.eci_system_name,  Server,     8);
            EciParms.eci_commarea                          = CommArea;
            EciParms.eci_commarea_length                   = ECI_SYNC_SIZE;
            EciParms.eci_extend_mode                       = ECI_NO_EXTEND;
            EciParms.eci_luw_token                         = ECI_LUW_NEW;
            EciParms.eci_timeout                           = 0;

            Rc = CICS_ExternalCall (&EciParms);

            if (Rc == ECI_NO_ERROR)
            {
               CommArea[(ECI_SYNC_SIZE-1)] = '\0';
               Print ("CommArea Returned: %s", CommArea);
            } /* endif */

            Print ("%s complete", Name);

            Print ("---------------------------");
            Print ("ECI Sample Program Completed");

         } /* EciGetReply */

         /******************************************************************/
         /* CallBackProc                                                   */
         /******************************************************************/
         /* This is the function that was registered on the ECI_ASYNC call. */
         /* It gets called when there is a reply ready.                    */
         /******************************************************************/
         void CICSEXIT CallBackProc (cics_ushort_t idx)
         {
            /* In the OS/2 Presentation Manager application, it puts a message
               to the system message queue, the main body of the PM application
               will process these messages in the queue and will know the reply
               from the CICS server is ready.
            */
            /* In non-PM application, it could change value of a global variable,
               the main body of the application will evaluate the value of this
               variable will know the reply is ready.
            */

            :::

         } /* CallBackProc */
```

Server Program for the ECI Sample

```c
/**********************************************************************/
/*                                                                    */
/* MODULE NAME         EC01.CCS                                       */
/*                                                                    */
/* DESCRIPTIVE NAME    CICS External Call Interface                   */
/*                     Server Program - C Source                      */
/*                                                                    */
/* Statement:          17H7605, 17H7616, 17H7627, 17H7638             */
/*                     (C) Copyright IBM Corporation 1994             */
/*                                                                    */
/* Status:             Version 1 Release 0                            */
/*                                                                    */
/**********************************************************************/

/* Structure to build up the data and time to be output. Note that */
/* the front end ECI calling program expects to pass and receive a */
/* comm area of size 18 bytes.                                     */
typedef struct
{
/* char DateArea??(8??);       */
   char DateArea[8];
   char Space;
/* char TimeArea??(8??);       */
   char TimeArea[8];
   char LowValue;
} CommAreaDetail;

/* Transaction entry point, to be invoked by CICS. No parameters. */
void main( void )
{

    /* Variable to recieve response codes from CICS. */
    long RespCode;

    /* Variable to hold the number of milliseconds returned by CICS. */
    /* change the original ??( to [ and the ??) to ]
    char AbsTime??(8??);
    */
    char AbsTime[8];

    /* Declare pointer to the comm area. */
    CommAreaDetail * pConsoleMessage;

    /* Get addressability to the EIB to validate the expected comm  */
    /* area length. If the comm area length was not of the expected */
    /* length, write an error message to the console and exit,      */
    /* otherwise get the date and time to pass back.                */
    EXEC CICS ADDRESS EIB( dfheiptr );

    /* Get addressability to the comm area. */
    EXEC CICS ADDRESS
        COMMAREA( pConsoleMessage );

    /* Initialise the padding character and the terminating null in */
    /* the ConsoleMessage structure.                                */
    pConsoleMessage->Space = ' ';
    pConsoleMessage->LowValue = '\0';
```

```
/* Get the number of milliseconds from CICS. */
EXEC CICS ASKTIME ABSTIME( AbsTime );

/* Use CICS to convert the elapsed milliseconds to a displayable */
/* date and time format.                                         */
EXEC CICS FORMATTIME
    ABSTIME( AbsTime )
    DDMMYY( pConsoleMessage->DateArea )
    DATESEP( '/' )
    TIME( pConsoleMessage->TimeArea )
    TIMESEP( ':' );

/* Write the date and time to the CICS message log. Note that 1    */
/* is subtracted from the size as a terminating 0 is not required */
/* on the CICS call.                                               */

/* This function is not supported by CICS/6000
EXEC CICS WRITE OPERATOR
    TEXT( pConsoleMessage )
    TEXTLENGTH( sizeof(CommAreaDetail)-1 )
    RESP( RespCode );
*/

EXEC CICS WRITEQ TD
    QUEUE( "CSMT" )
    FROM( pConsoleMessage )
    LENGTH( sizeof(CommAreaDetail)-1 )
    RESP( RespCode );

/* Transaction completed, return control to CICS */
EXEC CICS RETURN;
}
```

Client Program for the EPI Sample

This section lists only the code relevant to the EPI calls.

```c
/**********************************************************************/
/*                                                                    */
/* MODULE NAME        EPIC01.C                                        */
/*                                                                    */
/* DESCRIPTIVE NAME   CICS External Presentation Interface            */
/*                    OS/2 PM Sample - C Source                       */
/*                                                                    */
/* Statement:         (C) Copyright IBM Corporation 1994, 17H7627     */
/*                                                                    */
/* Status:            Version 1 Release 0                             */
/*                                                                    */
/**********************************************************************/

/**********************************************************************/
/* HEADER FILES                                                       */
/**********************************************************************/

   :::

#include <cics_epi.h>

   :::

/**********************************************************************/
/* DEFINES                                                            */
/**********************************************************************/
   #define BUFFER_SIZE 50                 /* Datastream buffer size */
   #define LIST_SIZE   10                 /* Used by EpiListSystems - maximum */

/**********************************************************************/
/* Global Variables                                                   */
/**********************************************************************/
   CICS_EpiSystem_t    ServerList[LIST_SIZE];
   CICS_EpiDetails_t   Details;           /* Details of autoinstalled */
   CICS_EpiEventData_t EventData;         /* Receives EPI event details */
   term_index_t        TermIndex;                 /* EPI Terminal Index */
   char                *DataPointer;

   typedef struct                                 /* Format of 3270 datastream */
   {
      char              AIDKey;
      char              Byte0;
      char              Byte1;
      char              TransactionCode[4];
      char              Data[BUFFER_SIZE];
   } DataStream;
   DataStream          TestData;

   BOOL                MoreEvents = FALSE;
/**********************************************************************/
/**********************************************************************/
/* main() - Sample Entry Point                                        */
/**********************************************************************/
/**********************************************************************/
int main(void)
{

   :::

} /* main */
```

```c
/***************************************************************************/
/* Initialize                                                              */
/***************************************************************************/
/* Issue a CICS_EpiInitialize call                                         */
/*                                                                         */
/***************************************************************************/
void Initialize (void)
{
   char           *Name = "CICS_EpiInitialize()";
   short          Rc;

   Print ("EPI Sample Program");
   Print ("------------------");

   Print ("%s test", Name);

   Rc = CICS_EpiInitialize (CICS_EPI_VERSION_100);

} /* Initialize */

/***************************************************************************/
/* ListSystems                                                             */
/***************************************************************************/
/* Issue a CICS_EpiListSystems call                                        */
/*                                                                         */
/***************************************************************************/
void ListSystems (void)
{
   char           *Name = "CICS_EpiListSystems()";
   short          Rc;
   unsigned short Count;
   unsigned short i;

   Print ("%s test", Name);

   Count = LIST_SIZE;
   Rc = CICS_EpiListSystems (NULL,         /* Get array of connectable systems */
                             &Count,
                             ServerList);

   if (Rc == CICS_EPI_NORMAL)
   {
      for (i = 0; i < Count; i++)
      {
         Print ("Server system is \"%s\" (\"%s\")",
                ServerList[i].SystemName,
                ServerList[i].Description);
      } /* endwhile */
   } /* endif */

} /* ListSystems */

/***************************************************************************/
/* AddTerminal                                                             */
/***************************************************************************/
/* Issue a CICS_EpiAddTerminal call                                        */
/*                                                                         */
/***************************************************************************/
void AddTerminal (void)
{
   char           *Name = "CICS_EpiAddTerminal()";
   short          Rc;

   Print ("%s test", Name);

   Rc = CICS_EpiAddTerminal (NULL,
                             ServerList[0].SystemName,
                             NULL,                    /* Autoinstall the terminal */
                             NULL,                    /* Use supplied TCT model  */
```

Client Program for the EPI Sample

```
                            (CICS_EpiNotify_t)&CallBackProc,
                            &Details,
                            &TermIndex);                /* Receives TermIndex */

} /* AddTerminal */

/***************************************************************************/
/* StartTransaction                                                        */
/***************************************************************************/
/* Issue a CICS_EpiStartTran call, to the trasaction EP01, passing a string */
/* of data                                                                 */
/***************************************************************************/
void StartTransaction (void)
{
    char            *Name = "CICS_EpiStartTran()";
    short           Rc;

    Print ("%s test", Name);

    TestData.AIDKey = 0x27;                             /* ENTER key */
    TestData.Byte0  = 0x20;                             /* Buffer address byte 0 */
    TestData.Byte1  = 0x20;                             /* Buffer address byte 1 */
    memcpy (TestData.TransactionCode, "EP01",4);        /* Transaction EP01 */
    memcpy (TestData.Data, "HELLO SERVER",BUFFER_SIZE); /* Put in data */
    DataPointer = &TestData.AIDKey;  /* Point to beginning of the  datastream */

    Rc = CICS_EpiStartTran (TermIndex,
                            NULL,
                            DataPointer,
                            sizeof (TestData));

} /* StartTransaction */

/***************************************************************************/
/* EventSend                                                               */
/***************************************************************************/
/* Some data has been sent, so display it                                  */
/*                                                                         */
/***************************************************************************/
void EventSend (void)
{
    int             Index;
    int             TheSize = EventData.Size;
    char            Output[255];

    if (TheSize > 0)
    {
      memset (Output, 0, 255);
      Print ("The following message was received from CICS:");
                                    /* Don't print the control chars */
      for (Index = 2; Index < TheSize; Index++)
      {
         strncpy (Output+Index-2, DataPointer+Index,1);
      } /* endfor */
      Print (Output);
    } /* endif */

} /* EventSend */

/***************************************************************************/
/* EventConverse                                                           */
/***************************************************************************/
/* Issue a CICS_EpiReply call, to the transaction EP01, with another string */
/*                                                                         */
/***************************************************************************/
void EventConverse (void)
{
    char            *Name = "CICS_EpiReply()";
    short           Rc;
```

Client Program for the EPI Sample

```c
    Print ("%s test", Name);

    EventSend ();      /* This allows for 6000 server which gets the data first */
    TestData.AIDKey = 0x27;                                /* ENTER key */
    TestData.Byte0  = 0x20;                     /* Buffer address byte 0 */
    TestData.Byte1  = 0x20;                     /* Buffer address byte 1 */
    memcpy (TestData.TransactionCode, "EP01",4);        /* Transaction EP01 */
    memcpy (TestData.Data, "This is my reply",BUFFER_SIZE);    /* Put in data */
    DataPointer = &TestData.AIDKey;  /* Point to beginning of the  datastream */

    Rc = CICS_EpiReply (TermIndex,
                        DataPointer,
                        sizeof (TestData));

    Print ("Reply sent, Rc=%d", Rc);

} /* EventConverse */
/**************************************************************************/
/* DelTerminal                                                            */
/**************************************************************************/
/* Issue a CICS_EpiDelTerminal call                                       */
/*                                                                        */
/**************************************************************************/
void DelTerminal (void)
{
    char            *Name = "CICS_EpiDelTerminal()";
    short           Rc;

    Print ("%s test", Name);

    Rc = CICS_EpiDelTerminal (TermIndex);

} /* DelTerminal */

/**************************************************************************/
/* Terminate                                                              */
/**************************************************************************/
/* Issue a CICS_EpiTerminate call                                         */
/*                                                                        */
/**************************************************************************/
void Terminate(void)
{
    short           Rc;
    char            *Name = "CICS_EpiTerminate()";

    Print ("%s test", Name);

    Rc = CICS_EpiTerminate();

    Print ("---------------------------");
    Print ("EPI Sample Program Completed");

} /* Terminate */

/**************************************************************************/
/* GetEvent                                                               */
/**************************************************************************/
/* Issue a CICS_EpiGetEvent, the reply will indicate what to do next      */
/*                                                                        */
/**************************************************************************/
cics_ubyte_t GetEvent (void)
{
    char            *Name = "CICS_EpiGetEvent()";
    short           Rc;
    cics_ubyte_t    State;

    Print ("%s call", Name);
```

Client Program for the EPI Sample

```
        EventData.Data = DataPointer;
        EventData.Size = sizeof (TestData);
        Rc = CICS_EpiGetEvent (TermIndex,
                              CICS_EPI_WAIT,
                              &EventData);

        if (Rc == CICS_EPI_ERR_MORE_EVENTS)
        {
           MoreEvents = TRUE;
        } /* endif */

        if ( (Rc == CICS_EPI_NORMAL) ]] (Rc == CICS_EPI_ERR_MORE_EVENTS) )
        {
           State = EventData.Event;
        } /* endif */

        Print ("Event (%d) retrieved, Rc= (%d)", EventData.Event, Rc);
        return State;

} /* GetEvent */
/****************************************************************************/
/* CallBackProc                                                             */
/****************************************************************************/
/* This is the function that was registered on the CICS_EpiAddTerminal call. */
/* It gets called when there is an event pending.                            */
/****************************************************************************/
void CICSEXIT CallBackProc (cics_ushort_t idx)
{

     /* In the OS/2 Presentation Manager application, it puts a message
        to the system message queue, the main body of the PM application
        will process these messages in the queue and will know the event
        pending.
     */

     /* In non-PM application, it could change value of a global variable,
        the main body of the application will evaluate the value of this
        variable will know the event pending.
     */

     :::

} /* CallBackProc */
```

Server Program for the EPI Sample

```
***********************************************************************
*                                                                     *
* MODULE NAME       EP01.CCP                                          *
*                                                                     *
* DESCRIPTIVE NAME  CICS External Presentation Interface              *
*                   Server Transaction - COBOL Source                 *
*                                                                     *
* Statement:        17H7605, 17H7616, 17H7627, 17H7638                *
*                   (C) Copyright IBM Corporation 1994                *
*                                                                     *
* Status:           Version 1 Release 0                               *
*                                                                     *
***********************************************************************

 IDENTIFICATION DIVISION.
 PROGRAM-ID. EP01.

 ENVIRONMENT DIVISION.
 DATA DIVISION.

 WORKING-STORAGE SECTION.
 01  OUTBOUND-DATA             PIC X(32).
 01  INBOUND-DATA.
     02  IN-TRANSACTION-CODE   PIC X(4).
     02  IN-MESSAGE            PIC X(50).
 01  WORKING-LENGTHS.
     02      INBOUND-DATA-LENGTH-1  PIC S9(4) COMP.
     02      INBOUND-DATA-LENGTH-2  PIC S9(4) COMP.
 LINKAGE SECTION.

 PROCEDURE DIVISION.
*********************************************************************
*    Main section                                                   *
*********************************************************************
 A-MAIN SECTION.
 A1.
     PERFORM Y-INITIALISATION.
     PERFORM B-RECEIVE-INITIAL-DATA.
     PERFORM C-SEND-MSG-TO-CLIENT.
     PERFORM D-RECEIVE-CLIENT-MSG.
     PERFORM Z-TERMINATE.
 A-END.
     EXIT.

*********************************************************************
*  Receive datastream passed from client with EpiStartTran.         *
*  Transaction code is in the first 4 bytes, display message        *
*  on the Message Log.                                              *
*********************************************************************
 B-RECEIVE-INITIAL-DATA SECTION.
 B1.
     EXEC CICS
         RECEIVE
         INTO(INBOUND-DATA)
         LENGTH(INBOUND-DATA-LENGTH-1)
         END-EXEC.
```

Appendix E. Sample ECI and EPI Source Code

Server Program for the EPI Sample

```
            * This command is not support by the CICS/6000.
            *
            *      EXEC CICS WRITE OPERATOR
            *                 TEXT(IN-MESSAGE)
            *                 TEXTLENGTH(LENGTH OF IN-MESSAGE)
            *                 END-EXEC.
                 EXEC CICS WRITEQ TD
                      QUEUE("CSMT")
                      FROM(IN-MESSAGE)
                      LENGTH(LENGTH OF IN-MESSAGE)
                      END-EXEC.
             B-END.
                 EXIT.

            *******************************************************************
            * Sends our message back to the client.                            *
            *******************************************************************
             C-SEND-MSG-TO-CLIENT SECTION.
             C1.
                 EXEC CICS
                      SEND
                      ERASE
                      FROM(OUTBOUND-DATA)
                      LENGTH(LENGTH OF OUTBOUND-DATA)
                      END-EXEC.
             C-END.
                 EXIT.

            *******************************************************************
            *  Clear buffer and set length, then                               *
            *  receives user keyed message from the client. No transaction*
            *  code at the beginning this time. Display message on the        *
            *  Message Log.                                                    *
            *******************************************************************
             D-RECEIVE-CLIENT-MSG SECTION.
             D1.
                 MOVE SPACES TO INBOUND-DATA.
                 MOVE 100 TO INBOUND-DATA-LENGTH-2.
             D2.
                 EXEC CICS
                      RECEIVE
                      INTO(INBOUND-DATA)
                      LENGTH(INBOUND-DATA-LENGTH-2)
                      END-EXEC.
             D3.
            * This command is not support by the CICS/6000.
            *
            *      EXEC CICS WRITE OPERATOR
            *                 TEXT(INBOUND-DATA)
            *                 TEXTLENGTH(LENGTH OF INBOUND-DATA)
            *                 END-EXEC.

                 EXEC CICS WRITEQ TD
                      QUEUE("CSMT")
                      FROM(INBOUND-DATA)
                      LENGTH(LENGTH OF INBOUND-DATA)
                      END-EXEC.
             D-END.
                 EXIT.
```

```
      ****************************************************************
      *  Set up big enough length value and message we'll send       *
      *  to the client.                                              *
      ****************************************************************
       Y-INITIALISATION SECTION.
       Y1.
           MOVE 100 TO INBOUND-DATA-LENGTH-1.
           MOVE "GREETINGS FROM TRANSACTION EP01" TO OUTBOUND-DATA.
       Y-END.
           EXIT.

      ****************************************************************
      *  Termination.                                                *
      ****************************************************************
       Z-TERMINATE SECTION.
       Z1.
           EXEC CICS RETURN END-EXEC.
           GOBACK.
       Z-END.
           EXIT.
```

Server Program for the EPI Sample

F

CM/2 .NDF and APPC NS/Windows NSD.INI Files

This appendix contains the network definition files used for the SNA configurations.

CM/2 .NDF files:

- Chapter 3, "CICS/ESA • CICS Client for OS/2 Using CM/2," on page 29
- Chapter 6, "CICS/VSE • SDLC • CICS Client for OS/2 Using CM/2," on page 77
- Chapter 9, "CICS/VSE • CM/2 APPN Gateway • APPC NS/Windows," on page 131

APPC Networking Services for Windows NSD.INI files:

- Chapter 4, "CICS/ESA • Token-Ring • Client Using APPC NS/Windows," on page 49
- Chapter 7, "CICS/VSE • SDLC • Client Using APPC NS/Windows," on page 95
- Chapter 8, "CICS/VSE • Ethernet • Client Using APPC NS/Windows," on page 111
- Chapter 9, "CICS/VSE • CM/2 APPN Gateway • APPC NS/Windows," on page 131

CM/2 .NDF File: CICS/ESA-CICS Client for OS/2 Using CM/2

This .NDF file contains definitions used for the configuration in Chapter 3, "CICS/ESA • CICS Client for OS/2 Using CM/2," on page 29.

```
DEFINE_LOCAL_CP   FQ_CP_NAME(USIBMSC.SJA2072 )
                  CP_ALIAS(SJA2072 )
                  NAU_ADDRESS(INDEPENDENT_LU)
                  NODE_TYPE(EN)
                  NODE_ID(X'05DA2072')
                  NW_FP_SUPPORT(NONE)
                  HOST_FP_SUPPORT(YES)
                  HOST_FP_LINK_NAME(CICSESA )
                  MAX_COMP_LEVEL(NONE)
                  MAX_COMP_TOKENS(0);

DEFINE_LOGICAL_LINK  LINK_NAME(CICSESA )
                  DESCRIPTION(Token Ring connection via 3745 network controller)
                  FQ_ADJACENT_CP_NAME(USIBMSC.SCMCICSA )
                  ADJACENT_NODE_TYPE(LEN)
                  DLC_NAME(IBMTRNET)
                  ADAPTER_NUMBER(0)
                  DESTINATION_ADDRESS(X'40000821020004')
                  ETHERNET_FORMAT(NO)
                  CP_CP_SESSION_SUPPORT(NO)
                  ACTIVATE_AT_STARTUP(YES)
                  LIMITED_RESOURCE(USE_ADAPTER_DEFINITION)
                  LINK_STATION_ROLE(USE_ADAPTER_DEFINITION)
                  SOLICIT_SSCP_SESSION(YES)
                  NODE_ID(X'05DA2072')
                  MAX_ACTIVATION_ATTEMPTS(USE_ADAPTER_DEFINITION)
                  USE_PUNAME_AS_CPNAME(NO)
                  EFFECTIVE_CAPACITY(USE_ADAPTER_DEFINITION)
                  COST_PER_CONNECT_TIME(USE_ADAPTER_DEFINITION)
                  COST_PER_BYTE(USE_ADAPTER_DEFINITION)
                  SECURITY(USE_ADAPTER_DEFINITION)
                  PROPAGATION_DELAY(USE_ADAPTER_DEFINITION)
                  USER_DEFINED_1(USE_ADAPTER_DEFINITION)
                  USER_DEFINED_2(USE_ADAPTER_DEFINITION)
                  USER_DEFINED_3(USE_ADAPTER_DEFINITION);

DEFINE_LOCAL_LU   LU_NAME(SJA2072I)
                  DESCRIPTION(Local LU)
                  LU_ALIAS(SJA2072I)
                  NAU_ADDRESS(INDEPENDENT_LU);
```

```
            DEFINE_PARTNER_LU    FQ_PARTNER_LU_NAME(USIBMSC.SCMCICSA )
                                 DESCRIPTION(Partner definition for CICS/ESA V3.3 region)
                                 PARTNER_LU_ALIAS(SCMCICSA)
                                 PARTNER_LU_UNINTERPRETED_NAME(SCMCICSA)
                                 MAX_MC_LL_SEND_SIZE(32767)
                                 CONV_SECURITY_VERIFICATION(NO)
                                 PARALLEL_SESSION_SUPPORT(YES);

            DEFINE_PARTNER_LU_LOCATION  FQ_PARTNER_LU_NAME(USIBMSC.SCMCICSA )
                                        DESCRIPTION(Partner definition for CICS/ESA V3.3 region)
                                        WILDCARD_ENTRY(NO)
                                        FQ_OWNING_CP_NAME(USIBMSC.SCMCICSA )
                                        LOCAL_NODE_NN_SERVER(NO);

            DEFINE_MODE    MODE_NAME(LU62APPB)
                           DESCRIPTION(Mode name LU62APPB defined with 8 sessions)
                           COS_NAME(#CONNECT)
                           DEFAULT_RU_SIZE(YES)
                           RECEIVE_PACING_WINDOW(7)
                           MAX_NEGOTIABLE_SESSION_LIMIT(32767)
                           PLU_MODE_SESSION_LIMIT(8)
                           MIN_CONWINNERS_SOURCE(4)
                           COMPRESSION_NEED(PROHIBITED)
                           PLU_SLU_COMPRESSION(NONE)
                           SLU_PLU_COMPRESSION(NONE);

            DEFINE_DEFAULTS  IMPLICIT_INBOUND_PLU_SUPPORT(YES)
                             DEFAULT_MODE_NAME(BLANK)
                             MAX_MC_LL_SEND_SIZE(32767)
                             DIRECTORY_FOR_INBOUND_ATTACHES(*)
                             DEFAULT_TP_OPERATION(NONQUEUED_AM_STARTED)
                             DEFAULT_TP_PROGRAM_TYPE(BACKGROUND)
                             DEFAULT_TP_CONV_SECURITY_RQD(NO)
                             MAX_HELD_ALERTS(10);

            DEFINE_TP  TP_NAME(CRSR)
                       DESCRIPTION(TP for ATI support. Filename is: CCLSNOTP.EXE)
                       PIP_ALLOWED(NO)
                       FILESPEC(C:\CICSCLI\BIN\CCLSNOTP.EXE)
                       PARM_STRING(CRSR)
                       CONVERSATION_TYPE(ANY_TYPE)
                       CONV_SECURITY_RQD(NO)
                       SYNC_LEVEL(EITHER)
                       TP_OPERATION(NONQUEUED_AM_STARTED)
                       PROGRAM_TYPE(BACKGROUND)
                       RECEIVE_ALLOCATE_TIMEOUT(INFINITE);

            START_ATTACH_MANAGER;

            CNOS       LOCAL_LU_ALIAS(SJA2072I)
                       FQ_PARTNER_LU_NAME(USIBMSC.SCMCICSA)
                       MODE_NAME(LU62APPB)
                       SET_NEGOTIABLE(NO)
                       PLU_MODE_SESSION_LIMIT(8)
                       MIN_CONWINNERS_SOURCE(4)
                       MIN_CONWINNERS_TARGET(4)
                       AUTO_ACTIVATE(4);
```

CM/2 .NDF File: CICS/VSE-SDLC-CICS Client for OS/2 Using CM/2

This .NDF file contains definitions used for the configuration in Chapter 6, "CICS/VSE • SDLC • CICS Client for OS/2 Using CM/2," on page 77.

```
DEFINE_LOCAL_CP      FQ_CP_NAME(DEIBMIPF.CCLICAPU)
                     CP_ALIAS(CCLICAPU)
                     NAU_ADDRESS(INDEPENDENT_LU)
                     NODE_TYPE(EN)
                     NODE_ID(X'05D00000')
                     NW_FP_SUPPORT(NONE)
                     HOST_FP_SUPPORT(YES)
                     HOST_FP_LINK_NAME(HOST0001)
                     MAX_COMP_LEVEL(NONE)
                     MAX_COMP_TOKENS(0);

DEFINE_LOGICAL_LINK  LINK_NAME(HOST0001)
                     FQ_ADJACENT_CP_NAME(DEIBMIPF.IPFV2B    )
                     ADJACENT_NODE_TYPE(LEN)
                     DLC_NAME(SDLC    )
                     ADAPTER_NUMBER(0)
                     DESTINATION_ADDRESS(X'FF')
                     CP_CP_SESSION_SUPPORT(NO)
                     INIT_WITH_SNRM(NO)
                     ACTIVATE_AT_STARTUP(NO)
                     LIMITED_RESOURCE(USE_ADAPTER_DEFINITION)
                     LINK_STATION_ROLE(USE_ADAPTER_DEFINITION)
                     SOLICIT_SSCP_SESSION(YES)
                     MAX_ACTIVATION_ATTEMPTS(USE_ADAPTER_DEFINITION)
                     USE_PUNAME_AS_CPNAME(NO)
                     EFFECTIVE_CAPACITY(USE_ADAPTER_DEFINITION)
                     COST_PER_CONNECT_TIME(USE_ADAPTER_DEFINITION)
                     COST_PER_BYTE(USE_ADAPTER_DEFINITION)
                     SECURITY(USE_ADAPTER_DEFINITION)
                     PROPAGATION_DELAY(USE_ADAPTER_DEFINITION)
                     USER_DEFINED_1(USE_ADAPTER_DEFINITION)
                     USER_DEFINED_2(USE_ADAPTER_DEFINITION)
                     USER_DEFINED_3(USE_ADAPTER_DEFINITION);

DEFINE_LOCAL_LU      LU_NAME(CCLICALU)
                     LU_ALIAS(CCLICALU)
                     NAU_ADDRESS(INDEPENDENT_LU);

DEFINE_PARTNER_LU    FQ_PARTNER_LU_NAME(DEIBMIPF.CICSSA22)
                     PARTNER_LU_ALIAS(CICSSA22)
                     PARTNER_LU_UNINTERPRETED_NAME(CICSSA22)
                     MAX_MC_LL_SEND_SIZE(32767)
                     CONV_SECURITY_VERIFICATION(NO)
                     PARALLEL_SESSION_SUPPORT(YES);

DEFINE_PARTNER_LU_LOCATION  FQ_PARTNER_LU_NAME(DEIBMIPF.CICSSA22)
                            WILDCARD_ENTRY(NO)
                            FQ_OWNING_CP_NAME(DEIBMIPF.IPFV2B    )
                            LOCAL_NODE_NN_SERVER(NO);

DEFINE_DEFAULTS      IMPLICIT_INBOUND_PLU_SUPPORT(YES)
                     DEFAULT_MODE_NAME(BLANK)
                     MAX_MC_LL_SEND_SIZE(32767)
                     DIRECTORY_FOR_INBOUND_ATTACHES(*)
                     DEFAULT_TP_OPERATION(NONQUEUED_AM_STARTED)
                     DEFAULT_TP_PROGRAM_TYPE(BACKGROUND)
                     DEFAULT_TP_CONV_SECURITY_RQD(NO)
                     MAX_HELD_ALERTS(10);
```

```
START_ATTACH_MANAGER;

CNOS    LOCAL_LU_ALIAS(CCLICALU)
        FQ_PARTNER_LU_NAME(DEIBMIPF.CICSSA22)
        MODE_NAME(BLANK)
        SET_NEGOTIABLE(NO)
        PLU_MODE_SESSION_LIMIT(8)
        MIN_CONWINNERS_SOURCE(4)
        MIN_CONWINNERS_TARGET(4)
        AUTO_ACTIVATE(4);
```

CM/2 .NDF File: CICS/VSE-CM/2 APPN Gateway-APPC NS/Windows

This .NDF file contains definitions used for the configuration in Chapter 9, "CICS/VSE • CM/2 APPN Gateway • APPC NS/Windows," on page 131.

```
DEFINE_LOCAL_CP     FQ_CP_NAME(DEIBMIPF.CCLICAPU)
                    CP_ALIAS(CCLICAPU)
                    NAU_ADDRESS(INDEPENDENT_LU)
                    NODE_TYPE(NN)
                    NODE_ID(X'05D00000')
                    NW_FP_SUPPORT(NONE)
                    HOST_FP_SUPPORT(YES)
                    HOST_FP_LINK_NAME(HOST0001)
                    MAX_COMP_LEVEL(NONE)
                    MAX_COMP_TOKENS(0);

DEFINE_LOGICAL_LINK LINK_NAME(HOST0001)
                    FQ_ADJACENT_CP_NAME(DEIBMIPF.IPFV2B  )
                    ADJACENT_NODE_TYPE(LEN)
                    DLC_NAME(SDLC   )
                    ADAPTER_NUMBER(0)
                    DESTINATION_ADDRESS(X'FF')
                    CP_CP_SESSION_SUPPORT(NO)
                    INIT_WITH_SNRM(NO)
                    ACTIVATE_AT_STARTUP(NO)
                    LIMITED_RESOURCE(USE_ADAPTER_DEFINITION)
                    LINK_STATION_ROLE(USE_ADAPTER_DEFINITION)
                    SOLICIT_SSCP_SESSION(YES)
                    MAX_ACTIVATION_ATTEMPTS(USE_ADAPTER_DEFINITION)
                    USE_PUNAME_AS_CPNAME(NO)
                    EFFECTIVE_CAPACITY(USE_ADAPTER_DEFINITION)
                    COST_PER_CONNECT_TIME(USE_ADAPTER_DEFINITION)
                    COST_PER_BYTE(USE_ADAPTER_DEFINITION)
                    SECURITY(USE_ADAPTER_DEFINITION)
                    PROPAGATION_DELAY(USE_ADAPTER_DEFINITION)
                    USER_DEFINED_1(USE_ADAPTER_DEFINITION)
                    USER_DEFINED_2(USE_ADAPTER_DEFINITION)
                    USER_DEFINED_3(USE_ADAPTER_DEFINITION);

DEFINE_PARTNER_LU   FQ_PARTNER_LU_NAME(DEIBMIPF.CICSSA22)
                    PARTNER_LU_ALIAS(CICSSA22)
                    PARTNER_LU_UNINTERPRETED_NAME(CICSSA22)
                    MAX_MC_LL_SEND_SIZE(32767)
                    CONV_SECURITY_VERIFICATION(NO)
                    PARALLEL_SESSION_SUPPORT(YES);

DEFINE_PARTNER_LU_LOCATION  FQ_PARTNER_LU_NAME(DEIBMIPF.CICSSA22)
                            WILDCARD_ENTRY(NO)
                            FQ_OWNING_CP_NAME(DEIBMIPF.IPFV2B  )
```

```
                              LOCAL_NODE_NN_SERVER(YES);

         DEFINE_DEFAULTS  IMPLICIT_INBOUND_PLU_SUPPORT(YES)
                          DEFAULT_MODE_NAME(BLANK)
                          MAX_MC_LL_SEND_SIZE(32767)
                          DIRECTORY_FOR_INBOUND_ATTACHES(*)
                          DEFAULT_TP_OPERATION(NONQUEUED_AM_STARTED)
                          DEFAULT_TP_PROGRAM_TYPE(BACKGROUND)
                          DEFAULT_TP_CONV_SECURITY_RQD(NO)
                          MAX_HELD_ALERTS(10);

         START_ATTACH_MANAGER;
```

APPC Networking Services for Windows NSD.INI File in a Token-Ring Environment

This NSD.INI file contains definitions used for the configuration in Chapter 4, "CICS/ESA • Token-Ring • Client Using APPC NS/Windows," on page 49.

```
[Configuration]
DLCTYPE=LAN
LANGUAGE=2924
STARTPROGRAMLAUNCHER=TRUE
LOCALLUNAME=USIBMSC.SJA2072I
NODEID=05DA2072
DIRECTORY=C:\NSW\

[LAN]
TRLD1=CICSESA, 400008210200

[REMOTE]
SDDI=66

[MODES]
SNASVCMG= 512, 7, 2, 1
BLANK=  , 3, 8, 4
#BATCH=  , 3, 8, 4
#INTER=  , 7, 8, 4
QPCSUPP= 1024, 2, 32, 16
LU62APPB= 256, 7, 8, 4

[DEFINETP]
APINGD=C:\NSW\SAMPLES\APINGD.EXE, 120, 30, am_started,
ATELLD=C:\NSW\SAMPLES\ATELLD.EXE, 120, 30, am_started,
CRSR=C:\CICSCLI\BIN\CCLSNWTP.EXE, 0, 30, AM_STARTED, CRSR
```

APPC Networking Services for Windows NSD.INI File in an SDLC Environment

This NSD.INI file contains definitions used for the configuration in Chapter 7, "CICS/VSE • SDLC • Client Using APPC NS/Windows," on page 95.

```
[Configuration]
DLCTYPE=SDLC
LANGUAGE=2924
STARTPROGRAMLAUNCHER=TRUE
LOCALLUNAME=DEIBMIPF.CCLICALU
NODEID=07500000
DIRECTORY=C:\NSW\

[REMOTE]
SDLD=CCLICAPU, C1, , , , secondary,
SDDI=66
SDMT=NULMODEM
SDLT=NONSWTPP
ASPN=MPAO

[MODES]
SNASVCMG= 512, 7, 2, 1
BLANK= , 3, 8, 4
#BATCH= , 3, 8, 4
#INTER= , 7, 8, 4
QPCSUPP= 1024, 2, 32, 16

[DEFINETP]
APINGD=C:\NSW\SAMPLES\APINGD.EXE, 120, 30, am_started,
ATELLD=C:\NSW\SAMPLES\ATELLD.EXE, 120, 30, am_started,
```

APPC Networking Services for Windows NSD.INI File: CICS/VSE-Ethernet-APPC NS/Windows

This NSD.INI file contains definitions used for the configuration in Chapter 8, "CICS/VSE • Ethernet • Client Using APPC NS/Windows," on page 111.

```
[Configuration]
DLCTYPE=LAN
LANGUAGE=2924
STARTPROGRAMLAUNCHER=TRUE
LOCALLUNAME=DEIBMIPF.CCLXL001
NODEID=05DE000B
DIRECTORY=C:\NSW\

[LAN]
TRLD1=CICSVSE, 020004040820

[REMOTE]
SDDI=66

[MODES]
SNASVCMG= 512, 7, 2, 1
BLANK=  , 3, 8, 4
#BATCH=  , 3, 8, 4
#INTER=  , 7, 8, 4
QPCSUPP= 1024, 2, 32, 16

[DEFINETP]
APINGD=C:\NSW\SAMPLES\APINGD.EXE, 120, 30, am_started,
ATELLD=C:\NSW\SAMPLES\ATELLD.EXE, 120, 30, am_started,
```

APPC Networking Services for Windows NSD.INI File: CICS/VSE-CM/2 APPN Gateway-APPC NS/Windows

This NSD.INI file contains definitions used for the configuration in Chapter 9, "CICS/VSE • CM/2 APPN Gateway • APPC NS/Windows," on page 131.

```
[Configuration]
DLCTYPE=LAN
LANGUAGE=2924
STARTPROGRAMLAUNCHER=TRUE
LOCALLUNAME=DEIBMIPF.CCLICAL1
NODEID=07500000
DIRECTORY=C:\NSW\

[LAN]
TRLD1=CICSVSE, 10005A910821

[REMOTE]
SDDI=66
```

```
[MODES]
SNASVCMG= 512, 7, 2, 1
BLANK= , 3, 8, 4
#BATCH= , 3, 8, 4
#INTER= , 7, 8, 4
QPCSUPP= 1024, 2, 32, 16

[DEFINETP]
APINGD=C:\NSW\SAMPLES\APINGD.EXE, 120, 30, am_started,
ATELLD=C:\NSW\SAMPLES\ATELLD.EXE, 120, 30, am_started,
```

G

IBM 3172 Customization

VSE/ESA supports an Ethernet adapter through an IBM 3172 Interconnect Controller. If your VSE/ESA system is running as a guest machine under VM/ESA, the 3172 must be defined to VM/ESA. In our case, we used the IBM 9221 machine's **I/O configuration data set** (IOCDS) and VM/ESA R2.1's automatic device sensing and dynamic configuration capability. In our configuration, the VSE virtual machine, *V132A80K*, owns the IBM 3172.

The following steps must be taken to permit VSE/ESA to control the IBM 3172:

1. The IBM 3172 must be defined to the VSE machine. This involves:
   - An appropriate DEDICATE statement in the VM directory for V132A80k.
   - A change in the VSE IPL procedure.
2. The IBM 3172 Interconnect Control Program (ICP) must be configured to reflect its operating environment.

- In our case we used the customization parameters in Figure 88 on page 119.
3. VSE/VTAM must be customized adequately to provide for network access to and from the CICS/VSE server as shown in "VTAM" on page 115.

IOCDS and VM/ESA Definitions

In this section we present the IOCDS and VM/ESA definitions.

The IBM 3172 is a channel-attached device and is defined in the IBM 9221 IOCDS. Figure 212 shows the entries in the IOCDS that describe the IBM 3172.

```
CHPID PATH=((29)),TYPE=BL
CNTLUNIT CUNUMBR=3172,PATH=(29),UNIT=3172,UNITADD=((60,32)),      X
         SHARED=N,PROTOCOL=S4
IODEVICE ADDRESS=(2960,32),CUNUMBR=(3172),UNIT=3172
```

Figure 212. IBM 3172 IOCDS Entries

VM/ESA R2.1 uses dynamic configuration and automatic device sensing. Static device definition is not required. The statements shown in Figure 213 are included in the VM SYSTEM CONFIG file to activate and auto-sense device addresses 0000-FFFF during system initialization.

```
Devices,
   Online_at_IPL 0000-FFFF,
   Sensed        0000-FFFF
```

Figure 213. VM/ESA Auto-Sense Definitions in SYSTEM CONFIG File

VSE/ESA Definitions

For the IBM 3172 to be owned by VSE/ESA, it must be attached or dedicated to the VSE/ESA virtual machine. In our environment, we used the **DEDICATE** statement shown in Figure 214, where **2961** is the real address and **961** the virtual address.

```
USER V132A80K PASSWORD 0032M 64M G
  ACCOUNT V132A80K V132A80K
  OPTION MAXCON 150
  MACHINE ESA
  CONSOLE 0009 3215
      .
      .
  DEDICATE 960 2960
  DEDICATE 961 2961
      .
      .
```

Figure 214. VM Directory Entry for VSE/ESA Machine

The IBM 3172 is added using the IPL procedure as shown in Figure 215 . VSE/ESA is to treat it as a channel-to-channel adapter (CTCA). The device is not to be sensed at IPL time (EML). This mechanism guarantees that the device characteristics implied by CTCA are not changed dynamically at IPL time by VSE/ESA.

```
    CATALOG $IPLBOE.PROC REPLACE=YES
009,$$A$SUPX,VSIZE=120M,VIO=512K,VPOOL=128K,LOG
ADD 009,3277
ADD 00C,2540R
      .
      .
      .
ADD 960,CTCA,EML
ADD 961,CTCA,EML
      .
      .
ADD FFF,CONS
      .
      .
SVA SDL=300,GETVIS=768K,PSIZE=640K
```

Figure 215. VSE IPL Procedure to Add the IBM 3172

VSE/ESA Definitions

H Configuration Worksheets

In this appendix we provide worksheets for each configuration discussed in the book.

CICS/ESA • CICS Client for OS/2 Using CM/2

The following tables are associated with Chapter 3, "CICS/ESA • CICS Client for OS/2 Using CM/2," on page 29:

VTAM Definitions on the Server	Ref. Key	Your Value
XID (IDBLK+IDNUM)	1	
PU		
LU	2	
Logmode	3	
APPL	4	
NETID	5	

CICS/ESA V3.3 Definitions on the Server	Ref. Key	Your Value
ISC SIT override		
DFHISC group		
Applid	4	
Netname in the LU6.2 connection definition	2	
Modename in the LU6.2 sessions definition	3	

CM/2 Definitions on the Workstation	Ref. Key	Your Value
Network ID	5	
Local node name		
Local node ID	1	
LAN Destination Address		
Local LU	2	
Partner LU	4	
Mode name	3	
Transaction program (CRSR)		
CNOS (session establishment, optional)		

CICS/ESA • CICS Client for OS/2 Using CM/2

CICS Client for OS/2 CICSCLI.INI Definitions on the Workstation	Ref. Key	Your Value
Server		
Network.Netname	5,4	
Protocol		
LocalLUName	2	
Modename	3	
Driver		
DriverName		

Matching	VTAM	CICS/ESA V3.3	CM/2	CICSCLI.INI	Your Value
1	XID	-	Local node ID	-	
2	LU	Netname	Local LU	LocalLUName	
3	Logmode	Modename	Mode name	Modename	
4	APPL	Applid	Partner LU	Netname	
5	NETID	-	Network ID	Network	

Appendix H. Configuration Worksheets

CICS/ESA • Token-Ring • Client Using APPC NS/Windows

The following tables are associated with Chapter 4, "CICS/ESA • Token-Ring • Client Using APPC NS/Windows," on page 49:

VTAM Definitions on the Server	Ref. Key	Your Value
XID (IDBLK+IDNUM)	1	
PU		
LU	2	
Logmode	3	
APPL	4	

CICS/ESA V3.3 Definitions on the Server	Ref. Key	Your Value
ISC SIT override		
DFHISC group		
Applid	4	
Netname in the LU6.2 connection definition	2	
Modename in the LU6.2 sessions definition	3	

APPC NS/Windows Definitions on the Workstation	Ref. Key	Your Value
Network ID	5	
Local LU	2	
Connection Type		
Link Name		
LAN Destination Address		
Mode name	3	
Transaction program (CRSR)		
Node ID (in NSD.INI file)	1	
CNOS (session establishment, optional)		

CICS/ESA • Token-Ring • Client Using APPC NS/Windows

CICS Client for OS/2 CICSCLI.INI Definitions on the Workstation	Ref. Key	Your Value
Server		
Network.Netname	5,4	
Protocol		
LocalLUName	2	
Modename	3	
Driver		
DriverName		

Matching	VTAM	CICS/ESA V3.3	APPC NS/Windows	CICSCLI.INI	Your value
1	XID	-	Node ID	-	
2	LU	Netname	Local LU	LocalLUName	
3	Logmode	Modename	Mode name	Modename	
4	APPL	Applid	-	Netname	
5	-	-	Network ID	Network	

Appendix H. Configuration Worksheets

CICS/ESA • NetWare for SAA Gateway • CICS Clients

The following tables are associated with Chapter 5, "CICS/ESA • NetWare for SAA Gateway • CICS Clients," on page 65:

VTAM Definitions on the Server	Ref. Key	Your Value
NETID	1	
LU	2	
APPL	3	
Logmode	4	
XID	5	

CICS/ESA V3.3 Definitions on the Server	Ref. Key	Your Value
ISC SIT override		
DFHISC group		
Netname in the LU6.2 connection definition	2	
Applid	3	
Modename in the LU6.2 sessions definition	4	

NetWare for SAA Definitions on the Gateway	Ref. Key	Your Value
SNA Network ID	1	
BlockID/PUID	5	

CICS Client CICSCLI.INI Definitions on the Workstation	Ref. Key	Your Value
Server		
Netname	3	
Protocol		
LocalLUName	2	
Modename	4	
Driver		
DriverName		

Matching	VTAM	CICS/ESA V3.3	NWSAA	CICSCLI.INI	Your value
1	NETID	-	SNA Network ID	-	
2	LU	Netname	-	LocalLUName	
3	APPL	Applid	-	Netname	
4	Logmode	Modename	-	Modename	
5	XID	-	BlockID/PUID	-	

CICS/VSE • SDLC • CICS Client for OS/2 Using CM/2

The following tables are associated with
Chapter 6, "CICS/VSE • SDLC • CICS Client for OS/2 Using CM/2,"
on page 77:

VTAM Definitions on the Server	Ref. Key	Your Value
ADDR	1	
PU		
LU	2	
APPL	3	
NETID	4	

CICS/VSE V2.2 Definitions on the Server	Ref. Key	Your Value
ISC SIT override		
DFHISC group		
Applid	3	
Netname in the LU6.2 connection definition	2	

CM/2 Definitions on the Workstation	Ref. Key	Your Value
Local station address	1	
Network ID	4	
Local node name		
Local LU	2	
Partner LU	3	
Transaction program (CRSR)		
CNOS (session establishment, optional)		

CICS Client for OS/2 CICSCLI.INI Definitions on the Workstation	Ref. Key	Your Value
Server		
Network.Netname	4,3	
Protocol		
LocalLUName	2	
Driver		
DriverName		

Matching	VTAM	CICS/VSE V2.2	CM/2	CICSCLI.INI	Your value
1	ADDR	-	Local Station Address	-	
2	LU	Netname	Local LU	LocalLUName	
3	APPL	Applid	Partner LU	Netname	
4	NETID	-	Network ID	Network	

Appendix H. Configuration Worksheets

CICS/VSE • SDLC • Client Using APPC NS/Windows

The following tables are associated with Chapter 7, "CICS/VSE • SDLC • Client Using APPC NS/Windows," on page 95:

VTAM Definitions on the Server	Ref. Key	Your Value
PU		
ADDR	**1**	
LU	**2**	
APPL	**3**	
NETID	**4**	

CICS/VSE V2.2 Definitions on the Server	Ref. Key	Your Value
ISC SIT override		
DFHISC group		
Applid	**3**	
Netname in the LU6.2 connection definition	**2**	

APPC NS/Windows Definitions on the Workstation	Ref. Key	Your Value
Network ID	**4**	
Local LU name	**2**	
Connection Type		
Link Name		
Local Station Address	**1**	
Transaction program (CRSR)		

CICS Client for Windows CICSCLI.INI Definitions on the Workstation	Ref. Key	Your Value
Server		
Network.Netname	**4**,**3**	
Protocol		
LocalLUName	**2**	
Driver		
DriverName		

CICS/VSE • SDLC • Client Using APPC NS/Windows

Matching	VTAM	CICS/VSE V2.2	APPC NS/Windows	CICSCLI.INI	Your value
1	ADDR	-	Local Station Address	-	
2	LU	Netname	Local LU name	LocalLUName	
3	APPL	Applid	-	Netname	
4	NETID	-	Network ID	Network	

CICS/VSE • Ethernet • Client Using APPC NS/Windows

The following tables are associated with Chapter 8, "CICS/VSE • Ethernet • Client Using APPC NS/Windows," on page 111:

VTAM Definitions on the Server	Ref. Key	Your Value
CUADDR	1	
XID (IDBLK+IDNUM)	2	
PU		
LU	3	
APPL	4	
DIALNO	5	
NETID	7	

ICPR Definitions required in the 3172 Interconnect Controller	Ref. Key	Your Value
Node address	6	
Subchannel	1	

CICS/VSE V2.2 Definitions on the Server	Ref. Key	Your Value
ISC SIT override		
DFHISC group		
Applid	4	
Netname in the LU6.2 connection definition	3	

LAN Support Program Definitions on the Workstation	Ref. Key	Your Value
MAC address	5	

APPC NS/Windows Definitions on the Workstation	Ref. Key	Your Value
Network ID	7	
Local LU name	3	
Connection Type		
Link Name		
Remote Address	6	
Transaction program (CRSR)		
Node ID (in NSD.INI file)	2	

CICS Client for Windows CICSCLI.INI Definitions on the Workstation	Ref. Key	Your Value
Server		
Network.Netname	7,4	
Protocol		
LocalLUName	3	
Driver		
DriverName		

Matching	VTAM	ICP 3172	CICS/VSE V2.2	LAN Support Program	APPC NS/ Windows	CICSCLI. INI	Your value
1	CUADDR	Subchannel	-	-	-	-	
2	XID	-	-	-	Node ID	-	
3	LU	-	Netname	-	Local LU	LocalLUName	
4	APPL	-	Applid	-	-	Netname	
5	DIALNO	-	-	MAC address	-	-	
6	-	Node Address	-	-	Remote Address	-	
7	NETID	-	-	-	Network ID	Network	

Appendix H. Configuration Worksheets

CICS/VSE • CM/2 APPN Gateway • APPC NS/Windows

The following tables are associated with Chapter 9, "CICS/VSE • CM/2 APPN Gateway • APPC NS/Windows," on page 131:

VTAM Definitions on the Server	Ref. Key	Your Value
NETID	**1**	
ADDR	**2**	
PU		
LU	**3**	
APPL	**4**	

CICS/VSE V2.2 Definitions on the Server	Ref. Key	Your Value
ISC SIT override		
DFHISC group		
Applid	**4**	
Netname in the LU6.2 connection definition	**3**	

CM/2 Definitions on the Gateway	Ref. Key	Your Value
Local station address	**2**	
Local node name		
Partner network ID	**1**	
Partner LU	**4**	

APPC NS/Windows Definitions on the Client	Ref. Key	Your Value
Network ID	**1**	
Local LU name	**3**	
Connection Type		
Link Name		
Remote Address		

CICS Client for Windows CICSCLI.INI Definitions on the Workstation	Ref. Key	Your Value
Server		
Network.Netname	1,4	
Protocol		
LocalLUName	3	
Driver		
DriverName		

Matching	VTAM	CICS/VSE V2.2	CM/2	APPC NS/Windows	CICSCLI.INI	Your value
1	NETID	-	Partner network ID	Network ID	Network ID	
2	ADDR	-	Local station address	-	-	
3	LU	Netname	-	Local LU name	LocalLUName	
4	APPL	Applid	Partner LU	-	Netname	

Appendix H. Configuration Worksheets

CICS for OS/2 • CICS Client Using TCP/IP for OS/2

The following tables are associated with Chapter 10, "CICS for OS/2 • CICS Client Using TCP/IP for OS/2," on page 153:

TCP/IP Definitions on the Server Workstation	Ref. Key	Your Value
IP address of workstation	1	
IP address of Domain Nameserver	4	
IP address of router		
Subnet Mask		
Hostname	2	
Port number	3	

CICS for OS/2 Multi-user Definitions on the Server Workstation	Ref. Key	Your Value
TCP/IP Local Host Name	1 or 2	
TCP/IP Local Host Port	3	
Maximum TCP/IP Systems		

TCP/IP Definitions on the Client Workstation	Ref. Key	Your Value
IP address of workstation		
IP address of Domain Nameserver	4	
Subnet Mask		
IP address of router		

CICSCLI.INI Definitions for the CICS Client for OS/2 on the Client Workstation	Ref. Key	Your Value
Server		
Protocol		
Netname	1 or 2	
Port	3	
Driver		
DriverName		

Matching	TCP/IP on Server	CICS for OS/2 on Server	TCP/IP on Client	CICSCLI.INI on Client	Your Value
1	IP address	TCP/IP Local Host Name	-	Netname	
2	Hostname	TCP/IP Local Host Name	-	Netname	
3	Port number	TCP/IP Local Host Port	-	Port	
4	IP address of Domain Nameserver	-	IP address of Domain Nameserver	-	

CICS for OS/2 • CICS Client for Macintosh • TCP/IP

The following tables are associated with Chapter 11, "CICS for OS/2 • CICS Client for Macintosh • TCP/IP," on page 165:

TCP/IP for OS/2 V1.2.1 Definitions on the Server Workstation	Ref. Key	Your Value
IP address of workstation	1	
IP address of Domain Nameserver	4	
IP address of router		
Subnet Mask		
Hostname	2	
Port number	3	

CICS for OS/2 Multi-user Definitions on the Server Workstation	Ref. Key	Your Value
TCP/IP Local Host Name	1 or 2	
TCP/IP Local Host Port	3	
Maximum TCP/IP Systems		

MacTCP Definitions on the Client Workstation	Ref. Key	Your Value
IP address of workstation		
IP address of Domain Nameserver	4	
Subnet Mask		
Gateway Address (IP address of router)		

CICSCLI.INI Definitions for the CICS Client for Macintosh on the Client Workstation	Ref. Key	Your Value
Server		
Protocol		
Netname	1 or 2	
Port	3	
Driver		
DriverName		

Matching	TCP/IP on Server	CICS for OS/2 on Server	TCP/IP on Client	CICSCLI.INI on Client	Your Value
1	IP address	TCP/IP Local Host Name	-	Netname	
2	Hostname	TCP/IP Local Host Name	-	Netname	
3	Port number	TCP/IP Local Host Port	-	Port	
4	IP address of Domain Nameserver	-	IP address of Domain Nameserver	-	

CICS/6000 • CICS Client for OS/2 Using TCP/IP for OS/2

The following tables are associated with
Chapter 12, "CICS/6000 • CICS Client for OS/2 Using TCP/IP for OS/2," on page 179:

TCP/IP on AIX/6000 Definitions on the Server	Ref. Key	Your Value
HOSTNAME	1	
Internet ADDRESS	2	
Network MASK	3	
Client Hostname	4	
Client Address	5	
TCP/IP service name	6	
Port number	7	
Protocol type (TCP only)		

CICS/6000 V1.2 Definitions on the Server	Ref. Key	Your Value
Listener Identifier		
Protocol type (TCP only)		
TCP adapter address	2	
TCP service name	6	

TCP/IP for OS/2 Definitions on the Client Workstation	Ref. Key	Your Value
Host name	4	
IP Address	5	
Subnet Mask	3	
Route Type		
Metric		
Server IP Address	2	
Server Hostname	1	

CICS Client for OS/2: CICSCLI.INI Definitions	Ref. Key	Your Value
Server		
Protocol		
Netname (host name)	1	
Netname (IP address)	2	
Port	7	
Driver		
DriverName		

Matching	TCP/IP for AIX/6000	CICS/6000	TCP/IP for OS/2	CICSCLI.INI	Your value
1	HOSTNAME	-	Server Hostname	Netname (host name)	
2	Internet ADDRESS	TCP adapter address	Server IP Address	Netname (IP address)	
3	Network MASK	-	Subnet Mask	-	
4	Client Hostname	-	Hostname	-	
5	Client Address	-	IP Address	-	
6	TCP/IP service name	TCP service name	-	-	
7	Port number	-	-	Port	

CICS/6000 • Client for DOS/Windows • TCP/IP for DOS

The following tables are associated with
Chapter 13, "CICS/6000 • Clients for DOS and Windows • TCP/IP for DOS," on page 191:

TCP/IP on AIX/6000 Definitions on the Server	Ref. Key	Your Value
HOSTNAME	1	
Internet ADDRESS	2	
Network MASK	3	
NAMESERVER Internet ADDRESS	4	
DOMAIN Name	5	
TCP/IP service name	6	
Port number	7	
Protocol type (TCP only)		

CICS/6000 V1.2 Definitions on the Server	Ref. Key	Your Value
Listener Identifier		
Protocol type (TCP only)		
TCP adapter address	2	
TCP service name	6	

TCP/IP for DOS Definitions on the Client Workstation	Ref. Key	Your Value
Host name		
IP Address		
Subnet Mask	3	
Domain name server address (DNSA)	4	
Domain name	5	

CICS Client: CICSCLI.INI	Ref. Key	Your Value
Server		
Protocol		
Netname (host name)	1	
Netname (IP address)	2	

CICS Client: CICSCLI.INI	Ref. Key	Your Value
Port	**7**	
Driver		
DriverName		

Matching	TCP/IP for AIX/6000	CICS/6000	TCP/IP for DOS	CICSCLI.INI	Your value
1	HOSTNAME	-	-	Netname (host name)	
2	Internet ADDRESS	TCP adapter address	-	Netname (IP address)	
3	Network MASK	-	Subnet Mask	-	
4	NAMESERVER Internet ADDRESS	-	DNSA	-	
5	DOMAIN Name	-	Domain name	-	
6	TCP/IP service name	TCP service name	-	-	
7	Port number	-	-	Port	

CICS for Windows NT • PC/TCP • Clients Using TCP/IP for OS/2 V1.2.1

The following tables are associated with Chapter 14, "CICS for Windows NT • PC/TCP • Clients Using TCP/IP," on page 205:

TCP/IP for Windows NT Definitions on the Server	Ref. Key	Your Value
Host Name	1	
IP Address	2	
Subnet Mask	3	
Domain Name Server	4	
Domain Name	5	

CICS for Windows NT Definitions on the Server	Ref. Key	Your Value
Maximum TCP/IP Systems		

PC/TCP for DOS/Windows Definitions on the Client Workstation	Ref. Key	Your Value
Hostname		
IP Address		
Router		
Subnet Mask	3	
DNS Server Address	4	
Domain Name	5	

CICSCLI.INI Definitions for CICS Client on the Client Workstation	Ref. Key	Your Value
Server		
Protocol		
Netname (host name)	1	
Netname (IP address)	2	
Port		
Driver		
DriverName		

Matching	TCP/IP for Windows NT	CICS for Windows NT	PC/TCP for DOS/Windows	CICSCLI.INI	Your value
1	Host Name	*	-	Netname (host name)	
2	IP Address	*	-	Netname (IP address)	
3	Subnet Mask	-	Subnet Mask	-	
4	Domain Name Server	-	DNS Server Address	-	
5	Domain Name	-	Domain Name	-	

CICS for Windows NT • LAN WorkPlace • TCP/IP

The following tables are associated with Chapter 15, "CICS for Window NT • LAN WorkPlace • TCP/IP," on page 215:

TCP/IP for Windows NT Definitions on the Server	Ref. Key	Your Value
Host Name	1	
IP Address	2	
Subnet Mask	3	
Domain Name Server	4	
Domain Name	5	

CICS for Windows NT Definitions on the Server	Ref. Key	Your Value
Maximum TCP/IP Systems		

LAN WorkPlace Definitions on the Client Workstation	Ref. Key	Your Value
Hostname		
IP Address		
Router		
Subnet Mask	3	
DNS Server Address	4	
Domain Name	5	

CICSCLI.INI Definitions for CICS Clients on the Client Workstation	Ref. Key	Your Value
Server		
Protocol		
Netname (host name)	1	
Netname (IP address)	2	
Port		
Driver		
DriverName		

Matching	TCP/IP for Windows NT	CICS for Windows NT	LAN WorkPlace	CICSCLI.INI	Your value
1	Host Name	*	-	Netname (host name)	
2	IP Address	*	-	Netname (IP address)	
3	Subnet Mask	-	Subnet Mask	-	
4	Domain Name Server	-	DNS Server Address	-	
5	Domain Name	-	Domain Name	-	

CICS for OS/2 • CICS Client for OS/2 • NetBIOS

The following tables are associated with Chapter 16, "CICS for OS/2 • CICS Client for OS/2 Using NetBIOS," on page 225:

CICS for OS/2 Definitions on the Server	Ref. Key	Your Value
Local System Appl ID	1	
NetBIOS Listener Adapter	2	
Maximum NetBIOS Systems		

CICSCLI.INI Definitions for CICS Client for OS/2 on the Client Workstation	Ref. Key	Your Value
Server		
Protocol		
Netname	1	
Adapter	2	
Driver		
DriverName		

Matching	CICS for OS/2 Multi-user	CICSCLI.INI	Your value
1	Local System Appl ID	Netname	
2	NETBIOS Listener Adapter	Adapter	

CICS for OS/2 • CICS Client for DOS/Windows • NetBIOS

The following tables are associated with
Chapter 17, "CICS for OS/2 • CICS Client for DOS/Windows • NetBIOS," on page 233:

CICS for OS/2 Definitions on the Server	Ref. Key	Your Value
Local System Appl ID	1	
NetBIOS Listener Adapter	2	
Maximum NetBIOS Systems		

CICSCLI.INI Definitions for CICS Client for DOS on the Client Workstation	Ref. Key	Your Value
Server		
Protocol		
Netname	1	
Adapter	2	
Driver		
DriverName		

Matching	CICS for OS/2 Multi-user	CICSCLI.INI	Your value
1	Local System Appl ID	Netname	
2	NETBIOS Listener Adapter	Adapter	

Appendix H. Configuration Worksheets

Glossary

A

abend. Abnormal ending of transaction.

API. Application programming interface. A set of calling conventions defining how a service is invoked through a software package.

APPC. Advanced Program-to-Program Communication. An implementation of SNA's LU6.2 protocol that allows interconnected systems to communicate and share the processing of programs.

application manager. A CICS run-time process that manages a pool of application servers.

application server. A CICS run-time process that executes CICS tasks.

application unit of work. A set of actions within an application that the designer chooses to regard as an entity. It is up to the designer to decide how, if at all, an application should be subdivided into application units of work, and whether any application unit of work will consist of one, or many, logical units of work (LUWs). Typically, but not exclusively, an application unit of work corresponds to a CICS transaction.

asynchronous. Without regular time relationship; unexpected or unpredictable with respect to the execution of program instruction. See synchronous.

C

CEMT. A CICS-supplied transaction that invokes all master terminal functions. These functions include inquiring about and changing the value of parameters used by CICS, altering the status of system resources, and terminating tasks.

cicsprnt. A CICS-supplied program that provides the ability to define a printer terminal on the client workstation. The program enables CICS applications running on the server to direct output to the client-attached printer. It is supplied with the CICS Clients.

cicsterm. A CICS-supplied program that provides 3270 emulation and enables connection to a CICS region. It is provided as part of the CICS Clients.

CICS. Customer Information Control System (CICS). A distributed online transaction processing system—an online system controller and some utilities that are capable of supporting a network of many terminals. The CICS family of products provides a range of application platforms on many operating system platforms.

client. As in client-server computing, the application that makes requests to the server and, often, handles the interaction necessary with the user.

client/server computing. A form of distributed processing, in which the task required to be processed is accomplished by a client portion that requests services and a server portion that fulfills those requests. The client and server remain transparent to each other in terms of location and platform. See client, distributed processing, and server.

commit. An action that an application takes to make permanent the changes it has made to CICS resources.

conversational. Communication model where two distributed applications exchange information by way of a conversation; typically, one application starts (or allocates) the conversation, sends some data, and allows the other application to send some data. Both applications continue in turn until one decides to finish (or deallocate). The conversational model is a synchronous form of communication.

cooperative processing. The process by which a single application is divided between two or more hardware platforms. Very often the term is used to reflect a tightly coupled relationship between the parts of the application.

D

database. (1) A collection of interrelated data stored together with controlled redundancy according to a scheme to serve one or more applications. (2) All data files stored in the system. (3) A set of data stored together and managed by a database management system.

DCE. Distributed Computing Environment. Adopted by the computer industry as a de facto standard for distributed computing. DCE allows computers from a variety of vendors to communicate transparently and share resources such as computing power, files, printers, and other objects in the network.

distributed processing. Distributed processing is an application or systems model in which function and data can be distributed across multiple computing resources connected on a LAN or WAN. See client/server computing.

DPL. Distributed program link. Provides a remote procedure call (RPC)-like mechanism by function shipping EXEC CICS LINK commands. In CICS/6000, DPL allows the linked-to program to issue unsupported CICS/6000 function shipping calls, such as to DB2 and DL/I, and yields performance improvements for transactions that read many records from remote files.

DTP. Distributed transaction processing. Type of intercommunication in CICS. The processing is distributed between transactions that communicate synchronously with one another over intersystem links. DTP enables a CICS application program to initiate transaction processing in a system that supports LU6.2 and resides in the same or a different processor.

E

ECI. external call interface. An application programming interface (API) that enables a non-CICS client application to call a CICS program as a subroutine. The client application communicates with the server CICS program using a data area called a COMM-AREA.

Encina. Enterprise computing in a new age. A set of DCE-based products from Transarc Corporation that are available on the RISC System/6000. The Encina family of online transaction processing products includes:

❑ Encina Toolkit Executive
❑ Encina Server
❑ Encina Structured File Server (SFS)
❑ Encina Peer-to-Peer Communication Executive (PPC)

EPI. External presentation interface. An application programming interface (API) that allows a non-CICS application program to appear to the CICS system as one or more standard 3270 terminals. The non-CICS application can start CICS transactions and send and receive standard 3270 data streams to those transactions.

environment. The collective hardware and software configuration of a system.

F

file server. A centrally-located computer that acts as a storehouse of data and applications for numerous users of a local area network.

G

GUI. Graphical user interface. A style of user interface that replaces the character-based screen with an all-points-addressable, high-resolution graphics screen. Windows display multiple applications at the same time and allow user input by means of a keyboard or a pointing device such as a mouse, a pen, or a trackball.

H

host. (1) In a computer network, a computer providing services such as computation, database access, and network control functions. (2) The primary or controlling computer in a multiple computer installation.

I

intercommunication. Communication between separate systems by means of Systems Network Architecture (SNA), Transmission Control Protocol/Internet Protocol (TCP/IP), and Network Basic Input/Output System (NetBIOS) networking facilities.

L

LU type 6.2 (LU 6.2). Type of logical unit used for CICS intersystem communication (ISC). LU 6.2 architecture supports CICS host-to-system-level products and CICS host-to-device-level products. APPC is the protocol boundary of the LU6.2 architecture.

LUW. Logical unit of work. An update that durably transforms a resource from one consistent state to another consistent state. A sequence of processing actions (for example, database changes) that must be completed before any of the individual actions can be regarded as committed. When changes are committed (by successful completion of the LUW and recording of the syncpoint on the system log), they do not need to be backed out after a subsequent error within the task or region. The end of an LUW is marked in a transaction by a syncpoint that is issued by either the user program or the CICS server, at the end of task. If there are no user syncpoints, the entire task is an LUW.

M

macro. An instruction that, when executed, causes the execution of a predefined sequence of instructions in the source language in which the macro is embedded. The predefined sequence can be modified by parameters in the macro.

O

OLTP. Online transaction processing. A style of computing that supports interactive applications in which requests submitted by terminal users are processed as soon as they are received. Results are returned to the requester in a relatively short period of time. An online transaction processing system supervises the sharing of resources for processing multiple transactions at the same time, minimizes compute time and duration of locks, and separates user think-time from the use of storage and other resources.

P

partner LU. In SNA, one of an LU pair between which a session is established.

portability. The ability to move application software components from one system for use on another system. Perfect portability would permit such movement without modification of the components.

protocol. (1) A formal set of conventions governing the format and control of data. (2) A set of procedures or rules for establishing and controlling transmissions from a source device or process to a target device or process.

pseudoconversational. A type of CICS application design that appears to the user as a continuous conversation, but consists internally of multiple tasks.

R

recovery. The use of archived copies to reconstruct files, databases, or complete disk images after they are lost or destroyed.

recoverable resources. Items whose integrity CICS maintains in the event of a system error. These include individual files and queues.

S

server. Any computing resource dedicated to responding to client requests. Servers can be linked to clients through LANs or WANs to perform services, such as printing, database access, fax, and image processing, on behalf of multiple clients at the same time.

synchronous. (1) Pertaining to two or more processes that depend on the occurrence of a specific event such as a common timing signal. (2) Occurring with a regular or predictable time relationship.

syncpoint. A logical point in execution of an application program where the changes made to the databases by the program are consistent and complete and can be committed to the database. The output, which has been held up to that point, is sent to its destination, the input is removed from the message queues, and the database updates are made available to other applications. When a program terminates abnormally, CICS recovery and restart facilities do not back out updates prior to the last completed syncpoint.

T

transaction. A unit of processing (consisting of one or more application programs) initiated by a single request. A transaction can require the initiation of one or more tasks for its execution.

transaction manager. Provides the function to begin, end, commit, and roll back transactions.

transaction monitor. Provides a total environment for transactional applications. In addition to transaction manager functions, provides services to aid development, execution, and operation of transaction applications.

transaction processing. A style of computing that supports interactive applications, in which requests submitted by users are processed as soon as they are received. Results are returned to the requester in a relatively short period of time. A transaction processing system supervises the sharing of resources for processing multiple transactions at the same time.

W

workstation. A configuration of input/output equipment at which an operator works. A terminal or microcomputer, usually one that is connected to a mainframe or a network, at which a user can perform applications.

List of Abbreviations

AIX	Advanced Interactive eXecutive (IBM's flavor of UNIX)	*FDDI*	Fiber Distributed Data Interface
API	application programming interface	*FTP*	file transfer program
		GUI	graphical user interface
ATI	automatic transaction initiation	*HP*	Hewlett-Packard Corporation
APPC	Advanced Program-to-Program Communication	*IBM*	International Business Machines Corporation
ASLM	Apple Shared Library Manager	*ICP*	interconnect control program
CD-ROM	Compact Disk-Read Only Memory	*ILU*	independent logical unit
CICS	Customer Information Control System	*IOCDS*	input/output configuration data set
CRSR	CICS-supplied transaction	*IPX*	Internet Packet Exchange
CM/2	Communications Manager/2	*ISC*	intersystem communication
CNOS	change number of sessions	*ITSO*	International Technical Support Organization
COMMAREA	communication area		
DCE	Distributed Computing Environment	*LAN*	local area network
		LSP	LAN Support Program
DEC	Digital Equipment Corporation	*LU*	logical unit
		LUW	logical unit of work
DLC	data link control	*MAC*	medium access control
DLU	dependent logical unit	*MVS*	Multiple Virtual Storage
DNS	domain name server		
DOS	Disk Operating System	*NDF*	node definition file
		NDIS	Network Driver Interface Specification
ECI	external call interface		
EPI	external presentation interface	*NetBIOS*	Network Basic Input/Output System
ESA	Enterprise Systems Architecture	*NLS*	national language support
		NS	Networking Services

415

NSD	Networking Services definition file	*Windows NT*	Windows New Technology
NTS/2	Network Transport Services/2	*XCA*	external communication adapter
ODI	open data-link interface	*XID*	exchange identifier
OS/2	Operating System/2		
OSF	Open Software Foundation Inc.		
PC	personal computer		
PCT	program control table		
PD	program definition		
PLU	partner logical unit		
PM	Presentation Manager		
PPT	processing program table		
PU	physical unit		
RDO	resource definition online		
SAA	Systems Application Architecture		
SDLC	Synchronous Data Link Control		
SIT	system initialization table		
SNA	Systems Network Architecture		
TCP/IP	Transmission Control Protocol/Internet Protocol		
TCS	connection and session table		
TCT	terminal control table		
TD	transaction definition		
TDD	transient data definition		
VSE	Virtual Storage Extended		
VTAM	Virtual Telecommunications Access Method		
WAN	wide area network		

Index

Numerics

3172 Interconnect Controller, See IBM 3172 Interconnect Controller
3270 Terminal Emulator, See CICS 3270 terminal emulator
802.2 interface support 51, 239

A

APPC 8
APPC configurations, See SNA
APPC Networking Services for Windows 49, 95, 111, 131
    CRSR 59
    mode definition 59
    NSD.INI sample files 367
    partner LU 52
    trace 304
Apple Shared Library Manager, See ASLM
AppleTalk LAN 20
application development tools 23
application portability 335
application server 2
application server model 6
APPN OS/2 gateway 131
architecture 10
ASLM 340
associated tools 23
ATI 342
autoinstall 9
automatic transaction initiation, See ATI

B

benefits of using CICS Clients 13

C

CCIN 340
CCLSNOTP.EXE 342
CCLSNWTP.EXE 342
CEMT 316
change number of sessions 92
change number of sessions, See CNOS
CICS 3270 Client printer support 12, 246
CICS 3270 terminal emulator 12
CICS Client 298
    error log 298
    starting 321
    status 322
    stopping 321
    trace 297
    trace analysis 305
CICS Client for DOS
    memory requirements 332
    starting 340
CICS Client for Macintosh
    Administration utility 323
    operation 323
    startup problems 340
CICS Clients 7
    configurations 25
    messages 346
CICS for DEC OSF/1 AXP 180
CICS for HP 9000 180
CICS for OS/2 153, 165, 225, 233
    configurations 25
CICS for Windows NT 205, 215
    configurations 25
CICS servers 7
CICSCLI commands 321
CICSCTSR 321
CICSCTSR.EXE 340
CICSDOSC.BAT 321, 340
CICSPRNT 248
CICSTERM commands 322
CICS/6000 179, 191
    configurations 25
CICS/ESA 29, 49
    configurations 25
CICS/MVS
    configurations 25
CICS/VSE 77, 95, 111, 131
    configurations 25
client control 13
client-server models 3
CM/2 29, 77, 131
    dumps 304
    gateway 19
    mode definition 42
    subsystem management 316
    trace 303
CM/2 gateway, See APPN OS/2 gateway
CM/2 NDF sample files 367
CNOS 45
COBOL stacksize 346
COMMEXEC 66

Communications Manager/2 , See CM/2
compatibility 334
compilers supported 349
configuration worksheets 381
configurations, list of 25
CRSR for CM/2 43
CTIN 340

D

data conversion 326, 337
database server model 4
dependent LU 343
DFHCNV , See data conversion
differences between CICS for OS/2 and CICS for Windows NT 335
disk space 332
distributed feature clients 22, 334
distribution of clients 15
documentation, online 347
DOS client configurations 25

E

ECI 11, 257
    asynchronous call with callback example 274
    asynchronous program link calls 262
    asynchronous status information calls 267
    concurrent transactions 334
    eci_transid 337
    facilities for managing LUWs 269
    managing logical units of work 269
    maximum COMMAREA size 336
    model 258
    multiple asynchronous calls 273
    program link calls 258
    reply solicitation calls 268
    sample implementation 277
    sample source code 351
    sequence of calls within one LUW 271
    status information calls 265
    synchronous program link calls 259
    synchronous status information calls 266
EPI 11, 283
    application flow 284
    concurrent transactions 334
    EPI model 284
    sample implementation 288
    sample source code 351
error log , See CICS Client
Ethernet 111, 180
Ethernet adapter 377
Ethernet configurations 25
external call interface , See ECI
external presentation interface , See EPI

F

FAARQ.INI 23
FAATPPCI 341
FDDI 180

G

gateways 18
    CM/2 19
    NetWare for SAA 19
    SNA 19
    SNA 20

H

hardware requirements 332

I

IBM 3172 Interconnect Controller 111, 377
    IBM 3172 customization 377
IBMTOK.DOS 239
IBMTOK.NIF 239
internet xxxiii
IPX 16

L

LAN Adapter and Protocol Support , See LAPS
LAN Distance 21
LAN support program , See LSP
LAN WorkPlace 215
languages supported 349
LAPS 228, 236
LSP 51, 233
LU6.2 communication 8

M

Macintosh client configurations 25
memory requirements 332
migration 22, 334
mobile communications 21
modem 22
multiple printers 253
multiple protocol configurations 21

N

national language support , See NLS
NDF sample files 367
NDIS MAC driver 239
NetBIOS 7, 225, 233
    configurations 28
    emulation over IPX 16
    listener 345
    over IPX 310
NetWare for SAA gateway 19
network configurations
    APPC 17
    gateways 18
    NetBIOS 16
    TCP/IP 16
Network Transport Services/2 , See NTS/2
NLS 15
Novell LAN WorkPlace , See LAN WorkPlace
NSD.INI sample files 367
NTS/2 225, 233

O

OS/2 client configurations 25
OS/2 gateway , See APPN OS/2 gateway

P

partner LU for APPC NS/Windows 97
performance 22
ping utility 327
port selection 328
printer configurations 28, 245
problem determination 293
    CICS server dumps 301
    CICS server message logs 301
    communication traces and dumps 303
    CSMT 301
    sources of information 295
    tools 294
problems, common 339

R

RDO for CICS LU6.2 connections 35
RDO for CICS sessions 35
remote data access 3

S

sample configurations 25
SDLC 77, 95
    configurations 25
security 15
SNA 8
    configurations 27
    gateways 19
SNA s gateway 20

T

TCP/IP 8
    IBM TCP/IP for AIX 179, 191
    IBM TCP/IP for DOS 191
    IBM TCP/IP for OS/2 153, 165, 179
    MacTCP for Macintosh 165
    Windows NT TCP/IP 215
TCP/IP configurations 27
TCP/IP port selection , See port selection
terminal emulator , See CICS 3270 terminal emulator
token-ring configurations 25
TokenTalk LAN 20

U

user exit 21 (CICS for OS/2) 248
user exit 22 (CICS for OS/2) 253

V

vendors 23
VTAM 29, 49, 77, 95, 111, 131

buffer trace 303

W

WAN 192, 336
Windows client configurations 25
WIN-OS/2 343
WINSOCK 344
wireless communications 21
worksheets 381
workstation
 customization 15
World Wide Web xxxiii

X

X.25 180